W9-DDT-857

"The Women Will Howl"

"The Women Will Howl"

The Union Army Capture of Roswell and New Manchester, Georgia, and the Forced Relocation of Mill Workers

MARY DEBORAH PETITE

McFarland & Company, Inc., Publishers
Jefferson, North Carolina, and London

LIBRARY OF CONGRESS CATALOGUING-IN-PUBLICATION DATA

Petite, Mary Deborah.
"The women will howl" : the Union Army capture of Roswell
and New Manchester, Georgia, and the forced relocation
of mill workers / Mary Deborah Petite.
p.   cm.
Includes bibliographical references and index.

ISBN-13: 978-0-7864-3168-7
illustrated case binding : 50# alkaline paper ∞

1. Roswell (Ga.)—History, Military—19th century.   2. New Manchester
(Ga.)—History, Military—19th century.   3. Women—Georgia—Social
conditions—19th century.   4. Children—Georgia—Social conditions—19th
century.   5. Women textile workers—Georgia—History—19th century.
6. Sherman, William T. (William Tecumseh), 1820–1891.   7. United States.
Army—History—Civil War, 1861–1865.   8. United States—History—Civil
War, 1861–1865—Women.   9. United States—History—Civil War,
1861–1865—Children.   10. United States—History—Civil War,
1861–1865—Social aspects.   I. Title.
F294.R75P48   2008   355.009758'23—dc22   2007033704

British Library cataloguing data are available

On the cover: vine-covered Sweetwater Mill ruins
(courtesy Dan Emsweller); cotton art (©2007 clipart.com);
Martha Louise Eldredge (courtesy descendants of Olney Eldredge)

Manufactured in the United States of America

*McFarland & Company, Inc., Publishers
Box 611, Jefferson, North Carolina 28640
www.mcfarlandpub.com*

For Nikki, Shani, Deja and Destiny:
you light up my life

Table of Contents

Preface

In July 1864, Union General William T. Sherman ordered the arrest and deportation of hundreds of women and children who worked in the cotton mills in Roswell, Georgia. Torn from their homes and transported hundreds of miles to Northern soil, these helpless victims were forced to fend for themselves in towns overrun by refugees where food was scarce and jobs were few. These women and children were not war criminals nor did they pose a serious threat to the Union army. Nevertheless, they were charged with treason for working in mills that supplied cloth to the Confederate government, jobs which provided their only means of support.

The Roswell mill workers were not the first women arrested and forcibly removed from their homes by Federal authorities. Hundreds of individual women were charged with various crimes of disloyalty throughout the war. Some were sent to prison, some into the Confederate lines, and others sent north. But never had an entire community of women been arrested and deported — at least not until General Sherman arrived in North Georgia and determined that the Roswell mill workers were deserving of such a fate. And they would not be the only ones so charged. Only a few days later, Sherman ordered the arrest of workers at the New Manchester cotton mill on Sweetwater Creek. Women and children from the two villages, along with a few men too young, too old, or too sick to fight, were sent to Marietta where trains would carry them to an uncertain destiny.

I was intrigued by the story of the mill workers from the time I learned of it. This is a tragic and little known example of innocent civilians swept up in the whirlwind of war. Too often historians focus on the soldiers and battles while overlooking the sufferings and sacrifices of civilians, particularly poor Southern women, who became unwitting and unwilling participants in a war brought to their very doorstep.

Very little was known about the actual events and much less had been written. Not surprisingly, the events were mired in myth and controversy. Stories of unarmed male factory hands shot in cold blood, of mill employees sold into slavery, and of the cruelty suffered by female workers at the hands of an evil doctress were widely circulated, but simply not true. Sorting fact from fiction would not prove an easy task. Few first-hand

1

accounts were ever written. Most of the young women who worked in the mills were illiterate and unable to leave behind any record of their heartbreaking ordeal, and yet their silence speaks volumes on the hardships of mill life as well as the profoundness of their tragedy. Pieces of the puzzle are found in family histories, period newspapers, and the letters and diaries of Union soldiers. The truth is a compelling story of women and children who lost everything and endured more than we can possibly imagine, and yet, unlike the men in uniform, their names and experiences were all but lost to history.

From the founding of the village to the war that brought widespread loss, death, and destruction, the stories of Roswell, her mills and her people are woven together in a rich tapestry of color and character. Many people played significant parts in shaping that history, perhaps no one more so than Roswell King, a transplanted Yankee whose early experiences prepared him for his central role as the founder of the village that continues to bear his name. Attitudes towards class, master-slave, owner-workers, regardless of southern or northern born, were formed early on and continued to play a role in the fate of our main characters.

I spent several years researching and writing this book, a journey I now refer to as my road to Roswell. I moved from California to Roswell in the summer of 2000 to complete some research at various state and local archives and libraries. But more importantly, I wanted to discover and experience the town that I had come to know so well through the accounts of others. During my brief stay, I visited most of the homes built by the founding families and toured Bulloch Hall, the Smith Home, the Bricks, and the old store, which now houses a popular restaurant. I attended church services in the original sanctuary of the Roswell Presbyterian Church and had an opportunity to see the checkerboard drawn on one of the church cabinet doors by a Union soldier so many years ago. I walked up the streets on Factory Hill where some of the original mill cottages still stand, many still recognizable after all these years. I climbed down the steep creek banks and explored the kudzu-covered machine shop and the rusted pipes, crumbling brick walls, and foundation stones that line the creek, humble reminders of the prosperous Roswell factories. I walked along the town square following the footsteps of the women and children who stood there in the summer of 1864 waiting for the wagons that would carry them far from home.

This journey into the heart and history of Roswell provided me with invaluable insight and perspective. These are memories I will always treasure.

This book could never have been written without the help and cooperation of many wonderful people. While there is not enough time or space to properly thank each and every one, there are some individuals and institutions I must at least mention.

I spent countless hours at the National Archives in Washington, D.C., and I would like to thank their knowledgeable and courteous staff, especially Michael Musick, former military archivist, who was particularly helpful in tracking down some new and important information. Thanks also to the staff of the Library of Congress; the U.S. Army Military History Institute in Carlisle, Pennsylvania; the Indiana Historical Society and the Indiana State Archives in Indianapolis; the Indiana Room at the New Albany–Floyd County Library; the Filson Historical Society and the Louisville Free Public Library in Louisville, Kentucky; the Kentucky State Archives in Frankfort; and the Tennessee State Library and Archives in Nashville.

I discovered a wealth of information in various state and local historical institutions in Georgia. The archivists at the Georgia State Archives rendered valuable assistance time and time again. Thanks also to the staff of the Atlanta Historical Society and the Bulloch Hall Research Library in Roswell; to Robert Bohanan, deputy director of the Jimmy Carter Library and Museum in Atlanta; to the librarians at the Cobb County Library in Marietta; and to Michael Garland of the Etowah Valley Historical Society. Darlene Walsh and Elaine DeNiro of the Roswell Historical Society were very generous with their time and expertise, and Elaine was especially helpful in locating the right photographs for this book.

My heartfelt thanks to the Roswell Mills Camp #1547 of the Sons of Confederate Veterans. John Cobb, Phillip Cochran and Sam Allen took me on my first tour of the Roswell mill ruins back in 1998, and Joe Walls was the first to show me around the historic Roswell Presbyterian Church. In addition, John Cobb and George Thurmond kept me updated on current events while I was still in California, and both were instrumental in passing on contacts for many of the mill worker descendents. Thanks to all the members of the Roswell Mills Camp for your support and encouragement.

It would have been impossible to write about New Manchester without the help of Bill Cahill and Dan Emsweller of the Friends of Sweetwater Creek State Park. Bill met with me on several occasions and gave me an extensive tour of the mill ruins and the surrounding area. Dan Emsweller, the park historian, helped me sort through much of the myth that surrounds the New Manchester events, and provided me with a tremendous amount of material from the park's history files. Dan was always willing to answer what must have seemed like endless questions by telephone and e-mail. Thank you both for your patience and indispensable assistance.

Michael Rutherford, Perry County, Indiana, historian, kindly provided me with a copy of his unpublished manuscript on the Cannelton Cotton Mill, along with many other items of interest. Ted Brooke of Cumming, Georgia, helped me unravel the mystery of the Adeline Buice story. Kenneth H. Thomas, Jr., was kind enough to include a couple of articles about my project in his genealogy column in the *Atlanta Journal–Constitution*, which produced some excellent contacts.

My sincere appreciation and gratitude to Richard M. McMurry and William C. "Jack" Davis, both distinguished authors and Civil War historians. Richard patiently waded through an early draft with pencil in hand. Thank you for the constructive helpful advice. Jack has been a source of encouragement and inspiration from the very beginning. He also took the time to critique an early draft and offered many insightful suggestions. His guidance and direction have been invaluable.

Thanks also to the staff of the Library of Congress, the U.S. Army Military History Institute in Carlisle, Pennsylvania, the Indiana Historical Society and the Indiana

State Archives in Indianapolis, the Indiana Room at the New Albany–Floyd County Library; the Filson Historical Society and the Louisville Free Public Library in Louisville, Kentucky; the Kentucky State Archives in Frankfort; and the Tennessee State Library and Archives in Nashville.

In a special category are all the descendants I've been blessed to meet along the way. So many have given generously of their time, their family histories and their cherished photographs. They have provided the heart and soul of this story, and their interest and enthusiasm have been a constant source of inspiration. Thanks to John Allen, Hazel Bailin, Michael E. Brown, Thomas Farr, David Floyd, Anna Gross, Betty Helms, Vickie Herring, Deborah Howard, David Jones, Mauriel Joslyn, Jack Hopkins, Tommie Phillips LaCavera, Bonnie Weed Malburg, Mary Stewart Newton, and Lyn Pewitt. Special thanks to George and Elizabeth Kendley, who invited me into their home and shared so much about the Kendley family; to Carmel Boswell for sharing the fascinating story of Lucinda Wood Shelly; and to Charlene Herreid for her assistance with the Humphries family. I owe a special debt of gratitude to the Eldredge family for helping me tell the story of Olney Eldredge. My thanks to Paul Eldredge, great-grandson of Olney Eldredge; Eleanor J. Eldredge, wife of Paul Eldredge; Mattie Lisenby, great-granddaughter of Olney; and Walter and Michael Eldredge, Olney's great-great-grandsons. Thanks especially to Michael and Mattie for taking the time to meet with me personally, and for sharing so many priceless family keepsakes.

I also want to thank my dear friend Caroline Matheny Dillman, an author and local historian, who provided me with a great deal of historical background. She also directed me to a number of important sources and offered many valuable insights.

My father, Harold Gordon, first told me the story of the Roswell mill workers and later generously provided the support I needed in order to finish my research in Roswell. I am especially thankful to Cindy Gordon for her unwavering confidence and her boundless enthusiasm. I will never forget you.

I could not have finished this manuscript without the help and support of my husband, Randy, who first suggested that I write a book about the "women." He assisted me with much of the research, but more importantly, he made innumerable sacrifices to see this to fruition without ever issuing one word of complaint. Thank you for sharing this long and often times frustrating journey with me.

And thanks most of all to Nikki, Shani, Damian, Jordan, Isaiah, Deja and Destiny, whom I virtually abandoned for the last six years in pursuit of this story. Your support and understanding has been the greatest gift I've ever received. I've missed so much, and will do my best to make it up to all of you.

And finally to my mother who always believed in me, even when I didn't believe in myself. I wish you were here.

It is my hope that this work will, in some small part, give voice to the women and children who have not been able to speak for themselves.

Introduction

No longer a small village by any definition, the lovely and thriving town of Roswell, Georgia, clings passionately to her past while eagerly embracing her future. Magnificently preserved historic homes and churches tell the story of a community that has stood the test of time. The town square, small cottages on Factory Hill, and familiar streets, now paved, exist much as they did some 175 years ago. Along Vickery Creek, most of the mill buildings are long gone, but old stone piers, earthen platforms, and granite walls bear witness to a rich history that was by turns courageous, turbulent and tragic.

Before the white settlers arrived, most of the land in and around Roswell belonged to the Cherokee, but white men had been removing Indians since their first contact and North Georgia would be no different. In 1817 white men negotiated a treaty that included provisions for Indian removal with the government promising assistance to those who chose to go. Less than 2000 Indians made that choice, and those who remained fought to maintain possession of the land that the whites were so desperate to take for themselves.

To earn the respect and favor of the white men, many Cherokee began to adopt the white culture while preserving their tribal integrity. Some quit hunting and turned to farming, raised livestock and planted crops, while Cherokee women took up spinning and weaving. The Indians established schools, developed written laws, and established a newspaper written in English and Cherokee. By 1827 they had established a supreme court and a constitution very similar to that of the United States. They soon proved that a Cherokee could do everything a white man could do. Still it was not enough. In their desire for land, many of the white men refused to see the Cherokee as anything but savages.

The discovery of gold in 1828 sealed the fate of the Cherokee who remained in Georgia. Gold fever spread like wildfire, and almost overnight 4,000 men were prospecting for gold in the headwaters of the Chattahoochee, Chestatee, and Etowah Rivers. The gold fields lay on and adjacent to Cherokee land, land Georgia now claimed for its own. On May 28, 1830, the state of Georgia passed the Indian Removal Act, which transferred possession of the Cherokee lands to the state. The act provided for the exchange of American Indian lands for lands west of the Mississippi River and removal to those lands. All laws and customs of the Cherokee were now null and void. As far as the state of Georgia was concerned, the Cherokee Nation had ceased to exist. Still some 9,000 Indians remained in Georgia.

Cherokee Georgia covered more than 6,000 square miles. The greater portion of this ill-gotten land was to be raffled off in a statewide lottery, from which the Indians themselves were barred. In preparation for the land lotteries of 1832 and 1833, surveyors arrived in late 1831 to begin partitioning the land into sections which would then be divided into 160-acre farm lots and 40-acre gold lots. In a futile effort to retain their lands, the Cherokee pursued action to protect their rights through the courts. President Andrew Jackson, ignoring a mandate by the Supreme Court upholding the Indian land rights, approved the removal of the Cherokee.

In 1835 the United States negotiated a treaty with only a small minority party of Indians who believed removal was inevitable. More than 16,000 opposed the treaty and refused to sign but the United States, ignoring the majority of the Indian nation, ratified the Treaty of New Echota in 1836. The Indians were given two years to emigrate or face forced removal. By 1838, the majority, stubbornly holding on to their rights, remained with only 2,000 moving west. The government sent in 7,000 armed militia and volunteers to forcibly remove those who remained. Given little or no time to gather their possessions, nearly 17,000 Cherokee were rounded up at bayonet point and herded into stockades constructed on their own land.

The initial plan would gather the Cherokee at three points from where they would be transported down the Tennessee and Ohio rivers to the Mississippi River and then sent overland to Indian Territory. In June of 1838, a few thousand were so removed, but this removal in the hottest part of the year was met with so much sickness and mortality that the Cherokees petitioned for and received permission to remove themselves in the fall after the sickly season had ended. But even in the cooler months, many would not survive the long, difficult journey west. Deaths occurred almost every day from disease, cold, hardship and accidents. The path was literally marked with the graves of those who died on the way, and the Cherokee named the journey the "Nunna dual Isunyi," literally the "Trail Where We Cried." We now know it as the Trail of Tears.

Ironically, the gold rush era survived the Cherokee by only a few years. Soon after the last of the Cherokee had been removed, the reason for their removal began to disappear as the gold began to play out. One historian wrote that it was "almost as if cursed by the exiled natives." But in outlying areas like Roswell, which lay some distance from the producing mines, the men awarded the 40-acre gold lots in 1832 and 1833, began trying to sell their land long before the removal of the Indians. It did not take long to realize that there was little gold to be found in the region. Moreover, the lots were not particularly suitable for farming as it was still a sparsely settled rural land without good roads to markets.

It would take a man of vision to see the potential of the land that lay on the north side of the Chattahoochee River at Vickery Creek. Enter Roswell King, a prosperous businessman, landowner, and slaveholder. King had no dreams of gold, at least not in the traditional sense, but he was a man of lofty ambitions, even in the twilight of his years. One of the few men of his time to recognize the importance of southern cotton manufacturing, King planned to bring the textile industry to a land of small farmers. This King would build his castles in the wilderness.

King worked hard to bring his dreams to fruition. Buying up a large number of the gold lots, King founded the village of Roswell and offered home sites and investment opportunities to his wealthy friends along the Georgia coast who would help establish the new settlement. With the help of his family and friends, King laid out the plans for the village, built magnificent homes, a church, a school and the cornerstone of the village: the cotton mill. He hired mill workers and built cottages for them on a hill overlooking Vickery Creek.

The mill employees, primarily women and children, lived in company houses on Factory Hill, their board deducted from their meager wages. What little was left was paid in company scrip redeemable at the company store. While the company yielded a considerable profit, the women and children spent most of their waking hours in the mills, under difficult and unhealthy conditions. Since they did not possess the skills or the education to find other employment, there was little hope of improving their circumstances. Far from a life of luxury, the factories did provide the workers with honest employment and the means to support themselves and their families. Resting at the bottom of the Roswell social ladder, the founding families often referred to them as "that class of people."

King's manufacturing experiment was an overwhelming success. The mills prospered and expanded, and the colony, as it came to be known, grew as more families arrived. Soon new textile mills were springing up in North Georgia. Thirty miles to the west, Col. James Rogers and Charles McDonald, a former Georgia governor, built a cotton mill on Sweetwater Creek in a village later known as New Manchester. In full operation by 1849, the mill was soon known throughout the south for its superior yarn and fabric. Times were good, but the bright days of promise were short lived for just ahead lay secession and the bloody Civil War.

With the outbreak of hostilities, young men from Roswell and New Manchester rushed to enlist in a wave of patriotic fervor. Many of the men from Roswell joined the Roswell Guards, a local unit commanded by one of Roswell King's grandsons. After drilling on the town square, the unit marched off to a distant field at Manassas Junction where the Roswell Guards suffered heavy casualties. Many more men died in other battles on other fields. Whether it was the loss of a loved one or the sufferings from widespread shortages, no one would be untouched by the harsh realities of war.

Although far removed from the early battles, the Roswell and New Manchester mills made a significant contribution to the Confederate war effort by supplying the Rebel armies with sheeting, tent cloth, rope and wool for uniforms. The factories received large military contracts and soon found they were hard pressed to keep up with the demand. Their production was so necessary that many of the male employees were exempt from conscription and detailed to work in the mills.

As the fighting drew closer, Roswell's citizens of wealth grew increasingly anxious, understanding that their factories were sure to be targeted by General William T. Sherman, commander of the vast Army of the Mississippi. Waging a war that sought to demoralize and thus defeat an entire population, Sherman's army swept through the towns and villages north of Roswell, leaving a wide path of destruction and desolation in their wake. Southern newspapers warned of the outrages committed by the Union Army and fueled the fears of the people who lay in Sherman's path. Fearing the worst, most of Roswell's elite removed as much of their property as possible and fled to what they prayed would be safer places, a luxury not available to the mill workers who had no means to leave. Instead, they would remain behind and work in the factories until driven out by the enemy.

Roswell faced some of her darkest days during the last terrible year of the Civil War. And while she would be forever changed, she was not destroyed. The legacy of Roswell King would survive, and indeed has endured through all of the years that have followed. We shall begin then, with the man who had the most profound influence on the town that continues to bear his name: Roswell King.

On July 6, 1864, Brigadier General Kenner Garrard, commander of the Second Division Cavalry Corps, Army of the Cumberland, sent a detailed report to Major General William T. Sherman, along with a map of the small mill town of Roswell, Georgia. Having drawn the map on his arrival the day before, Garrard had made a brief notation along the right hand side, "Roswell is a very pretty factory town of about four thousand inhabitants. Mills & private property not injured by me." But before handing the map to the courier, the cavalry commander took a pencil and crossed out the word "Mills." For Garrard did indeed put the factories to the torch, and as the mill workers, primarily women and children, stood on the bank of Vickery Creek and watched the mills go up in smoke, not one could have foreseen the tragic fate that lay before them.

1

Roswell King

He was the founder of the village which bears his name. A man of great energy,
industry and perseverance of rigid integrity, truth and justice. He early earned
and long enjoyed the esteem and confidence of his fellow men.
— Inscription from the tombstone of Roswell King

The "very pretty factory town" of Roswell, Georgia, sat on a high bluff overlooking the Chattahoochee River near the mouth of Vickery Creek, twenty miles north of Atlanta. Unlike the traditional mill villages throughout the South, Roswell was a community of prominent families, stately mansions and grand churches. Arriving in the 1830s, Roswell King carved his colony out of an untamed wilderness and in so doing created a lasting legacy. The small colony would become a thriving and prosperous village that would forever stand as a monument to the vision and tenacity of a man who would be king.

Roswell King, patriarch of the "Royal Family" and founder of the Roswell Colony, may not have been of noble birth, but he could boast of impressive lineage nevertheless. A distant ancestor, Lord Edward King, served as the first archbishop of Ireland after the reformation, and his son, Sir John King, was secretary of Ireland during the reign of James I. Sir John's grandson and Roswell King's great-grandfather, John King, was born in Ireland in 1629. He attended school in North Hampton, England, but left for the colonies at the age of sixteen, arriving in America in 1645. The first of the line to set foot on American soil, John was instrumental in the founding of Northampton, Massachusetts. Timothy King, Roswell King's father, achieved fame as the commander of the United States brig *Defiance* during the American Revolution. Roswell could also claim kinship with a number of prominent Americans including Noah and Daniel Webster and John Fitch, the American steamboat pioneer.[1]

Born in Windsor, Connecticut, in 1765, Roswell King left his New England home to seek his fortune in Georgia at the age of 23. He settled in the small river town of

Darien, which bore little resemblance to his native home. Instead of large cities and factories, King found extensive rice plantations scattered along the coast and on the Sea Islands. Cultivated by slave labor, the lowland plantations produced abundant crops of rice for domestic and world markets.[2]

Possessing generous amounts of Yankee enterprise and ingenuity, King soon proved himself a successful and prosperous commission merchant dealing in lumber, cotton and rice. He achieved some fame as a building contractor, and was well known for his skill in the use of tabby, a regional building material made of lime, shells and sand mixed with water. King constructed a number of stores and warehouses along the waterfront, as well as a large hotel later taken over by the Darien Academy. King also supervised the construction of Thomas Spalding's home on Sapelo Island in the early 1800s, one of the first Georgia homes with towering white columns.[3]

King impressed the locals with his energy and integrity, earning their trust and respect. Within a short time, King had served as a county surveyor, a justice of the peace and a justice of the inferior court. Commissioned a lieutenant in the Georgia Militia in 1793, he also served as a member of the Georgia House of Representatives in 1794 and 1795.[4]

Roswell married genuine royalty when he wed Catherine Barrington in 1788. The daughter of Colonel Josiah and Sarah Williams Barrington, Catherine is said to have possessed the same ancestry as the royal Tudors. Catherine's family also claimed ties with Oliver Cromwell, and the distinguished General James Oglethorpe, founder of the colony of Georgia. The royal union of Roswell King and Catherine Barrington produced ten children, of whom five boys and two girls lived to adulthood.[5]

Although King had long since made a name for himself and was successful and prosperous in his own right, he set aside his personal business affairs and accepted a lucrative position from Major Pierce Butler in 1802 as overseer of his plantations on Butler and St. Simons Islands. Butler preferred to live in Philadelphia and wanted a manager who would free him "from the necessity of ever going to see my estate." Butler believed he found such a manager in Roswell King. Finding him to be of good judgment, Butler gradually gave him more control over the day-to-day operations.[6]

King's many responsibilities included overseeing the hundreds of black slaves living and working on the Butler plantations. The slaves represented a large capital investment and King understood the importance of protecting these valuable *possessions*. Their health and wellbeing was a primary concern since strong, healthy slaves could work harder and longer and generally produced healthier children, children who would eventually replace the old and infirm. Consequently, King made sure they were, at least, adequately fed and clothed, but he demanded strict obedience in return. He would not allow anything or anyone to threaten his success and under his management, the slaves frequently met with harsh treatment.

Both Butler and King professed to be fair and humane in their handling of the slaves and claimed that any punishments they inflicted were necessary. But King was a stern disciplinarian and had no qualms about resorting to the whip or other cruel measures to exact obedience. Butler's biographer, Malcolm Bell, claimed that even Butler seemed troubled by the "frequency and severity" of King's punishments. In addition to the brutal whippings, slave families were often broken up in order to punish them or silence quarrels. The worst offenders were whipped and then banished to a horrible swamp in a remote corner of St. Simons Island, a penal colony called Five Pound Tree.[7]

Even obedient slaves fared worse under King's management than did slaves on other nearby plantations. King kept the slaves isolated and away from the influence of others. Religious pursuits were discouraged. Neighboring slaveholders encouraged their slaves to attend church services, believing that religion provided the slaves with a sense of hope and purpose. After all, contented slaves were far less likely to run away. King saw things differently. Not long after his arrival, he informed Butler that the slaves were spending too much time in their religious pursuits. King had a plan, which would not be "much expense." If Butler would send him a dozen fiddles, "which should not cost more than one or two dollars each," King would use them to "break up so much preaching as there is on your Estate," believing that dancing would give the Negroes "a better appetite for sleep than preaching."[8]

Butler and King came to a parting of the ways in 1820, but relations between the two had been strained for several years. Butler blamed King for losing a number of slaves during the British invasion of St. Simons Island in 1815. King had viewed the British with apprehension, but felt more at ease after meeting with the secretary of the admiral leading the invasion. The secretary advised King that they would use all possible means to induce the Negroes to join them but "declared upon his honr [sic] that they would take no negro that had rather live with their master." Confident of their loyalty, King assured Butler that the slaves would not leave the plantation. He would soon regret those words. One hundred and thirty-eight slaves left with the British who promised them the one thing they wanted above all else: their freedom.[9]

King could not comprehend the slaves' willingness to leave the plantation and thought them "foolish and ungrateful." In a letter to Butler, he expressed his frustration, writing that the Negroes had "neither honr [sic] or Gratitude." King continued, "God cursed the Negroe by making him Black. I Curse the Man that brot the first from Africa, and the Curse of God is still on them, to send them away to die a miserable death." King believed that the slaves would return in time of peace, but confided to Butler, "Who can look at Negroes that have been so humanely treated as yours." He closed his letter, "I cannot write, I am in too much pain."[10]

Furious with King, Butler held him responsible for the loss of his valuable property, a loss King himself estimated at $61,450. Believing that his overseer should have moved the slaves out of reach of the British, Butler gave thought to replacing King and became increasingly dissatisfied with his work, frequently complaining about him in letters to William Page, King's predecessor. Eager to return to his own interests, and growing tired of Butler's constant criticism, King tendered his resignation in 1821, leaving his son, Roswell King Jr., as manager of Butler's estate. Living conditions for the slaves would only grow worse under the management of the younger King.[11]

After his resignation from Butler's employ, Roswell King Sr. returned to Darien to look after his varied business interests. He had done well for himself during the years he worked for Butler, amassing vast land holdings and a number of slaves. As a prosperous businessman in his own right, King had acquired a keen understanding of the southern economy and was one of a handful of industrialists who believed that the prosperity and independence of the South depended on the growth of domestic industry. So long as the South clung tightly to her agricultural status and depended on the North for all of her manufactured goods, she would never achieve any measure of independence. Some men, most northern born like Roswell King, turned to the textile industry, believing there was money to be made by building mills in the south, where they could take full advantage of cheap labor, abundant raw material, and the necessary waterpower. A forerunner of a new era, King sought an opportunity to build a cotton mill of his own.

Sixty-three-year-old Roswell King made a trip on horseback through the Carolinas and northeast Georgia in 1832 as a representative of the Bank of Darien. Riding through rugged, mountainous country still occupied by Indians and with few roads and only scattered settlements, King was to investigate the bank's interests in the gold fields of Goldsboro, North Carolina; Kingsville, South Carolina; and Dahlonega, Georgia. As he crossed the Chattahoochee River and climbed the hill along Vickery Creek, he was taken with the beauty of the unspoiled wilderness, high hills covered with virgin pine and oak and swift-flowing streams of crystal-clear water. Envisioning a cotton mill on the west bank of the Chattahoochee River, King realized this was the place and opportunity he had been seeking. This place, which the Cherokee called "the enchanted land," would one day be his home.[12]

King returned to North Georgia in 1833 and spent several months in the

Roswell King (1765–1844). Founder of the Roswell Colony, King built his castles in the midst of a wilderness. He established the Roswell Manufacturing Company in 1839 (courtesy the Roswell Historical Society).

12

town of Auraria, working for the Bank of Darien. The bank had established a new branch in the small gold mining town and King worked as a cashier and served as a member of the board of directors. Sometime in 1834 or early 1835, King headed south to the Chattahoochee River and returned to the place that had captured his heart and imagination.[13]

2

The Colony

The Colony people were as distinct almost from the ordinary settlers of the country as from the Indians, who had lately been removed. Most of the "colony people" had handsome houses, plenty of servants, carriages and a plantation. They were an educated and exclusive society. They had their own church with an educated pastor who was one of them and a good school, while the others had log cabins and cultivated small patches or worked in the cotton mill built by the colony, and many of them had no education except what they got in the colony Sunday school.
— Archibald Smith Jr., member of the Roswell colony

King's new home was little more than a wilderness sparsely inhabited by small farmers. There were a few distant plantations, some along the river and the larger creeks, and only a few slaves, but the next few years would bring great change to this wild, unsettled land. That change would begin with Roswell King. After purchasing a number of 40-acre gold lots from men who had acquired them by way of the Georgia land lotteries in 1832 and 1833, King enlisted the help of his son Barrington, along with local workmen and slaves brought from the coast, in clearing the land and building a log house for Roswell and his family. Enlarged several times to make room for the arrival of new settlers, King's log cabin soon became known as the castle.[1]

The Cherokee in and around Roswell were primarily farmers and maintained cordial relations with the white settlers until most of them were removed in 1838. King traded with the local Indians and may have hired some of them to help build the mill. According to family folklore, the Cherokee called King "The Proud Man."[2]

King offered land lots and investment opportunities to his friends and family who were then living along the Georgia coast. A mild, healthy climate, the choice of a home site, and the option to buy stock in the new cotton mill were enough to entice the low country planters to leave their homes and make the long, difficult journey to an upcountry forest broken up by a few small farms. The new settlers lived in the castle with the

"Royal Family," while they constructed log cabins which they would occupy until their permanent homes were complete.[3]

Most of the founding families arrived in 1838, including two of King's children. Barrington arrived in May with his wife, Catherine Margaret Nephew King, nine children, eight servants and six horses. Eliza King Hand, Roswell's daughter, and her three children arrived in the fall. King had already drawn up the plans for the town; the newly arriving families had only to select their sites and build their new homes. King's wife, Catherine, died in 1839 without visiting the village that was to bear her husband's name and was buried near Darien in a small brick-walled graveyard.[4]

Roswell patterned his colony after a New England town with wide streets leading from the town square, the square separating the mill village from the homes of the newly arrived aristocracy. After selecting sites for the church and school, the work on the houses began. Barrington King sent for Willis Ball, a Connecticut architect, who supervised the construction of a number of the Roswell homes including the majestic Barrington Hall.[5]

The first permanent home was built for Roswell's recently widowed daughter, Eliza. The site adjoined her brother Barrington's property and sat across from land reserved for the Presbyterian Church. Work on Primrose Cottage began in January 1839, and Eliza and her children moved into the two-story white clapboard, New England-style home in August of that year. Roswell King later moved into the house with his daughter and lived there until his death.[6]

Barrington King chose the site for his home carefully. Built on six acres on the highest point in the area and directly across from the town square, the Greek revival mansion with fourteen fluted columns and a porch extending on three sides had a commanding view of the village. From the captain's walk on the roof, he could see the mill, Vickery Creek and the Chattahoochee River in the distance. A circular drive bordered by cedars led from the street down to a handsome, tall, white, arched gate inscribed with the name "Barrington Hall."

A reporter from the *Atlanta Journal* described the estate in 1923:

> The tall white columns, glimpsed through the dark green of cedar foliage, the wide veranda encircling the house, the stately silence engendered by the century old oaks evoke Thomas Nelson Page's Ole Virginia. The atmosphere of dignity, peace, and courtesy that was the soul of the Old South breathes from this old mansion, as it stands at the end of a long walk, bordered by old-fashioned flowers.

The reporter was none other than Margaret Mitchell, and it has often been suggested that the lovely Barrington Hall may very well have served as the inspiration for the legendary Tara.[7]

King persuaded an old friend, Major James Stephens Bulloch, to join his new settlement. Bulloch, his wife Martha Stewart Elliott Bulloch, six children, and four of their slaves left their home in Savannah in the spring of 1838 and set out on the 300-mile journey to Roswell. The Bulloch family joined the Kings in the castle until their

Completed circa 1842, Barrington Hall was the home of Barrington King and Catherine Margaret Nephew King (courtesy the Library of Congress, Prints and Photographs Division, Historic American Building Survey, L.D. Andrew, photographer, 1936).

home was finished. Inspired by the ancient Greek Parthenon, Bulloch built his beloved Bulloch Hall with four towering columns and an immense front verandah on a point west of the park overlooking Willeo Creek and the valley beyond. It was in this grand home that James and Martha's daughter, Mittie Bulloch, married Theodore Roosevelt Sr. on December 22, 1853.[8]

John Dunwody, a coastal planter from Liberty County, arrived next with his wife and their six children. John's wife, Jane Bulloch Dunwody, was the sister of Major Bulloch and they decided to build their home on land adjoining her brother's property. The house, a near twin of Bulloch Hall, burned to the ground on the night of the housewarming. A new home was built a few years later in a similar style and re-christened Phoenix Hall symbolizing its rise from the ashes. The home was most often referred to as Dunwody Hall until after the Civil War, when a subsequent owner changed the name to Mimosa Hall in reference to the numerous mimosa trees in the garden.[9]

Archibald Smith and his wife, Anne Magill Smith, came from Camden County, Georgia, in 1838 and settled in the nearby community of Lebanon before moving to Roswell. Although participants in the manufacturing experiment at Roswell, the Smiths were a simpler, less pretentious family. Their simple but spacious farmhouse was

Bulloch Hall, completed circa 1840, was the home of James Stephens Bulloch and Martha Stewart Elliott Bulloch. Their daughter, Mittie Bulloch, married Theodore Roosevelt Sr. in Bulloch Hall on December 22, 1853 (courtesy the Library of Congress, Prints and Photographs Division, Historic American Building Survey, Branan Sanders, photographer, 1934).

completed after the other homes and was set back some distance, a mile north of town, from the Greek revival mansions of the Kings, the Bullochs and the Dunwodys. Distance wasn't the only thing that set the Smith family apart. The Smiths' youngest son implied that some of the founding families were not always as religious as they might first appear. According to Archibald, Jr., "They [the Colony] proposed to keep the devil out of the town but most of them were willing for him to have a cat hole in the back door. Father did not know of the cat hole arrangement and tried to keep him [the devil] out altogether. This made for trouble." It's not clear what Archie is referring to, but it does make for interesting speculation.[10]

Religion played a central role in the lives of Roswell's first citizens, who were devout Presbyterians, although perhaps not as devout in practice as the Smith family might have preferred. The Roswell Presbyterian Church was established in 1839, the same year that the Roswell Manufacturing Company opened its doors for business. The first church services were held in Roswell's daughter's home at Primrose Cottage, but plans for a proper church building were soon underway.[11]

Mimosa Hall, completed circa 1847, was the home of John Dunwody and Jane Bulloch Dunwody. This house was originally called Phoenix Hall or Dunwody Hall but was renamed Mimosa Hall after the Civil War in reference to the numerous mimosa trees in the surrounding garden (courtesy the Library of Congress, Prints and Photographs Division, Historic American Building Survey, L.D. Andrew, photographer, 1936).

Completed in 1840, the Roswell Presbyterian Church occupied a prominent site on land donated by the King family. Described by a King family descendant as a "sentinel" on the "brow of a hill," the church, designed and built by Willis Ball, reflected the classic Greek revival form of architecture so popular with Ball, with four large columns and pedimented gables. An iron ship's bell, a gift from members of a Savannah church, hung in the short square steeple. Modeled after New England meeting houses, the interior of the church held box pews, a raised pulpit, and a gallery for the slave members in order that they might worship with, albeit physically apart from, their owners.[12]

In April 1839 the members of the colony invited Reverend Nathaniel Alpheus Pratt, pastor of the First Presbyterian Church in Darien, to become their pastor and to assist them in organizing the new church. Pratt, who was married to Roswell's daughter Catherine King Pratt, would serve in Roswell as pastor until his death in 1879. Directly across from the church, a gracious three-story Georgian colonial home was built for the Reverend and Mrs. Pratt. Although original plans for the home called for a clapboard structure with a design similar to Bulloch Hall, the wood caught fire two days before the construction began, and all the timber was burned. Pratt decided against using lumber the second time around. Testing the clay from a nearby creek, Pratt found the bricks, hand molded by slaves, to be of good quality, and Great Oaks became the first residence built entirely of hardened Georgia clay. Pratt's slaves tended the surrounding fields planted with corn, wheat and sorghum.[13]

The cornerstone of the colony, the church held its members to high moral standards. In July 1842 the minister of the Lebanon Baptist Church and Reverend Pratt met with a small group of villagers from both Lebanon and Roswell to form the Washington Total Abstinence Society, its members pledging "not to drink any Spirituous or Malt Liquors, wine or cider." Apparently some members found the requirement a bit too stringent, and the pledge was amended to exclude wine and cider in December of that year. The list of members included the names of both servants and masters. One year later, the society consisted of 295 members; 151 white males, 102 white females and 42 colored.[14]

The church members committed themselves to the "fostering of education" and constructed a school in 1838 to see to the educational needs of the colony's children. Built on church property, the two-room log academy was replaced by a brick building with shuttered windows and a Greek revival style portico after the church sanctuary was built in 1840. The school operated sporadically as a free school until it was deeded over to the town in the late 1870s. It seems that the school frequently suffered from a shortage of teachers, and there were several periods when the school was not in operation.[15]

Roswell King died on February 15, 1844, less than ten years after his arrival. Those last ten years had been perhaps the most rewarding of his life. A pioneer and a visionary, King brought an aristocracy and an experiment in domestic industry to a land of Indians and small farmers. He watched as his town grew and prospered and he lived long enough to see his dreams of dignified mansions and grand churches materialize before his eyes. Still, his crowning achievement, at least to Roswell King, was very likely the success of his cotton mill. Far ahead of his time, when few men were willing to take the risk, Roswell King proved that such a venture could succeed and prosper. Perhaps King's greatest legacy was the Roswell Manufacturing Company.

3

Roswell Mills

*That is exactly what the Southern factory almost invariably was, a plantation,
essentially indistinguishable in organization from the familiar plantation of the
cotton fields.*

— W.J. Cash, *The Mind of the South*

There were few cotton mills in Georgia when Roswell King began clearing the
land for his factory in the mid–1830s. The textile industry was not entirely new to the
South, but most of the early factories had been small affairs, producing primarily for
local use. A number of Northern industrialists had come south to build commercial
mills, but most Southern men clung fervently to their agricultural ways, leaving the
fledgling textile business to the transplanted Yankees.

The most ideal locations for cotton mills were beside the swift waters and along
the steep banks of streams in the upper Piedmont. Vickery Creek seemed the perfect
site for King's dream of a large textile mill in North Georgia. Here were all the necessary resources: cheap white labor from among the hard-pressed farm families, plentiful raw materials and an endless supply of waterpower. King had the means and
determination to see his manufacturing experiment succeed. The Roswell Manufacturing Company would be one of the first and largest commercial mills in Georgia, and
its success would inspire others throughout the state.

By 1840, one year after the Roswell Manufacturing Company began operation,
cotton mills had gained greater importance in the South, and there were nineteen textile mills in Georgia alone. This manufacturing trend echoed throughout the southern
states, and another industrialist, William Gregg, built one of the largest and most modern cotton mills in South Carolina during the late 1840s.[1]

Still, the fear of and distaste for industrialism would keep others away, at least until
after the Civil War. Concerned about the impact of industry on their agricultural and slave-
based dominance of the southern economy and society, Southern conservatives perceived
industrialism as a threat to what they believed was a superior Southern civilization.

Dependent on waterpower, 19th century textile mills were located near rivers, often in remote and undeveloped settings. The isolation of these mills did little to attract workers, and mill owners found it necessary to provide housing in order to draw operatives to their establishments. This would be especially true in Roswell, located in an area of scattered farms and small settlements, miles away from the next town.

Roswell King's position as manager of Butler's plantations had well prepared him for the day-to-day operations of overseeing a mill village. In truth, there was very little difference between the two tasks. The owners of the mill village controlled every aspect of the worker's life, just as the planters controlled the lives of their slaves. The company owned the cottages the workers lived in, the streets the houses stood on and the stores where the workers obtained their food and clothing. The operatives obeyed company temperance rules and worked long hours under the watchful eyes of strict overseers. The major difference was that the authority in the company was vested in a number of stockholders rather than an individual. Still, the stockholders had little to do with the daily operations, and the head of the mill typically had practical control of the corporation itself. Of course, there was one other important difference; the mill workers were free. On the other hand, their freedom often worked to their disadvantage. Mill owners had no vested interest in their workers, unlike the planters who had invested large sums of money in their human property. Mill owners, therefore, did not need to concern themselves with the health and well-being of their workers, for, unlike slaves, workers could be more easily dismissed and replaced.

Mill villages were paternalistic by design, sometimes to the benefit of the mill worker, most often to the benefit of the mill owner. Paternalism has been defined as a "policy or practice of governing or treating people in a fatherly way, especially by providing for them without giving them rights or responsibilities." By having his workers close by and dependent on him for all necessities, the mill owner maintained a captive labor force and was able to control the behavior of the operatives both inside and outside the workplace.[2]

Allegedly motivated by benevolent concerns, many factory owners claimed they were alleviating the suffering of the "ignorant, half-fed, ill-clothed" poor whites. At the same time, these benefactors paid low wages, often below the cost of living, for a day's work in the mills that ran from daybreak until dark. There were isolated cases of men such as Robert Owen and William Gregg who were dedicated to the betterment of their employees. More often than not, however, the motivations had far more to do with increased profits than with any humanitarian concerns.[3]

Based on his success at the New Lanark Mills in Scotland, Robert Owen emerged as a leader of social and education reform in the early 1800s. A generous and benevolent man, Owen was driven by a desire to benefit humanity, not only though productivity and profits, but also by bettering the lot of his employees. He instituted policies at the mill in Scotland that dramatically improved the quality of life for his workers. He raised the minimum age of employment, reduced the number of working hours, and founded the first infant school. The operation was a remarkable success, and educational and social reformers, dignitaries, statesmen and philanthropists journeyed from all over the world to see Owen's great social experiment. Over 20,000 guests visited the New Lanark factory in the ten years between 1815 and 1825.[4]

Owen's American counterpart, William Gregg, laid the cornerstone for his Graniteville factory in the spring of 1846, after a tour of prosperous cotton mills in the North. Gregg hoped to build a cotton mill and surrounding village that would be an object lesson to the South in terms of social reform and profitability. Unlike the mill owners in Roswell, and most mill owners throughout the South, Gregg placed a high premium on education, and made sure that a school for the mill children was one of the first buildings constructed. He is credited with starting the first compulsory education system in the South, and parents of children between the ages of six and twelve were required to keep their children in school. His workers gave up many freedoms, but in return they lived in handsome Gothic-style cottages, received cash wages, attended their own schools and churches, and had access to medical services. Gregg's brand of paternalism was indeed fatherly, humane, and designed to benefit the individual and society as a whole.[5]

It is not clear if Roswell King shared the humanitarian motives that inspired men like Robert Owen and William Gregg, but one thing is certain: King was eager to build his mill. Although it has been suggested that King's primary motive for moving north was to provide a retreat from the sickly climate of the coast, it was the mill that captured King's immediate attention. Before the fine houses and churches, even before most of the colony arrived, King set to work constructing his cotton factory. A page torn from a ledger in King's handwriting is entitled, "Expenses On and Near Vickery Creek since September 1835," with the first entry recording an expense for "building road, dam and race." Slaves brought from the coast constructed the road that ran down the steep slopes to the creek and provided most of the hard labor necessary to build the first mill.[6]

A 30-foot-high dam of logs, rock, and mud was erected with wooden flumes directing the water from the dam to the mill wheel, providing the power for the machinery. The water also powered the sawmill that cut wood for homes and offices. A kiln, constructed to supply brick for the various mill buildings, remained in operation for the next 50 years.[7]

Built into the hillside, the cotton mill was a long, narrow building of handmade brick shaped from the red clay that lined the stream. The imposing structure which stood just below the dam measured 48 feet by 88 feet and consisted of four stories, with the first story level with the creek bank and the fourth floor opening onto a village street. The picking and packing work of the mill was done on the top floor. The cotton was carded on the third floor, spun on the second and woven on the first, the looms being placed on the solid granite foundation floor to avoid excessive wear on the building by the motion of the massive machines.[8]

The cotton mill was in full operation by late 1839 and was incorporated in December as the Roswell Manufacturing Company. The stockholders of record were Roswell

King, his sons Barrington and Ralph, John Dunwody, James S. Bulloch, Henry Atwood, and the heirs of Bayard E. Hand. The charter also granted the corporation the privilege of erecting other factories for the spinning and weaving of cotton or wool. Barrington King was appointed as agent, James S. Bulloch as chairman of the stockholders, and John Dunwody as secretary.[9]

Henry Merrell, a textile manufacturer from New York, was hired as the first assistant agent in 1839. The factory building was complete by the time he arrived, but the foundation of the mill was not substantial enough to support the immense brick building. After replacing the portions of the foundation that had cracked and buckled with hewn granite blocks, Merrell began supervising the installation of the new machinery.[10]

Merrell settled into the community at Roswell and married Archibald Smith's sister-in-law in 1841. Merrell had few dealings with Roswell King, as Barrington King was in charge of operations by the time Merrell arrived. Although King was in his mid 70s, Merrell described him as quite active with a "great many good ideas" and "youthful in his feelings." But Merrell didn't seem particularly fond of the elder King and found him "opinionated." Some of his comments regarding Roswell King are vague and mysterious and leave much room for conjecture. When discussing his first year at the factory Merrell described Roswell King as someone "who was not my friend, at least he did not speak to me when we met." Elsewhere he writes, "For a long time he [Roswell King] did not speak to me because I had differed from him in some opinion.... I had reason, all the time, to think he bore me no ill will — but the contrary. He was by no means a Christian man, at that time, but found he was possessed of generous impulses."[11]

Merrell found Barrington more to his liking. "Barrington King, Esq., was very much of a man and gentleman. Every thing about him was firm and steady like his handwriting. He ruled his white family and his servants absolutely, but with dignity and a pleasant humor." It would seem that King ruled the company with an equally firm hand. Noting that King

Barrington King (1798–1866). Son of Roswell King and co-founder of the Roswell Colony, Barrington served as president of the Roswell Manufacturing Company until his death in 1866 (courtesy the Roswell Historical Society).

and Merrell "came to high words" on several occasions, Merrell added, "I have no doubt I had to encounter the roughest side of his character, for at the factory he was acting as agent for others, and with a severe idea of his duty."[12]

Merrell took on more and more responsibility, but received only one raise during his employment and that during his first year. He was not offered any additional increases to compensate for the increased workload, and Merrell claimed he was too proud to ask. Overworked and underpaid, with no chance for advancement or promotion, Merrell left the mills in 1845 to operate the Cutright Mill in Green County, Georgia, with his brother-in-law, George Camp, taking his place as Barrington's assistant agent. Still, Merrell was proud of his association with the Roswell Manufacturing Co., boasting that the factory's "machinery [was] of the latest improvements, its management on humane and Christian principles, and its great success, formed an era from which others took a fresh start."[13]

Roswell King's manufacturing venture at Roswell was an overwhelming success. Increasing demand for shirting, rope and yarn led Barrington King to recommend further expansion of the textile mill. After adopting plans to build a second mill and improve the original factory, a committee was appointed in 1852 to procure land and water titles for the construction of the new mill. The second factory, a new dam and a machine shop were built in 1854. The new four-story brick building measured 140 feet by 53 feet, its machinery powered by a sixteen-foot overshot iron wheel.[14]

Two of Barrington's sons constructed a moderately sized woolen mill in the mid–1850s. James King had studied the manufacturing business in the north, serving for two and one-half years in the shop of Rogers, Ketchum and Grosvenor at Paterson, New Jersey. On his return, he and his brother, Thomas Edward King, built their woolen factory below the cotton mills, near the mouth of Vickery Creek. The Ivy Woolen Mill produced jeans, jerseys and cassimeres, and most notably, a particularly well-made cloth called "Roswell Grey."[15]

Dividends of 22 percent in 1844 testified to the success of the Roswell mills and inspired others to follow in their footsteps. Textile mills began to spring up all over the state and soon Georgia was proclaimed "The New England of the South." By 1848 there were 32 cotton mills in Georgia supporting over six thousand operatives and their families, and two years later, the state ranked first in the South in textile manufacturing. The phenomenal success of the textile industry throughout the state prompted J.D. DeBow, superintendent of the sixth census and leading statistician of the South, to declare in 1855 that Georgia well deserved the sobriquet of the "Empire State of the South." Five years later, Georgia possessed nearly 21 percent of all cotton manufacturing establishments in the South, but despite the tremendous growth, Georgia remained predominantly agricultural.[16]

There were a number of reasons for the success of the textile industry in the south: nearness to the raw product, ever-present waterpower, and an abundant labor force.

Roswell Cotton Mills. Early wood engraving (circa 1853) of the Roswell Manufacturing Company. A portion of the first cotton mill can be seen in the foreground at the left. The second cotton mill is on the far right (courtesy the Kenan Research Center at the Atlanta History Center).

However, it was the low wages paid the workers that accounted, in large part, for the high profits. Early mills owed their success almost entirely to the exploitation of labor:

> *We're low, we're low — we're very, very low —*
> *Yet from our fingers glide*
> *The silken flow and the robes that glow,*
> *Round the limbs of the Sons of pride;*
> *And what we get, and what we give,*
> *We know, and we know our share*
> *We're not too low the Cloth to weave,*
> *but too low the Cloth to wear.*
> [From "Song of the Lower Classes"
> June 3, 1876, *The Socialist*, Ernest Jones[7]

The Roswell Manufacturing Company was blessed with a cheap and plentiful source of labor. The Georgia gold rush had brought hundreds of prospectors to North

Georgia in the late 1820s and 1830s. Since the Cherokee owned most of the land where gold was discovered, the Georgia legislature made immediate plans to remove the Indians. Cobb County was laid out from the Cherokee purchase and the land raffled off in the lottery of 1832 and 1833. Most of the land in the county was distributed as 40-acre gold lots and early settlers hurried to claim their territory. But when dreams of gold turned to naught, many found themselves on poor, unproductive farmland. Those with established homes and plantations elsewhere had no wish to be pioneers in Georgia's last frontier and most disposed of the land quickly and cheaply. The gold lots could be purchased for ten or twenty dollars and sometimes swapped for a horse.[18]

It was generally poorer people, seeking to better their conditions, who bought a great number of the inexpensive lots. Many invested everything they had in the forty-acre parcels and soon others began referring to them as the "forty-acre people." The families lived for the most part on self-sustaining farms, growing their own food, spinning and weaving their own clothing and handling but little money. The farms were located in a thinly settled, uncultivated region offering few economic opportunities. Even if there had been abundant crops, the rugged forested hills and poor roads would have made it difficult to get the produce to market. From these small struggling farms would come many of the Roswell mill workers.[19]

Young women and children made up a large part of the work force in the Roswell factories. In the homes throughout North Georgia, as well as homes in the villages, towns and big cities across the land, women had been involved in the production of cloth, long before the first textile mills appeared on American soil. Almost all of the yarn produced in the 18th century was made by women in the home. Women carded the cotton with hand carders and spun the fibers into yarn on their own spinning wheels, a staple in almost every household. The very first factories used traditional hand-powered spinning wheels, but it was not long before powered machinery revolutionized the textile industry. Soon the entire process from carding to weaving was done by machine, and as the production moved from home to factory, so too did many of the women.[20]

The mill owners welcomed women and children into the factories. Untrained and inexperienced workers could operate the simple spinning machines and powered looms with relative ease. More importantly, women and children would work for lower wages. As a result, textile manufacturing was one of the few industries that routinely employed more women than men. This would be no less true at Roswell. In 1860, women made up more than 70 percent of the workers over fifteen years of age.[21]

Although the wages for women were very low, millwork allowed the operatives to earn at least enough to be self-supporting. There were few employment opportunities available for women in the first half of the 19th century and most of those that did exist did not provide anything close to a living wage, especially for unskilled and uneducated women whose only hope of employment outside the home was domestic service. Factory work provided women with a measure of economic independence they could not find elsewhere, independence that would become increasingly important with the outbreak of the Civil War. A number of North Georgia farmers moved their loved ones closer to the mills so that every able-bodied member of the family could find employment in the factories while the farmer prepared to march off to war.[22]

Although children also became wage earners by virtue of their employment in the mills, the pay was so low that it was not enough to cover their own support. It is not known at what age children went to work in the Roswell factories. The 1840 census does not list occupations and both the 1850 census and 1860 census lists them only for workers over 15 years of age. But it was quite common for boys and girls as young as ten to be employed by Southern factories in the years prior to the Civil War.[23]

Whenever possible the mill owners recruited and hired entire families, the larger the better. More children meant more workers. Women and older children operated the machines in the carding, spinning and weaving departments, while men worked as clerks, managers, overseers and mechanics, positions requiring a certain amount of training. Experienced overseers and mechanics were always in great demand and usually the highest paid, for it was their skill and proficiency that kept the factory running smoothly.[24]

Southern factories tended to employ few slaves. Most factory owners believed it was far more practical and economical to employ poor whites. Englishman James Buckingham visited Georgia mills in 1842 and wrote about his findings in his book on the slave states. Paying particular attention to the mills at Augusta and Athens, Buckingham discovered that the labor force in the Augusta mills was composed almost entirely of poor white families, while the employees of the three cotton factories in Athens were divided equally between slaves and poor whites who worked side by side with little difficulty. The slaves were as easily trained as white operatives, but the mill owners complained that the slaves were more expensive to employ. The slaveholders hired them out at the same wages paid to whites — then seven dollars per month. In addition the mill owners had to feed and shelter the slaves, while whites were forced to fend for themselves on the wages they received from the mill. Local mill owners hoped that immigration would bring sufficient white people into the Augusta area so that they would no longer have to depend on slave labor.[25]

The mill owners in Columbus, Georgia, relied exclusively on white labor, hoping to render the factory work a more "genteel employment" for the white operatives. Sir Charles Lyell, a British geologist, visiting the Columbus factories in 1846, found this policy somewhat ironic since many of the "colored" mechanics were the most highly skilled artisans in the region.[26]

In rural areas, like Roswell, the white labor force was abundant, cheap and unlike the slaves, workers were easy to replace. Occasionally servants or freed Negroes were employed as janitors or hired for other menial tasks, but they rarely held the production jobs, traditionally reserved for white labor. According to the 1860 manufacturing census, the Roswell factories employed three slaves that year, but that was the exception rather than the rule. Throughout the South, uneducated and unskilled white women and children represented the majority of the labor force.[27]

Southern factories generally imported skilled workers from the north. In the early

1840s Henry Merrell was responsible for overseeing the mill operations and hiring many of the mill employees. One of his first duties was to hire experienced overseers. He encouraged several of his friends from New York to come south to work for the Roswell Manufacturing Company and called upon his brother-in-law, George Hull Camp, to fill a vacancy in the mill store.[28]

Later attempts to find overseers and mechanics proved much more difficult. Merrell looked to the young men of Southern birth but was disappointed in these efforts. As he saw it there were two sources to draw from, the sons of gentlemen and the factory boys themselves. But he found that the sons of gentlemen, including the "rich and poor, educated and ignorant," believed labor was disreputable. Merrell claimed that some of the young gentlemen from the low country informed him that they had "never seen a white man do a hand's turn of work." According to Merrell, "even the overseers and Negro drivers rode on horseback and were exempt from labor."[29]

The sons of Barrington King had some interest in carrying on the family business. Charles, the oldest, worked in the factory after school and according to Merrell had a "natural turn for mechanics." However, he went away to college, studied theology and became a Presbyterian minister. James King went to New Jersey to study the manufacturing business, and Thomas King learned the business in the office. Young Barrington pursued a different course, going north to learn shipbuilding, and later turning to the study of homeopathic medicine. The sons of Reverend Pratt and the sons of John Dunwody turned their attention to trade and mechanical affairs, but most of the aristocratic class, determined to be leaders, refused to work in subordinate positions. Nor would they submit to an apprenticeship of seven years as Merrell had done.[30]

Merrell was forced to look to the rank and file of his own operatives, those he referred to as "the lower class of white people at the South," a statement which bespoke his own prejudices. Merrell found that many of the young men had enough "practicable ability of the very highest style," but their lack of education and religious training "diluted and vitiated the whole."[31]

Although Merrell claimed he found his experiment only "tolerably" successful, the owners had considerable success in hiring and training their own operatives for skilled and supervisory positions in the years after Merrell left. By the early 1860s, at least six of the overseers were local men. Still, the majority of men in managerial positions were northern or European born.[32]

Roswell's mill village was located on a ridge known as Factory Hill, overlooking the mill and Vickery Creek. Compact rows of small single-story, single-family detached cottages lined each side of Mill Street. Most of the dwellings reflected a modified New England salt box design, several with central chimneys. The simple but functional houses were adequate for shelter but lacked the charm and ornamentation of the Graniteville cottages.[33]

Two apartment-style buildings were built to house factory employees, most likely the mill managers and their families. Known simply as The Bricks, one building contained four units, and the other had six. Each two-story apartment had a kitchen and living room on the first floor, and a bedroom on the second overlooking the creek.[34]

The company store was essential to the operation of the mill village. Unlike a number of New England factories and Gregg's South Carolina factory, the workers at Roswell and many other Southern mills were paid in scrip redeemable only at the company store. Merrell believed this system was absolutely necessary for their success. "By means of the store, we kept our hands close at their work & controlled labor that could not have been steadily controlled by wages in money. With the money, our hands would have spent their time, a great part of it, in straggling many miles away to make their purchases." By paying them in supplies, the owners were able to make a handsome profit while keeping the hands under their influence, a system quite similar to the "forced isolation" practiced by Roswell King on Pierce Butler's plantations. Merrell concluded that the business, "in that frontier location, could not have gone on without the store any more than a wheel without a hub."[35]

Paternalistic practices as evidenced by the payment of wages in company scrip were commonplace in the Roswell mills, and while these policies certainly paved the way for higher profits, they were generally viewed as beneficial to the welfare of the workers. Sometime after Barrington King's death, a family member described him as a man of the strictest of integrity. "He [Barrington] exacted the best from his hands in the mills and in return he made their welfare his earnest concern, protecting, advising, and *controlling* [italics author's] his people; a Christian gentleman of the 'old school,' using his power for the good of all."[36]

Although some of the mill villages provided schools and teachers for the younger children, attendance was generally not encouraged or enforced. Critics claimed that the cotton manufacturers had little interest in educating the boys and girls living in mill villages for fear they would be lost to the mill. The children represented an important labor force, entering the mills as young as ten years of age. There was no mill school in Roswell, and it is doubtful that any of the mill children attended the academy owned and operated by the Roswell Presbyterian Church. Archie Smith noted that the only schooling many of the village children received was in the church Sunday school. On the other hand, sons and daughters of the Roswell nobility went away to school or attended special classes held by Reverend Pratt in preparation for entering the universities. Whether it was due to lack of teachers or lack of encouragement, little attention was given to educating the children of the Roswell mill workers in 1860. While the census lists 231 children between the ages of seven and fourteen, only 33 attended school. Only two of these were children of factory hands.[37]

In all fairness, this was not unique to Roswell. The mill village in Roswell was probably no better and no worse than the traditional mill villages throughout the South. There were exceptions. William Gregg not only provided schools for the mill village at Graniteville, but he also fined the workers if their children did not attend. Unfortunately most mill owners never demonstrated that level of concern for the welfare of their workers.[38]

> *Ah! leave my harp and me alone*
> *My grief thou may'st not share,*
> *Responsive to its plaintive tone*
> *Will flow refreshing tears.*
>
> *Far from the factory's deaf'ning sound,*
> *From all its noise and strife,*
> *Would that my years might run their rounds*
> *In sweet retired life.*
>
> *But, if I still must wend my way,*
> *Uncheered by hope's sweet song,*
> *God grant that in the mills, a day*
> *May be blest, "Ten Hours" long.*
> [Untitled / anonymous factory worker
> *Voice of Industry*, February 20, 1846[39]]

Little is known about the actual working conditions in the Roswell mills, but the practices varied little from mill to mill. Women usually entered the mills at a young age, often as young as ten, and retired early, reaching the peak of their earning power before 30. The nature of much of the work required agility, nimble fingers and good eyesight and was not particularly difficult for a young girl, but long hours and poor working conditions exacted a heavy toll, and the young women grew old before their time. The female worker of 35 or 40 found her earning capacity decreasing rapidly. Forced to give up their jobs when they could not keep up with the physical demands, relatively young women were replaced with younger children. It was not uncommon for parents in their 40s to find themselves entirely dependent on the labor of their young children.[40]

Children worked the same hours and under the same conditions as the adult operatives and rarely saw the light of day in the long winter months. On their feet from morning to night, older children tended the machines and pieced together broken threads, while the younger ones performed jobs more suited for little fingers. Children oiled and cleaned the machinery, changed bobbins, removed loose threads from inside the moving parts and cleared accidental obstructions, since their small hands could fit into narrow places that adult hands could not.[41]

Children, in particular, had to be careful in working with the various machines. The work was not strenuous but the machines were dangerous with their exposed belts and pulleys, and the young workers had to be quick and alert. Flying spindles and broken belts frequently caused painful injuries to the eyes and face. Long hair proved particularly hazardous and women and young girls occasionally lost hair and scalp in the cogs and wheels. Although few of the injuries proved fatal, many led to permanent disability. Fingers, hands and even arms were sometimes caught up in the belting of the unforgiving machines, especially towards the end of the day when workers were tired and less observant.[42]

In addition to the dangers posed by the machinery, factories were breeding grounds for disease and other related health problems. Working twelve to fourteen hours per day, six days per week, men, women and children spent most of their waking lives in the gray light of glazed windows and poorly ventilated rooms, crowded with workers, amid flying lint and the deafening sounds of the machines. The small windows in the thick brick walls admitted little light and were rarely opened for fear that the cotton yarns would break in the slightest draft.

Without proper ventilation, the hot, humid, lint-filled air, heavy with the pungent odor of oil, was not safe to breathe. New workers often complained of feeling sick during the first few weeks in the factory. The initial reaction to factory pollution became known as mill fever. Many workers eventually became sick with tuberculosis and other respiratory diseases. The most common ailment associated with textile workers was byssinosis, a pulmonary affliction caused by the inhalation of cotton dust. More commonly known as brown lung after the brown dust of the leaves surrounding the cotton balls, the disease often lead to shortness of breath, coughing and permanent breathing problems. With continued exposure brown lung could become totally disabling and ultimately fatal. Operatives frequently complained of bad air and flying lint, with many of the female workers dipping snuff, believing that it would keep the lint out of their throats.[43]

Contagious diseases like the measles swept through the factories like wildfire. Production at the Roswell mills was nearly brought to a standstill after an outbreak in 1848 that nearly crippled the factory for three months. Barrington wrote his daughter in February 1848, "The measles are now on Factory Hill, about 100 children out of the factory, which interferes with our operatives."[44]

When James Buckingham visited the Georgia mills in 1842, he found that the poor working conditions often led to sickness and death. He described the workers as "miserably pale and unhealthy." Buckingham was told that the workers were "short-lived" and that they often fell victim to the first symptoms of fevers and dysenteries in the autumn, "sweeping numbers of them off by death."[45]

Fevers, dysentery, measles, lung disease, eyestrain, hearing loss, varicose veins from standing on their feet for long hours, and the potential for serious injury plagued the workers toiling in these factories without adequate sunshine, fresh air or sufficient rest. The sick and injured generally received no sick pay or medical assistance and frequently lost their jobs when the mill boss hired someone to take their place. It was 1911 before most states passed legislation requiring industries to pay compensation to injured employees.[46]

The conditions in most 19th century textile factories cried out for reform, but it would be some years before anything was done to alleviate the suffering of the factory workers. During the late 1800s, it was not uncommon for children as young as six to be employed in factories throughout the country. Overworked, underpaid and victim to unhealthful and unsafe working conditions, factory workers would have to wait until the early years of the 20th century before legislation was passed to protect their health and well-being.

Often viewed as philanthropic enterprises, textile mills provided desperately needed jobs. It is another thing to say that they were just and humane. Still, it was factory life in the 19th century and accepted as such. Uneducated, unskilled, paid in scrip, with every aspect of their lives under the control of the factory, the mill workers in Roswell lived lives little better than that of slaves. In many ways they were victims long before the Union army set foot on the red clay soil of Georgia.

4

Roswell Grey (1861–1863)

Hurrah! Hurrah! Hurrah! Hurrah! Hurrah! One for each sovereign State and independent Sovereignty. It was to day Resolved that Georgia has a right and should secede from the Union; passed at 4 o'clock P.M. by 35 majority. Our cannon are proclaiming it to the world.
—Thomas E. King, January 18, 1861

The election of Abraham Lincoln in 1860 by a purely sectional vote aroused the fears of Southern whites who believed the Republican Party was bent on destroying the Southern way of life. In public meetings throughout the state, Georgia citizens adopted resolutions urging the legislature to provide for the defense of the State "against the aggression to be feared" from the Republican president and party that would come to power in March 1861. The legislature responded by appropriating $1,000,000 for military defense, authorizing the acceptance of 10,000 troops by the governor, and the purchase of 1,000 rifles and carbines for coastal defense. The Georgia lawmakers called for an election of delegates on the first Wednesday of January 1861 to a convention that would determine the course of the state in the emergency.[1]

On December 20, 1860, news that South Carolina had adopted an ordinance of secession from the United States was telegraphed to cities and towns across Georgia and met with the firing of cannon, the ringing of bells and the lighting of bonfires. Volunteer companies of the state, organized under acts of the legislature, enthusiastically offered their services to the governor even as new companies were being formed.[2]

Georgia followed South Carolina's lead on January 18, passing a resolution to secede by a narrow margin of 166 to 130. The Ordinance of Secession was adopted the following day by a less divided vote of 289 to 89, effectively severing all ties to the Union. After the vote, the president of the convention, former governor George W. Crawford, informed the delegates that it was his "privilege and pleasure to declare that the state of Georgia was now free, sovereign, and independent." News of the momentous decision was received with cheers and applause from the great crowd assembled outside, while cannon thundered a salute.[3]

Six weeks later when the convention resumed in Savannah, the members ratified the Confederate Constitution on March 16, making Georgia the fifth state to join the new Confederacy; following South Carolina, Mississippi, Alabama and Florida. The convention adopted a new state constitution, authorized the issue of treasury notes and bonds for public defense, transferred the control of military operations as well as forts and arms to the new union, and provided for the organization, arming and training of the militia.[4]

Young men caught up in the surging patriotic tide rushed to enlist with heads and hearts filled with romantic notions of glory. More companies were offered than could initially be used, and many new recruits found themselves without arms. But with or without guns, the would-be warriors drilled on the town squares and village greens, in large cities, small towns and rural villages, preparing themselves for battle.

The opening salvos at Fort Sumter in April 1861 inspired another wave of enlistments. Able-bodied men from Roswell immediately volunteered for what most believed would be only a short but glorious struggle. Only five years earlier, a sermon delivered by Reverend Pratt on the "Perils of Dissolution of the Union" had brought such praise that the sermon had been published and widely circulated. But faced with the invasion of Yankee soldiers, Roswell men immediately rose to the occasion. Barrington King complained that the early enlistments had left the factories short of help in the offices. "All our young folk say they can stand it no longer and must go to defend their country — we old ones must work the harder to support our men on the battlefield."[5]

Three local units proudly bore the Roswell name: the Roswell Guards organized in the spring of 1861, the Roswell Troopers raised in March 1862, and the Roswell Battalion, a local defense unit organized in June 1863. The founding families would all send sons to distant fields under the Roswell banner. Serving in various companies and capacities, the Kings, Bullochs, Pratts, Dunwodys and Smiths all made their stand for Southern independence.[6]

The first enlistees joined the Roswell Guards, a volunteer company organized by the popular and widely esteemed Thomas Edward King, fourth son of Barrington King. The unit was mustered into Confederate service on May 31, 1861 as Company H, 7th Georgia Infantry Regiment. Tom had been offered a position as colonel in the quartermaster's department but was eager for field service. Charles Dunwody and Hugh Proudfoot, son of the factory bookkeeper, joined along with a number of mill workers, all eager to do their part. James Barker, James Dodgen, John Gossett, John Kendley, James Rowland, Randolph Sherman, John Simmons, Benjamin F. Smith and Ananias Wallace, all workers in the Roswell factories, took up arms to fight side by side with the sons of the Roswell aristocracy, with three of the factory hands, Kendley, Sherman and Gossett, serving as non-commissioned officers. The members of the newly formed company drilled on the town square as they readied themselves for war.[7]

Tom King's wife, Marie, and his sister-in-law, Fannie, quickly fashioned a flag for

John Robert Kendley (1837–?). John was serving in the Roswell Battalion when his brothers and sisters were arrested and sent to Indiana (courtesy George and Elizabeth Kendley).

the men to carry with them into battle. Fannie cut up her crimson crape shawl and Marie sacrificed two of her dresses to furnish white satin and blue silk. A blue silk field was adorned with "R.G" in large white satin letters and eleven satin stars. Tom's brother James Roswell King made the staff, and Tom's mother took blue silk tassels off her dressing gown to finish the lovely handmade flag, which James presented to the members of the battalion upon their departure.[8]

Fannie King boasted of the unit in a letter to her sister on May 29, the day the Guards left for Atlanta on their way to Richmond. "The company is a fine one, not a man among it but is a splendid marksman tho' of course they are not drilled well yet, but under a good Captain, one they love, one they doat on as they do Tom, they will make splendid soldiers." After tearful good-byes to their wives, mothers and children, and a last look at the village, the untrained and untried soldiers in dashing new uniforms marched out of town with bands playing and colors flying.[9]

Sent north to join the Confederate forces in Virginia, the Roswell Guards came face to face with Yankee soldiers in the fighting at Manassas. Ordered up to support General Barnard Bee, they found Bee's Brigade routed and took the lead. After four hours of desperate fighting, Colonel Francis Bartow, commanding the 8th Georgia Infantry, was ordered to lead the 7th Georgia and 17th Virginia in a movement to capture the detachment of General William T. Sherman's battery causing so much injury to the Confederate troops. Taking heavy fire, Bartow was shot and killed, but the men pressed on, "standing our ground against fearful odds" and driving back the gunners from the ten-piece battery. Reinforcements enabled them to hold the advantage, but they were now under fire of "near ten thousand men" and the air was dense with flying bullets. Captain Tom was in the front line encouraging his troops when he was shot, the bullet shattering his ankle. Unable to stand, the young captain had to be carried to the rear.[10]

A story is told about King's departure from the field, which, if not true, was certainly believed to be true by those who knew him best. Breaking out in a fervent prayer for a Confederate victory as he was carried to the rear, King was overheard in his loud supplication by a company of South Carolinians who turned to stare. Spying a body of Yankee Zouaves nearby, King stopped his prayers long enough to roar, "Forward Boys," upon which the Confederates executed a gallant charge, capturing the position and driving the Yankees from the field.[11]

Thomas Edward King (1829–1863), son of Barrington King. Still recuperating from wounds received at Manassas, Captain Tom rode out to Chickamauga to fight for independence and the "freedom of Georgia." Tom and Brigadier General Preston Smith unwittingly rode out into the front of a detachment of the enemy, and both were mortally wounded (courtesy the Roswell Historical Society).

Southerners celebrated their first major victory after the Confederate soldiers routed the Union forces in the fierce fighting at Manassas. But for many in Roswell, the news of the glorious conquest was overshadowed by reports that the Guards had taken heavy casualties. Soldier and citizen alike now came face to face with the tragic consequences of war.

Charles Dunwody was seriously wounded during the battle, along with a number of other Roswell men including Abraham Padget, Joel Pickens, Joshua Stephens, Hezekiah Roberts, and factory worker Peter Cobb. Benjamin Smith and James W. Paden were killed in the battle and James Burton and Sergeant John Gossett, both fatally wounded, died a few weeks later. Jesse Scoles died of wounds sustained at Manassas while on his way back to Roswell in September. Tom King's brother, Joseph Henry, a private in the 8th Georgia Infantry, was also wounded in the fight, taking a bullet in the hip. Both Joseph and Tom were sent to a hospital in Richmond for medical attention.[12]

Captain Tom returned to Roswell to recuperate but refused to let his disability prevent him from doing all that he could to serve the cause. The war hero and newly elected mayor of Roswell directed his attention to the war on the home front. North Georgia was suffering from widespread food shortages as early as 1862, especially corn, an all-important staple. Tom wrote "Jeff Davis" in February, introducing himself as one of the "fortunates" who had the honor of teaching the Yankees the "Bull Run quick step." He wished to advise the Confederate president of the large number of distilleries in the area. These "gates of hell" were driving up the price of corn and causing a severe shortage. Tom warned, "Unless a stop is put to this criminal waste of the staff of life, it will soon be out of the power of the families of our volunteers to get any and there will be suffering." Georgia's governor Joseph Brown had similar concerns. Two weeks later on February 28, 1862, he issued a proclamation prohibiting distillation of spirits to conserve grain for other uses.[13]

Tom had hoped to return to his company, but it was a year before he could lay down his crutches, and even then he was unable to walk without a staff. His commission expired in May 1862, and he was dropped from the rolls of the Roswell Guards. Tom continued to look after the needs of the community and to aid the war effort as best he could. In addition to his responsibilities as mayor, King assisted the wives of deceased mill workers with their applications for Confederate pensions, acting as their power of attorney and providing letters of reference.[14]

Eagerly awaiting his return to the field, Tom followed the battles as best he could, scanning the newspapers for any news from the front. After learning of the heavy losses of local men killed "by the first fire in charging one of the rascals batterys" at the Battle of Second Manassas, Tom declared his hatred for the Yankees, promising to disinherit his sons if any one of them ever married one of those "she-devils." Southern born and firmly entrenched into the Southern way of life, Tom seemed to forget that Yankee blood coursed through his veins. Rejoicing over the victory that had been "dearly dearly bought," but deeply saddened by the casualties, Tom was moved to write, "Oh God what joys and sorrows are daily mingled in our cup of life. How much the more should we love our country."[15]

As Georgia prepared to enter the second year of war, Governor Joseph Brown warned, "These are not ordinary times. We are in the midst of a revolution." The Confederacy would need additional soldiers to continue the battle and in February 1862, President Jefferson Davis called for twelve additional regiments from Georgia before the 15th of March to serve for three years or the duration of war. The request for additional troops ended hopes that the terrible conflict would be short-lived.[16]

Brown was confident that enough volunteers would come forward to fill the twelve regiments before the appointed date, but made a final appeal to Southern wives and mothers. Expressing his belief that "even should there not be an immediate response," he could not believe that "the noble women of the state who have done so much for the cause would ever tolerate such delinquency."[17]

Once again men from Roswell responded enthusiastically to the call. In early March factory workers Daniel and George T. Hopkins, Joseph Mackey, and T.R. Parks enlisted in the Roswell Guards, along with a number of other local men. Other recruits joined the Roswell Troopers, Company E of the famed Cobb's Legion Cavalry, commanded by Barrington King's fifth son and namesake, Barrington Simeral King. King had enlisted in the cavalry division of Cobb's Legion in September 1861 and was given permission to raise a new company when the unit was reorganized in 1862. The company was composed of men from the towns of Lawrenceville and Roswell and included farmers, brick masons, blacksmiths, and a few men from the Roswell factories including James Netherland, John Owens, and George Ridings. Sixteen-year-old mill worker James Dodgen had been discharged from the Roswell Guards in December 1862 for being too young. Determined to fight under a Roswell banner, he enlisted in the Roswell Troopers six months later and served with the unit until the end of the war.[18]

As Brown predicted, Georgia met her quota and then some, raising thirteen regiments and three battalions by the 15th of March. The new recruits were trained at several camps of instruction, the "boot camps" of the Civil War. Many of their instructors were young cadets from Marietta who had studied the art of war at the renowned Georgia Military Institute, otherwise known as the West Point of Georgia.[19]

Built on a hill, less than a mile from the town square, the institute opened in 1851 under the direction of Colonel Arnoldus V. Brumby with seven cadets and a staff of three instructors. Two years later, the number of students had increased to 180 with a teaching staff of six. By the mid–1850s, the academy was attracting boys, not just from Georgia, but from most of the other Southern states as well. The institute continued to thrive, enrollment rising with the threat of hostilities, until students had to be turned away for lack of accommodations.[20]

The young men enrolled at GMI would prove invaluable to the state and to the Confederacy during the four years of the war. Cadets, employed as instructors and drillmasters, quickly whipped the raw recruits into shape. Students, eager to join the fight, left school in early 1861 and enlisted in the Confederate army. Others followed their example in the spring of 1862 in response to the call for additional troops. Some cadets may have enlisted to avoid the embarrassment of being labeled one of "Joe Brown's Pets," after Governor Brown exempted the GMI cadets from conscription. Several young men from Roswell's founding families attended school at GMI. A former student, Charles Pratt, son of the Roswell Presbyterian minister, served as drillmaster with the grade of second lieutenant at a camp of instruction. Barrington's youngest son Clifford left GMI in the summer of 1861 and secured a position on General William Hardee's staff, after finally persuading his father to let him leave his studies. And Archie

Smith, the youngest son of Archibald and Anne Smith, remained at the institute, later serving with the GMI Cadet Battalion when it was called to active duty in 1864.[21]

Recognizing that the war would bring a great demand for the cotton and woolen goods produced by the Roswell factories, James Roswell King, third son of Barrington King, remained at home in Roswell to oversee the operations of the Ivy Woolen Mill. James yearned to join the army, but with most of his brothers gone to war, James stayed behind to serve the Confederacy in the best way he could, by supervising the manufacture of the wool cloth so urgently needed to clothe Confederate soldiers.

Wartime demand gave rise to a great expansion of industry in Georgia. This proved particularly true in Atlanta, already a major industrial center as well a vital railroad depot and junction. After the Nashville Ordnance and Arsenal works was moved to Atlanta in February 1862, the "Gate City" quickly evolved into a chief manufacturing center, serving as the headquarters for the Confederate Quartermaster and Commissary departments in the lower South, as well as one of the most important supply depots of the Confederacy.[22]

It was not long before manufacturing establishments sprang up all over North Georgia, particularly those producing military supplies. Factories in Dalton and Athens manufactured muskets, pistols, bayonets, swords, canteens, knapsacks and shoes, while foundries in Rome made cannons and batteries. Iron was in such high demand that iron manufacturers faced a coal shortage by 1862. The Etowah Iron Works near Cartersville, Georgia, received an advance of $500,000 in 1863 from the Confederate government for a contract to make munitions. Other well-established factories adapted their production to meet the increased demand. One of the largest paper producers in the state, the Marietta Paper Mills, located a few miles west of Roswell on Sope Creek, previously a major supplier of newsprint, now expanded its operation to include the manufacture of cartridge paper and stationery for the Confederacy.[23]

It took an enormous amount of cotton and woolen goods to supply and clothe the Confederate army. No new textile mills of any size opened during the war, so those already established were soon running at maximum capacity in an effort to meet the growing demand. The Roswell factories experienced an initial slowdown when they could no longer ship goods to standing clients in Baltimore, Philadelphia, and Newark through their agents in New York and began searching for new buyers in Alabama and Mississippi. George Camp, agent for the Roswell Manufacturing Company, was forced to lay off 30 factory hands in April. Orders continued to decrease and on May 7, Camp reported that the company was "entirely out of orders for goods and will commence piling up, to be ready for any demands."[24]

Still, Barrington King was not discouraged. That same month he advised his son-in-law that management had been preparing for war, and business matters were very "smug." Although they had large quantities of yarn on hand, there was still good local demand for all of the cloth. The factories were presently producing only one-half the normal amount of yarn, "merely to feed out hands." After all, King had "750 mouths

Roswell Manufacturing Company, circa 1853 to 1864 (courtesy the Roswell Historical Society).

to provide for" and all required "looking after." He was determined to prevent them from starving, but "they [factory hands] must be satisfied with bread and water." Barrington had advised some of the workers to "move off" until the troubles were over, but wrote that the workers preferred standing their chance of support at his factories with what work they could get.[25]

As it turned out King's business troubles were only temporary for the Roswell Manufacturing Company began receiving large military contracts as early as August 1861 and was soon providing the Confederacy with rope, candlewick, tent cloth, and large quantities of brown muslin sheeting.[26]

King believed the new contracts necessitated a change in management and quickly hired a new superintendent to oversee the operations of the two cotton factories. Olney Eldredge, a native of Massachusetts, had extensive experience in the textile industry. Eldredge left his job at the Chicopee Manufacturing Company and moved to Milledgeville, Georgia, in 1846. In 1850 he moved to Sparta and worked as a superintendent for the Hancock Manufacturing Company. Five years later, he moved to Jewell where he entered into a partnership and purchased the Rock Mills, located on the Ogeechee River between Sparta and Warrenton. Two years after the death of his wife

Olney Eldredge (1807–1879) and son Judson Work Eldredge (1855–1893). Olney was the supervisor of the Roswell cotton mills, and one of the favored few to be rehired after the war. Judson was only 8 when his family was loaded onto a mule wagon and sent to Marietta (courtesy the descendants of Olney Eldredge).

in 1859, Eldredge sold his interest in the Rock Mills partnership and moved to Roswell with his three children, Mary, Martha, and Judson. An upstanding citizen and devout Christian, Eldredge joined the Presbyterian Church on his arrival, serving as a ruling elder until his death. Well respected by the community, Eldredge also earned the trust and confidence of the "Royal Family," who considered the superintendent a family friend as well as a loyal employee.[27]

By 1862 the mills were doing a brisk business, but an arson fire set them back six to eight weeks in their production. A new employee confessed to setting the fire, claiming he was paid $500 by two unnamed men from Tennessee to burn the mills. The fire caused damage to the cotton house and pickers room, but factory workers, men, women, boys and girls brought water to the fire, and King credited them with saving the factory. The employee was tried and sent to a Marietta jail. King explained that it was hard work to keep the factory workers from hanging the men, since it was the employees who would most suffer from any slowdown in production. King immediately placed an eight-man guard at the factory to prevent any similar incidents.[28]

The Roswell factories struggled to keep pace with the increasing military and civilian demand for their goods while doing everything possible, according to Barrington King, to "keep down speculation." At the same time, the company looked for profits "large enough for reasonable men," but there was much disagreement during the course of the war as to just what constituted reasonable profits. Critics frequently turned to the newspapers to wage a battle of words, publicly accusing the manufacturers of preying on their own people by charging exorbitant prices. Responding to the charges, many of the owners and agents denied speculative practices and pledged to keep their prices low. A large number of factories began making generous charitable donations, which they hoped would demonstrate their concern for the poor and suffering.[29]

In September of 1862, George Camp wrote a letter to the editors of the *Atlanta Southern Confederacy,* on behalf of the Roswell Manufacturing Company, proposing a "gratuitous distribution" of 1000 bunches of yarn, to be divided among the needy poor in ten surrounding counties. An article in the *Mobile Register and Advertiser* took exception to the charitable offer. As a citizen of one of the ten specified counties, the writer was thankful, but suggested it was far from enough. "But this is not what we want. Reduce your prices greatly, Mr. Camp! Otherwise it will be truly said of your donation — 'With one hand he put a penny in the urn of poverty, and with the other took a shilling out.'"[30]

Most of the donations made on behalf of textile companies were met with similar criticism. The president of the Augusta Cotton Factory sent a check for $40,000 to the mayor of the city for the aid of soldiers' families and the poor of Augusta. An article in the *Athens Southern Banner* praised the company for the use of its profits, but submitted that the large amount that it was able to give away was "incontestable proof" that it had demanded extortionate prices from the public for its fabrics. Would it not have been better for all concerned if it had given less in charity and done more in setting fair prices?[31]

In November 1863 Barrington King complained there was too much speculation, and he no longer derived any satisfaction in doing business. But despite his commitment to keep prices low, he confessed that he was now forced to sell a portion of the company's goods at market rates in order to obtain needed supplies, rates which were three to four times their normal price and too expensive for the poor families so dependent on the yarn for clothing.[32]

The Ivy Woolen Mill had always fared well in the press. An article in December of 1861 praised them for their efforts to furnish goods to the soldiers at low prices. While the owners had "scarcely been making the usual manufacturing profits," the company had been furnishing an excellent article of "cadet gray" for the army, and in every instance where it was possible, directly to the soldiers. Commending the Messrs. Kings for their "patriotism and fidelity" to the common cause, the writer suggested they should stand as an "exception to sweeping assertions of venality."[33]

Production at the Roswell mills was so vital to the war effort that the Confederate authorities exempted a number of employees from the draft, and detailed soldiers to fill vacancies left by men who insisted on joining the army. In 1862 James King, owner of the woolen mill, wrote to Secretary of War George W. Randolph requesting additional exemptions for several of his employees. "We have to run our mill night and day and therefore require a double set of hands." King informed Randolph that he tried to hire their workers from those too young or too old for the militia, but it was not always possible because much of the work required skilled operators.[34]

While demand for woolen cloth increased, raw wool grew scarce. James King looked to the government to supply his woolen mill with the necessary raw materials. The Confederacy furnished most and eventually all of the raw wool for the Ivy Mill and required a certain amount of cloth in return, purchasing large quantities of the light gray-colored woolen cloth.[35]

The woolen mill sent their "cloth and pant" goods to Marietta by wagon and then by train to the Atlanta Depot where it was issued to the tailors and cut into required garments under the watchful eye of a superintendent. Once they were cut, the garments were given to trimmers, who supplied the necessary trimmings and then passed them on to the inspectors who issued them to some 3000 female operatives employed as seamstresses. Atlanta workers turned out large numbers of Confederate uniforms, sending many soldiers off to war in Roswell Grey.[36]

Increased production translated to higher stockholder profits. As a major supplier of cotton goods to the Confederate government, the stockholders of the Roswell Manufacturing Company were earning almost record dividends of 20 percent in 1863. In an effort to keep up with the increased demand, and with the full consent and approbation of the War Department, the Kings ordered additional machinery from England in the summer of 1863. When the machines arrived towards the end of the year,

Barrington Simeral King requested, and was granted, a 30-day furlough from his command of the Roswell Troopers. In requesting the leave of absence, King stated that the machines were not in service and required his personal attention to put them in "full & successful operation." King reminded his superiors that if he desired he could be exempted from all military duty in order to remain at home and superintend the machines, but he believed his first and greatest duty was to his country. All he asked was enough time to serve his own interest as well as his country's.[37]

In the summer of 1863, with no end to the war in sight and Union troops threatening the Georgia borders, Governor Joseph Brown organized the Georgia State Guard, drawing mainly from exempts and others not liable for conscription. Intended for local defense, these troops were "not to be called upon except to repel a raid of the enemy and not to be kept in service longer than necessary for that purpose." Captain Tom organized the Roswell Battalion, initially known as King's Company, in early June. More than half of the enlisted men were mill workers and exempt from regular service. Although the boys were supposed to be at least sixteen years of age, William Charles Hopkins was only 14 when he enlisted in the battalion alongside his father, George W. Hopkins, a local factory hand. Helen Zubly Magill described the battalion in glowing terms: "They have a grand military organization here now; Infantry, Cavalry, & Artillery; the three departments, commanded by three of the Royal Family. Have two cannon, and plenty of small arms."[38]

In 1863, 34-year-old Captain Tom King decided that it was time to return to the field of battle. Although he was still suffering from his injury and was unable to mount a horse without assistance, Tom insisted on riding to the front, despite his father's best efforts to persuade him to remain in Roswell. Tom explained, "The state is invaded — our family is not represented in the defending army — I must go." He requested a furlough from his duties in command of the Roswell Battalion in order to join the Confederate troops at Chickamauga. Colonel Marcus Wright, commander of the troops at Atlanta, sent his approval on the 12th of September, but expressed concern about the unsettled conditions in the immediate area. Wright advised King to caution the commander left in charge at Roswell to be vigilant in guarding the approaches to Roswell and Atlanta. Turning over command of the Roswell Battalion to his brother James, Tom headed north. "Left the dear ones at home again, having buckled on the sword to join the Army of Tennessee under General Bragg, to strike another blow for independence and the freedom of Georgia from the polluting tread of the Abolitionists." Tom did not believe he would survive this battle. Before leaving Roswell, he executed his will, and committed his children to the care of his father.[39]

Captain King hoped to find a position on General Leonidas Polk's staff, but General Polk had no need of King's services. Determined to serve, King sought a position elsewhere and the next day was invited to join the staff of Brigadier General Preston Smith as an acting aide-de-camp. At 5 P.M., during a lull in the battle, Tom wrote in his notebook:

Have seen the enemy once more.... Through the mercies of a kind Providence, who has shielded me with His wings, and covered me, I have been preserved without a wound, amidst the hundreds around me, and the thousands of shot and shell which sung the requiem of our dead boys. Thank God who gave me strength, I feel that so far as I am concerned I have done my duty.[40]

A fresh attack was made a half-hour later and the enemy driven back some two miles. Shortly afterwards, General Smith and Captain King rode to the front under the cover of darkness to find out why the advance had come to a halt. Coming upon soldiers in their immediate front, General Smith demanded to know who was in charge and soon discovered that they had unwittingly ridden into the front of a detachment of the enemy. Recognizing Smith as a Confederate officer, the Yankees fired a volley that mortally wounded the two horsemen. Sensing that his death was imminent, Tom delivered his notebook, pocket book, and the contents of his pockets to a nearby officer, requesting him to make a proper disposition of them. Upon his death, a staff officer from Polk's command recorded his own tribute to the captain in King's own war diary, "His gallantry upon the battle field was conspicuous; and since this war began, no nobler, braver or truer heart has been offered a sacrifice to the great cause." Unknown to many of the men on the field at the time of his death, for some time Tom was referred to as the "unknown hero."[41]

Tom's cousin, Doctor Charles Quintard, chaplain of the First Tennessee Regiment, arrived on the field shortly after Tom's death and escorted his body to Marietta, where he met James King, who took his brother home to Roswell. Tom's widow, Marie, was devastated by the death of her husband. She was not alone; the entire village joined in grieving over the death of their beloved Tom. On the 22nd of September Captain Tom was laid to rest in the cemetery behind the Roswell Presbyterian Church, followed and mourned by the whole community en masse, "bond and free."[42]

The Confederacy sustained heavy losses at Chickamauga, and soldiers loaded the wounded and dying men into straw-littered boxcars and sent them on to makeshift hospitals in Marietta. Local women assisted with the sick and wounded, preparing food and tending to the soldiers crowded into churches, stores, and buildings at the Georgia Military Institute. The battles were no longer confined to distant fields. The sight of so many wounded and dying soldiers brought home all the horror and cruelty of the war.[43]

Local citizens grew fearful for their safety and many gave serious thought to leaving. Sixteen miles away in Roswell, Archibald Smith buried his important papers and personal possessions under a walnut tree in his garden and talked to his wife about moving south. While others made plans to leave, Barrington King seemed determined to stay. Yankee cavalry burned the Trion Cotton Factory near Rome, Georgia, in mid–September. Convinced that the Roswell factories were in very real danger of enemy raids, King remained hopeful that the state forces would be effective in preventing the "vandals" from making further encroachments. For his part, he had no intention of moving until the "Yankees actually set fire to his house."[44]

News of the Confederate defeat at Missionary Ridge in November followed by the concentration of Union forces on the Tennessee border was disheartening. Southern newspapers did much to fan the flames of panic. Although most of the articles expressed confidence in General Joseph E. Johnston, appointed to the command of the Army of Tennessee in late December, others offered only dire predictions. An article in the *Augusta Daily Chronicle and Sentinel* warned of imminent danger. "An army of invasion will come down upon us, formidable [in] numbers and ferocious in its purposes of plunder and destruction. No man, woman or child will escape. One universal ruin awaits us all."[45]

By early 1864, many of the original founding families no longer lived in Roswell. Roswell King, John and Jane Dunwody, and James Bulloch had passed on and each had been laid to rest in Roswell's Founders' Cemetery on a small shady hill above the mill. Martha Bulloch stayed in town for a few years after her husband's death, but moved to New York City in 1857 to be near her daughter Mittie and her new husband, Theodore Roosevelt, Sr. Of the six founding families only Barrington and Catherine King, Nathaniel and Catherine Pratt, and Archibald and Anne Smith remained in Roswell. With preparations for the spring campaign already underway, each of these families would soon be forced to make a difficult decision: to stay in Roswell and prepare for the advance of the enemy, or to flee to safer places, leaving homes and possessions behind to an uncertain fate.[46]

5

Sherman Takes Command

They cannot be made to love us, but they can be made to fear us, and dread the passage of our troops through their country.
— William T. Sherman, October 4, 1862

The Atlanta Campaign of 1864 would bring ruin and devastation to the state of Georgia. The messenger of her fate; Major General William T. Sherman, newly appointed commander of the vast Military Division of the Mississippi.

Graduating sixth in a class of 43 from West Point in 1840, Sherman spent 13 years in the regular army before resigning in 1853 for a succession of civilian positions. Banking ventures in San Francisco and St. Louis proved to be disasters, although not wholly of Sherman's own doing. After a brief and unremarkable stint as a partner in a Kansas law firm, Sherman accepted a position as superintendent of the Louisiana Military Seminary in 1859 with the understanding that he would leave should Louisiana choose to secede.[1]

True to his word, Sherman tendered his resignation after Louisiana troops captured the U.S. Arsenal at Baton Rouge on January 10, 1861. He then served as president of the Fifth Street Railroad, a St. Louis streetcar company, but returned to the army after the outbreak of the Civil War and was appointed colonel of the 13th U.S. Infantry. Three months later he became the seventh-ranking brigadier general of volunteers in the service, outranking Ulysses S. Grant.[2]

Given a command in Kentucky in the fall of 1861, Sherman buckled under pressure and suffered a near breakdown. Sherman's gross exaggerations of enemy strength, constant demands for reinforcements and predictions of defeat led to his replacement by Don Carlos Buell, while newspapers widely circulated stories that he was both insane and incompetent.[3]

Despite the poor showing in Kentucky, Sherman was placed in command of a division of volunteers and fought under General Ulysses S. Grant at the Battle of Shiloh in April 1862. Ignoring repeated warnings of an impending attack, Sherman soon found his ill-prepared position overrun by Albert Sidney Johnston's Confederates. Sherman remained calm and handled his forces well, despite being wounded in the hand and having three horses shot out from under him. Sherman made serious errors, but the battle was a Federal victory, and his conduct won high praise and an appointment to major general. Perhaps his greatest achievement at Shiloh was the cultivation of a friendship with General Grant.[4]

Grant and Sherman developed a close relationship during the two years that preceded the Atlanta Campaign. The two commanders had a great deal in common; both

were born and raised in the Midwest, both were West Point graduates and both had served in the regular army. Each of them had tried his hand in civilian employment, but neither had been particularly successful. Although Sherman and Grant would achieve fame as army commanders, both were somewhat careless about their appearance and neither looked the part of a high-ranking military officer. Still, there were obvious differences. While Grant was calm, clear-headed and confident, Sherman was impulsive, restless, and an incessant talker. Whatever their differences, the men held each other in high regard and forged a lifelong bond. Sherman would later boast, "He [Grant] stood by me when I was crazy and I stood by him when he was drunk; and now we stand by each other always."[5]

Major General William T. Sherman (1820–1891). Commander of the Military Division of the Mississippi, U.S.A., Sherman ordered the arrest and deportation of the mill workers at Roswell and New Manchester (courtesy the Library of Congress).

Despite achieving a measure of success during the next two years, Sherman also experienced some dismal failures. In the early part of the Vicksburg Campaign in December 1862, Sherman launched a doomed assault at Chickasaw Bluff, Mississippi, and accepted personal responsibility for the costly defeat. The following November he directed an unsuccessful attack against the Confederate position near Missionary Ridge and once again failed to accomplish his objective. Fortunately for the Federals, General George Thomas's men routed the enemy and ended the siege of Chattanooga. Nevertheless, Grant's confidence in Sherman remained high.[6]

After leading a successful raid across central Mississippi in February 1864, Sherman was summoned to Nashville for an important meeting with General Grant, who had just been appointed general-in chief, a position which placed him in command of all the armies of the United States. As his successor, Grant looked to Sherman, and on March 18, 1864, Sherman replaced Grant as commander of the Military Division of the Mississippi.[7]

Forty-five years old in 1864 with red hair and short crisp whiskers, Sherman was tall and wiry with a face marked with deep lines and a furrowed brow. His men often described him as nervous and restless with an endless supply of energy. He was a constant smoker and was often found pacing with a cigar firmly between his lips. One staff officer described him as "neither excessively handsome nor painfully repulsive.... He has, perhaps, as great a disregard for his personal appearance as he pretends to have for what others may say or think of him." Sherman admitted to an uncommonly bad temper and made no attempt to control or correct it. It was said that he treated everyone with the same "sternness, abruptness, gruffness and roughness," which tended to alienate and offend some people, but "Uncle Billy" was genuinely loved and respected by the troops who fought under his command.[8]

In planning the spring campaigns of 1864, Grant's objective was to "work all parts of the army together and somewhat toward a common center." In this way he hoped to press the Confederates on all fronts while allowing no room for maneuver or concentration. Grant and the armies under his direct command would pursue Lee's army in such a way that Lee would not be able to come to the assistance of Confederate general Joseph E. Johnston. In the same manner, Sherman would lead his armies into Georgia, engaging Johnston's Confederates so "in no event could any part be detached to assist General Lee in Virginia." Sherman wrote, "Neither Atlanta, nor Augusta, nor Savannah, was the objective, but the army of Joseph Johnston, go where it might."[9]

Grant expected to combine the destruction of Southern armies with the destruction of Southern war resources. The success of these campaigns would depend on the elimination of the food, forage and ammunition necessary to maintain the Confederate armies in the field regardless of the impact on Southern civilians. Although Grant would leave the planning and the execution of the campaign to Sherman, he made it clear what he expected Sherman to accomplish. "You I propose to move against Johnston's army, to break it up, and to get into the interior of the enemy's country as far as you can, inflicting all the damage you can against their resources."[10]

Grant's order reflected the evolving changes in Federal war policy. The hard war policies of 1864 were far removed from the early practices of 1861. In the beginning, the hard hand of war was not to fall on the peaceable Southern population. Civilians were to be treated with respect, their property, including their slaves, free from confiscation. It was widely believed that the majority of white Southerners were merely pawns of a small but mighty slaveholding power and only half-hearted about secession. It seemed reasonable that a policy of conciliation would bring the "misguided" Southerners willingly back to the Union.

The early conciliatory policies adhered to commonly accepted laws and usages of war as defined by Emmerich de Vattel in his book, *The Law of Nations*. Published in 1758, the commentary remained a standard authority at the outbreak of the Civil War. In the section dealing with warfare, Vattel proposed that both combatants and noncombatants alike were enemies who could be subjected to "every measure necessary to weaken" the enemy, provided that the methods were not "of an odious kind, nor unjustifiable in themselves, and prohibited by the law of nature." However, "Women and children, feeble old men and sick persons" were enemies who made no resistance. All peaceful inhabitants who refrained from acts of hostility should be spared the hardships of war and left, whenever possible, to live in safety and to remain in possession of their property. The writer urged a "rule of moderation"; wars were struggles between armies, not wars against civilians. Unless specifically designed to punish an enemy, Vattel concluded that "all damage done to an enemy unnecessarily," every act of hostility, which did not "tend to procure victory and bring the war to the conclusion," was a "licentiousness condemned by the law of nature." Military necessity, then, was the deciding factor and this gave the commanders a great deal of latitude in their conduct, depending upon their own definition of necessity. Indeed the interpretation of military necessity would change dramatically as circumstances and perceptions dictated.[11]

Although most commanders adopted the conciliatory policies during the first year of the war, there were notable exceptions. The 9th Ohio Infantry of Colonel Robert L. McCook's brigade plundered and burned the town of Fayetteville, Virginia, in October 1861. A number of other towns and villages in Virginia and Missouri met a similar fate during that fall and winter, although most of these were acts of retaliation and not indiscriminate acts of destruction.[12]

One of the worst atrocities was committed in May 1862 by a brigade in the Army of the Ohio, under the command of Colonel John B. Turchin. Turchin "turned his back" for two hours in Athens, Alabama, while his men entered private homes and pillaged and plundered to their heart's content, destroying what they did not steal. Unrestrained soldiers stole money, food, jewelry, and in some cases, even the clothing of women and children. The insults and injuries were not limited to white women; a number of the men reportedly attacked and raped female slaves.

This time the abuse was too serious to ignore. Turchin was tried and convicted, but not removed from the army. Thanks largely to the efforts of his wife, instead of censure, Colonel Turchin was promoted to brigadier general and placed at the head of a new command in September of 1862.[13]

Federal reverses in the Shenandoah Valley combined with General George B. McClellan's failure to take Richmond in mid–1862 led to a cry for a more vigorous prosecution of the war. The conciliatory policies had failed to achieve the desired results. The Southerners had not lost the will to fight, nor were they flocking back to the Union. What many had believed would be only a short war now stretched out before them with no end in sight. Lincoln's Emancipation Proclamation signaled a dramatic shift in the war's focus, and while the primary objective remained the preservation of the Union, it was abundantly clear that the war would now be conducted with less regard for the Southern civilian population. Peaceable private citizens would be spared the burden of war whenever possible, but the new policies encouraged harsh retaliatory measures and many noncombatants would pay the price for acts of guerrilla bands that continued to plague the Union forces.

The harsher measures called for more aggressive guidelines, and in April 1863, the War Department issued general instructions for the conduct of the war, written in large part by Francis Lieber, an eminent international and military jurist. According to Mark Grimsley, author of *Hard Hand of War*, General Orders No. 100, more commonly known as the Lieber Code, represented the "western world's first formal set of guidelines for the conduct of armies in the field." While the Lieber Code called for moral and responsible conduct on the part of the soldiers, it also called for a bolder prosecution of the war: "The more vigorously wars are pursued the better it is for humanity. Sharp wars are brief." At the core was the definition of military necessity, which Lieber described as "those measures which are indispensable for securing the ends of the war, and which are lawful according to modern law and usages of war." Although it did not permit wanton destruction or wanton violence, the Lieber Code sanctioned the "destruction of property, and obstruction of the ways and channels of traffic, travel, or communication, and of all withholding of sustenance or means of life from the enemy," as well as the "appropriation of whatever an enemy's country affords necessary for the subsistence and safety of the Army." Firmly repudiating the early conciliatory policies, the Lieber Code failed to set specific limits, and once again, much was left to the local commander's perception of military necessity.[14]

The last twelve months of the conflict saw the emergence of the hard war policies, which signaled a marked change in the prosecution of the war. Military objectives expanded beyond the boundaries of the battlefields as Union armies sought to demoralize Southern civilians while destroying the Confederate economy, particularly its industrial and transportation resources. Still, northern troops were expected to distinguish between Unionist, passive and secessionist civilians, and the hard hand of war was to fall most heavily on public property and the property of private citizens who actively supported the Confederacy.

Sherman embraced the hard war policies, viewing citizen and soldier alike as the enemy. "We are not only fighting hostile armies, but a hostile people, and must make old and young, rich and poor, feel the hard hand of war, as well as their organized armies." To those who would submit to the "Rightful Laws & authority of their state & National Government" he promised all gentleness and forbearance. But a different fate awaited the "petulant and persistent" secessionist. "Why, death or banishment is a mercy, and the quicker he or she is disposed of the better."[15]

The invasion into Georgia gave Sherman the perfect opportunity to put his ideas into action as he embarked on a campaign of destruction that would bring the full burden of the war to the civilian population that lay in the path of his advancing army. While most generals would continue to seek victories on the battlefields, Sherman would seek to win his battles against the enemy's society. Needless slaughter on the battlefields was not the answer. Destruction of Southern crops and property would be far more effective and far less costly to his army. Sherman explained to his daughter Minnie, "Whenever a result can be accomplished without Battle I prefer it."[16]

Sherman had not always been an advocate of hard war. He, like most other Union commanders, had adopted and practiced the conciliatory policies in the early years of the war. In June 1862 Sherman went so far as to authorize summary punishments for stragglers committing depredations on private property. The next month he ordered daily patrols comprised of one officer and ten mounted men to patrol the country around the camps and shoot any soldier caught stealing or vandalizing. He was determined to put an end to the "demoralizing and disgraceful" practice of pillage, "else the country will rise on us and justly shoot us down like dogs and wild beasts."[17]

However, civilians in Randolph, Mississippi, did not find Sherman particularly "conciliatory." After bushwhackers fired on a Union riverboat near the village, Sherman ordered a detachment to burn the entire town save for one house "to mark the place." After the burning of Randolph, Sherman announced his intention to expel ten families for every attack on Union riverboats. When the attacks continued, Sherman issued orders for forty families to move beyond enemy lines, but only a few were actually forced to leave.[18]

Still Sherman was not yet waging war on the civilian population. In April 1863, Sherman sent Brigadier General Frederick Steele to Deer Creek, Mississippi, in response to recent acts by local bushwhackers. Steele was ordered to "let the planters and inhabitants on Deer Creek see and feel that they will be held accountable for acts of guerrillas and Confederate soldiers who sojourn in their country for the purpose of firing on our boats passing Greenville." Although Sherman authorized Steele's troops to seize all provisions that could be used by his men, he advised them to leave what the peaceful inhabitants needed to survive. Any surplus that might be of use to the Confederate army in Vicksburg was to be destroyed.[19]

Steele's troops disobeyed orders and destroyed most of the food supplies, not just the surplus that might have fed the Confederate troops. Union soldiers seized a thousand horses, mules and cattle, as well as wagons, buggies and farm tools, and burned about 500,000 bushels of corn. Sherman criticized the actions of the overzealous troops:

War at best is barbarism, but to involve all — children, women, old and helpless — is more than can be justified. Our men will become lawless unless this can be checked. We sure have [a right] to corn, cotton, fodder & c., used to sustain armies in war. Still I always feel that the store necessary for a family should be spared, and I think it injures our men to allow them to plunder indiscriminately the inhabitants of the country.[20]

Ironically, when the citizens of Warren County, Mississippi, complained about Steele's conduct at Deer Creek, Sherman referred to them as "little annoyances." In response to their request for protection and assistance, he explained that neither he nor Grant could give them any assurance or guarantees. "Of necessity, in war the commander on the spot is the judge, and may take your house, your fields, your everything, and, turn you all out, helpless, to starve. It may be wrong, but that don't alter the case." The only remedy, according to Sherman, was to "stop the war."[21]

Only three months later, in a sharp contrast with his previous policy, Sherman led a raid of extensive destruction on Jackson, Mississippi, "absolutely stripping" the country of corn, hogs, sheep, and poultry, leaving no food for the local inhabitants. Sherman's forces destroyed the railroad, wrecked factories, and burned cotton, while foragers roamed the countryside. Sherman's report failed to mention the indiscriminate destruction of churches, public buildings and private dwellings. The *Brandon Republican* reported the burning of the Catholic Church and parsonage along with a large number of private homes. Soldiers entered the Episcopal Church and damaged the interior. Grocery stores were burned, the newspaper office was broken into, the type thrown in the street, and the presses and furniture destroyed. Federal troops vandalized the post office and broke open the governor's mansion and destroyed pianos and furniture. Nearly all of the private residences were entered, trunks broken open, fine dresses torn to pieces, and all jewelry, silverware, and provisions taken. Unlike his previous operations, the extensive devastation was not committed in retaliation for guerrilla activity, nor could it be justified as military necessity. Sherman attributed it to the "scourge of war"; its purpose was to destroy and weaken the resources of the enemy. Indeed, the operations in and around Jackson marked a dramatic shift in Sherman's own policies toward the Southern civilian population.[22]

During his Meridian Campaign in February 1864, Sherman deliberately pursued a course of destruction intent on crippling both the enemy's ability and will to fight. Armed with "axes, crowbars, sledges, claw bars and with fire," Sherman's soldiers spent five days destroying Meridian's war resources and more than one hundred miles of railroad. Just as at Jackson, the destruction was not limited to war materials; soldiers ransacked and destroyed homes and public buildings, and crops and animals disappeared from farms along the route. Sherman boasted of their success. "Meridian, with its depots, store-houses, arsenal, hospitals, offices, hotels, and cantonments no longer exists." Leaving "a swath of desolation 50 miles broad across the state of Mississippi," Sherman pronounced the work "well done."[23]

Sherman assumed his new post as commander of the Military Division of the Mississippi with confidence, his previous struggles with doubt and personal insecurity seemingly behind him. As the second most powerful field commander in the Federal army, Sherman turned his attention to the organization and preparation of his forces for the spring campaign. One of the first items on his agenda was a meeting with his three commanders, Major Generals John McAllister Schofield, George Henry Thomas, and James Birdseye McPherson. Sherman instructed each of the generals "to make immediate preparations for a hard campaign." It was only a matter of time before they would begin the advance against the enemy firmly entrenched at Dalton, Georgia, some 30 miles distant.[24]

Sherman intended to invade Georgia with the largest force possible, supplying his men over a long and tenuous supply line. As a result, his greatest concern was the "troublesome question of transportation and supplies" which would determine his success or failure on the campaign. Procuring the necessary supplies at his base in Nashville was not the problem. The difficulty lay in the transporting those items to his soldiers on the march. The railroad would serve as his only supply line as they faced an enemy to his front and possibly hostile guerrillas and cavalry to his rear.[25]

When Sherman took command, the railroads provided little more than the daily wants of the armies then depending on them. The trains were already loaded with men returning from furlough, cattle, horses, and provisions for the suffering inhabitants of East Tennessee. In addition, citizens and charities added to the strain, with large numbers of them requesting passage daily. Sherman recognized that immediate and drastic changes had to be made. Not only would his men have to be well supplied with food, forage, clothing, medicine, and ammunition on the march, but they would also require an accumulation of the supplies at the front in case of an interruption to the railway, whether by act of enemy or common accident.

While Sherman worked out the logistics of acquiring additional trains, he sought and received permission to reserve the railroad exclusively for military use. On April 6, 1864, he issued General Orders No. 6, limiting the use of the railroad cars to transporting only essential articles of food, ammunition, and supplies for the army in the field. Trains would be closed to civilian traffic, cattle would be driven overland, troops would march, and provisions would no longer be issued to the starving citizens. The order alleviated the logistical problems, but "of course it naturally raised a howl." When the suffering citizens of East Tennessee pleaded with the president to intervene on their behalf, Lincoln asked Sherman if he would consider modifying or repealing the order. Sherman refused to make any concession. Military needs took priority over humanitarian concerns. "The railroad cannot supply the army and the people. One or the other must quit, and the army don't [sic] intend to, unless Joe Johnston makes us."[26]

As part of his preparations, Sherman reorganized his army, which actually consisted of three armies, each one acting more or less independently. The largest of the armies was Major General George Thomas's Army of the Cumberland, which numbered 72,938 officers and men on April 30. The command was made up of three infantry corps—the IV, XIV, and XX—and a cavalry corps. Major General James McPherson's Army of the Tennessee also comprised three corps, the XV, XVI and XVII, but some of the divisions were not up and at the end of April it numbered 24,380 officers and men. The smallest of the armies was the Army of the Ohio under Major General John McAllister Schofield. Consisting of the XXIII Army Corps and a division of cavalry, it numbered only 12,805 officers and men on the eve of the campaign. Since some of the cavalry divisions were absent collecting horses and would not join the army until later in the campaign, Sherman estimated his effective strength for offensive purposes on May 1 at 98,797.[27]

Sherman's cavalry would prove to be one of his greatest weaknesses. Rather than create a strong, effective, unified cavalry force, Sherman divided his horsemen into four divisions, each with its own commander, each treated as a separate unit. Three of the divisions belonged to the Army of the Cumberland and formed a corps headed at least nominally by Brigadier General Washington Elliott. The fourth division, under the command of Major General George Stoneman, belonged to the Army of the Ohio. Instead of employing his cavalry as a powerful attacking force, Sherman generally used his mounted forces on the extreme flanks, or for some special detached service.[28]

At noon on April 28, Sherman left Nashville, transferred his headquarters to Chattanooga, and prepared for taking the field in person. Grant had originally planned to begin the spring offensive on April 27, but bad weather forced him to postpone the opening date.

On May 5, "the great campaign was begun" as three Union armies, some 100,000 men, began their march. Thirty miles to the southeast, near the small town of Dalton, Georgia, General Joe Johnston and the 55,000 officers and men of the Army of Tennessee awaited their advance.[29]

Unlike Sherman, Johnston looked every bit the soldier. According to Benjamin Ewell, who served under Johnston for three years, Johnston "had more the appearance of a soldier than anyone I ever met in the Confederate or subsequently in the Union Army." Described as elegant and well mannered, Johnston was of slight build and "rather below middle height," although one reporter claimed "he looked taller on account of his erect carriage." One of the most controversial generals of the Civil War, Johnston's career was hampered by disputes with Jefferson Davis over rank and military protocol. Born and raised in Virginia, Johnston entered West Point with Robert E. Lee in 1825, graduating in 1829. Except for a brief stint in 1837 as a civilian engineer, he remained in the Army until 1861. Johnston's thirty-year military career included command or staff service in every branch of the army, during which time he was wounded nine times and received four brevet promotions for gallantry. Serving as quartermaster general of the U.S. Army in 1861 with the staff grade of brigadier general, Johnston remained in the regular army until the secession of his native state.[30]

As a result of his performance at First Manassas, the first significant victory for the Confederacy, Johnston was given command of the Army of the Potomac. A short time later Johnston became embroiled in a dispute with President Jefferson Davis over his rank and relations between the two would remain strained for the rest of the war. Johnston opposed General George McClellan in the Peninsula Campaign until he was severely wounded at Seven Pines in May 1862. On his return the following November, Johnston was appointed commander of the Department of the West, largely a supervisory command. Faced with a shortage of experienced and competent generals, Davis reluctantly assigned Johnston to the command of the Army of Tennessee to replace General Braxton Bragg in December 1863.[31]

Now Johnston prepared to face Sherman. Understanding that he was badly outnumbered, the Confederate commander planned to "spare the blood" of his soldiers, while slowing down Sherman's advance by preparing elaborate defensive positions, hoping to draw Sherman into direct frontal assaults on the Rebel fortifications. When possible he would attempt to draw Sherman away from his base of supplies and give battle only where he had the chance of success and where defeat to Sherman would be most disastrous.[32]

For his part, Sherman believed he was facing a formidable foe. Later when writing of Johnston, Sherman recalled, "Even then [May 1863] the ability of General Johnston was recognized, and General Grant told me that he was about the only general on that side whom he feared." Although Grant had ordered Sherman to move against Johnston's army and to break it up, Sherman preferred to fight a war of maneuver. Sherman knew he was facing a much smaller force, but he also knew Johnston's defensive strength and did not plan to shatter his armies in futile assaults against the Confederates. Instead he would use his superior numbers to flank his opponent out of one defensive position after another. Sher-

General Joseph E. Johnston (1807–1891). Commander of the Army of Tennessee, C.S.A., Johnston hoped to "spare the blood" of his soldiers while slowing down Sherman's advance. The general's willingness to sacrifice territory in order to save lives would cost him his command (courtesy the National Archives, photo no. 111-B-4246, Brady Collection).

man explained to Grant that he expected to maneuver Johnston across the Chatta-hoochee and, given the opportunity, move against Atlanta. He assured Grant that in any event, he would keep Johnston so busy that he could not send any part of his command against Grant.[33]

With Sherman's preference for maneuver and Johnston's willingness to sacrifice territory in order to preserve his forces, the stage was set for a "nice game of war," or as one Confederate officer described it, "a game of chess between two masters." The contest would not be confined to the field of battle; innocent civilians would become unwilling pawns in this not-so-nice game of war.[34]

6

Innocent Pawns

Madam, my soldiers have to subsist even if the whole country must be ruined to maintain them. There are two armies here; one in rebellion against the Union, the other is fighting for the Union — if either must starve to death, I propose it shall not be the army that is loyal. There is nothing too good for the soldiers who wear the blue.

— William T. Sherman, December 1863

Widespread acceptance of the final hard war policies set the stage for Sherman's grand entrance into the heart of Georgia. The kid gloves were off. It was time to bring the full burden of the war to those who neither wore uniforms nor shouldered guns: the women, the children, the old men, the young boys, the sick and infirm. Although strict orders forbade unauthorized pillaging and plundering, many unarmed and defenseless women, young and old, rich and poor, plantation mistress and mill-worker alike, would suffer cruelly at the hands of the Yankee invaders. It would be the officers and soldiers in blue who offered the most compelling evidence of the wanton acts of violence committed all along the advance.

While Sherman and Johnston made ready for the imminent campaign, the inhabitants of the towns and villages that lay along the railroad made preparations of their own. The fear of being caught between two armies set many to packing before the first shot was fired. For others, all too familiar with Sherman's earlier exploits, his name alone was enough to cause frightened citizens to evacuate homes and abandon belongings. "Time after time we had been told of the severity of General Sherman," said Mary Rawson of Atlanta, "until we came to dread his approach as [one] would that of a mighty hurricane which sweeps all before it caring naught for justice or humanity." Others deciding not to leave right away began making plans for a hasty departure should the Yankees troops draw near.[1]

The first fifty days of the Atlanta Campaign were marked by a series of flanking maneuvers and minor battles from Dalton to Kennesaw Mountain, with Johnston sacrificing precious ground as he withdrew from one position after another. With each foot of ground Johnston lost, Sherman advanced that much closer to Atlanta. Citizens along the railroads and river crossings anxiously searched the newspapers for reports from the front. As the front moved closer, and the sounds of distant guns grew much less distant, many began to question the wisdom of remaining at home. Even those determined to stay often experienced a change of heart once smoke began to fill the skies. Abandoning hope as well as possessions, men, women and children hurriedly packed their trunks and wagons and fled.

Soldiers discovered abandoned homes and towns all along the march. At Adairsville only three or four families remained in a town that had boasted a population of some 300 before the war. James Zearing, First Surgeon of the 57th Illinois, arrived in Rome and discovered a number of the families had moved away on the approach of the troops, giving the Union officers plenty of houses to occupy for their quarters. Realizing that their town was likely to be occupied by enemy forces, the inhabitants of Cassville fled, leaving only days before the Union troops arrived and causing one Confederate soldier to remark, "It is an ugly sight to see them leaving their homes and fleeing for a place of safety." The townspeople might have been better off had they stayed. Writing in his diary, Yankee sergeant Oliver Hascall described the fate that had befallen many of the abandoned homes in the "nice looking" town of Cassville, adding that "many of the citizens left their houses along with the rebles [sic] and the boys tore their things to pieces."[2]

Unoccupied homes were fair game. Sherman claimed a right to such property: "All houses left vacant by an inimical people are clearly our right, or such as are needed as store-houses, hospitals, and quarters." Any building near the fighting was subject to seizure for military use and houses were occasionally torn apart so that the boards could be used for fortifications. According to one Union officer, abandoned homes not confiscated by the military rarely escaped the torch of straggling troops: "strict orders restrained, although they did not entirely prevent, arson and pillage of dwellings." Indeed, flames and towering smoke become a common sight in the rear of the Union army. The brick chimneys, often all that remained of homes along the march, were commonly referred to as Sherman's sentinels.[3]

In the ensuing days, many of those who dared to remain in their homes found the war brought to their very doorstep. Fearing life as refugees more than they feared the enemy, they now hid in their homes, praying that closed doors would afford them some measure of safety. Sherman did instruct his men to leave the peaceful civilians alone. Noncombatants who remained in their homes and kept to their "accustomed business their opinions and prejudices" should not be noticed, but "if any one comes out into the public streets and creates disorder, he or she should be punished, restrained, or banished, either to the rear or front as the officer in command adjudges." While it is true that the majority of the civilians who remained in their homes had no problems with the Yankee troops, David Conyngham, Sherman's aide-de-camp and a war correspondent, claimed that many others endured great hardships:

> It is sad to witness the fearful sufferings of the people, particularly the women and children, in those parts of Georgia through which we have campaigned.... I am sorry to say that our men often wantonly burned down the houses, destroyed the contents, and drove forth their wretched inmates, houseless, homeless, starving outcasts, to perish of cold and hunger. It is true that such acts were not sanctioned, but stragglers and hangers-on, who bring up the rear of a large army, destroy everything, like a swarm of locusts, particularly when they find a place deserted. I have met ... frenzied groups of affrightened, starving women and children huddled together in the woods, where many of them perished of cold and want.[4]

Frances Howard later wrote of the harsh treatment her family received at the hands of Union soldiers during the occupation of Kingston in May 1864. Frances and her family watched as soldiers destroyed valuable belongings and works of art, stole books and ornaments, and smeared lard on the doors, walls, and windows. Nor was it just the whites that suffered. Frances claimed that everything was stolen from the slaves as well: pillows, sheets and what little food they had.[5]

Sherman for his part seems to have cared little what the men did in their idle hours and rarely enforced the rules he had established. His adjutant, Henry Hitchcock, offered this critique: "I am bound to say that I think Sherman lacking in enforcing discipline. Brilliant and daring, fertile, rapid and terrible, he does not seem to me to carry things out in this respect." Still, it was not simply a lack of discipline. Some years after the war, Sherman admitted that much of the pillaging was deliberately ignored:

> I know that in the beginning, I, too, had the old West Point notion that pillage was a capital crime and punished it by shooting, but the Rebels wanted us to detach a division here, a brigade there, to protect their families and property while they were fighting. This was a one-sided game of war, and many of us, kind-hearted, fair, just and manly ceased to quarrel with our own men about such minor things, and went in to subdue the enemy, leaving minor depredations to be charged up to the account of the rebels who had forced us into the war, and who deserved all they got and more.[6]

Sherman claimed his officers were powerless to prevent many of the abuses. Writing to his brother in January 1863, Sherman even then admitted that it was difficult to control the men. "Our armies are devastating the land ... it is sad to see the destruction that attends our progress — we cannot help it.... General officers make feeble efforts to stay the disorder, but it is idle." The rank and file resented the hostility they encountered from Southern citizens, and as Sherman's policies of directed severity conditioned the soldiers to view civilians as the enemy, the wanton destruction of private property increased. As Sherman predicted in April 1863, many of the soldiers grew "lawless" and ignored orders, while many officers chose to turn a blind eye.[7]

Brigadier General Jacob D. Cox, a division commander in the XXIII Corps, tried to justify the vandalism as an inevitable part of war in a hostile territory. "The tendency of war to make men relapse into barbarism becomes most evident when an army is living in any degree upon the enemy's country. Desolation follows in its track, and the utmost that discipline can do is to mitigate the evil." Cox claimed that "the legitimate exercise of the rules of war" was not easily distinguished from their abuse. Such acts as trampling crops, felling timber for breastworks and campfires, and dismantling houses to build bridges were necessary and lawful. Cox confessed, however, that officers often excused or overlooked even some of the more blatant abuses. "The best efforts of a provost marshal with his guard will be useless when superior officers, and especially colonels of regiments, encourage or wink at license." Cox explained that as long as the "habit of measuring right by might" continued unchecked, "pillage often became wanton and arson was committed to cover the pillage." He painted a vivid picture of the desolation and devastation often left behind by Sherman's armies. "A vacant house was pretty sure to be burned, either by malice or by accident, until, with fences gone, the roads are an impassable mire, the fields bare and cut up with innumerable wagon-tracks, no living thing to be seen but carrion birds picking the bones of dead horses and mules." Cox concluded, "Dante's Inferno could not furnish a more horrible and depressing picture than a countryside where war has swept over it."[8]

Some officers refused to ignore what they considered to be malicious acts of violence. On May 20, Major General John McAllister Schofield, commanding the Department and Army of the Ohio, called attention to an Indiana regiment left to guard the trains of the army. Schofield accused the men of violating orders in "straggling from their regiment, committing acts of violence and depredation on the defenseless inhabitants of the country through which we are passing, and thus neglecting to perform the important duty assigned them of protecting the train." Schofield ordered the commanding officer to be severely reprimanded and warned that future acts would be punished by arrest.[9]

Brigadier General Milo Smith Hascall, commanding a division in the XXIII Corps, did not hesitate to report to General Schofield what he called "barbarous practices" in a letter dated May 23:

> I consider it my duty to call the attention of the major general commanding the corps to the terrible state of things that exists in different parts of the grand army under Major-General Sherman, so far as the wanton destruction of private property and works of art is concerned. It has not been my fortune to march a single day during the last week without being compelled to witness sights which are enough to disgrace and render worthy of defeat any army in the universe. I have seen at some times as many as half a dozen houses and barns on fire at a time, and in too many cases the wanton destruction of fine paintings and other works of art and culture has been reported to me, and also come under my own observation.

Hascall explained that he had no problem with the soldiers taking everything that could be of service to the Union army, "if done in an orderly manner," but he would not tolerate the detestable behavior he had observed. "I have no desire to serve with an army where the fundamental principles of civilized warfare are so shockingly violated at every step in our progress." Fearing retribution, he added, "Should any untoward event happen to us, compelling us to retreat (which may God forbid), I fear that those of our men that might fall into the enemy's hands would neither receive nor deserve any other than barbarous treatment in their hands."[10]

Many of those who despaired over the devastation left by their armies more often than not shared the belief that the ends justified the means. A Union sergeant echoed similar sentiments in a letter to his father:

> Our men has [have] no mercy whatever — take anything they can lay their hands on, leave the country bare wherever they go. The houses near the road suffer the most — I have seen women crying and begging for them to leave a little for the children but their tears were of no avail. Some of our soldiers are a disgrace to the service. Such is war & the sooner the aristocracy or rather the ones who brought it on feel the effects, the sooner we will have peace.[11]

The abuses suffered by noncombatants were not limited to pillaging, plundering, and arson. Numerous accounts detail physical assaults on both men and women. A correspondent to the *Atlanta Daily Intelligencer* reported that in addition to being robbed of everything of value, many of the inhabitants near Kingston had been "hung up to limbs of trees" in order to force them to give up what money or other valuables they might have concealed. Duncan Murchison told his neighbors that the Yankee army had made three attempts to take him out to the woods to hang him for refusing to disclose the whereabouts of his property, but each time he was able to gain his release by identifying himself as a "Mason."[12]

Southern women most likely feared being raped by a Union soldier more than anything else. Tales and accusations of such crimes widely circulated and numerous accounts appeared in Confederate newspapers. One such article in the *Macon Telegraph* reported the rape of a widow and her two daughters by six Union soldiers at their home in Adairsville. While there is no evidence that rape was an official or unofficial policy, it did occur. Federal court-martial records document more than 350 trials for rape alone, not including those that may have been buried under assault or other charges. Eighteen-year-old private Charles Billingsley, of the 7th Indiana Light Artillery Battery committed "rape on a defenseless woman" near Dallas. Billingsley stood trial on May 30 for the assault on Louise Smith at Burnt Hickory, Georgia, but deserted the day the trial closed. His captain believed that Billingsley had gone over to the enemy, but the young private returned to Indiana and joined the 5th Indiana Cavalry, collecting a bounty for his enlistment. He was apprehended shortly thereafter and executed on December 23, 1864 — not for rape, but for desertion and "bounty jumping."[13]

The most widely known case of rape is probably the account of 27-year-old Kate Latimer Nichols, wife of Confederate captain James H. Nichols of Phillips' Georgia Legion. Confined to her sick bed, Kate was allegedly raped by two Federal soldiers who forced their way into her bedroom at gunpoint. A local resident wrote, "The worst of their acts was committed to poor Mrs. Nichols — violence done, and atrocity committed that ought to make her husband an enemy unto death. Poor woman I fear she has been driven crazy." Kate later died in an insane asylum.[14]

While Union army records document very few rapes committed against Southern women by Sherman's soldiers, there is no way of knowing how many unreported assaults occurred. Raped by a Yankee soldier, a white woman would likely be far too ashamed to ever report the attack outside of her family and even less likely to report it to the Union military authorities, no matter how cruel or violent the attack. In addition to the personal humiliation of admitting such an act occurred, she had no guarantee that she would be taken seriously, or that the soldier would be held accountable. Far less likely to have been reported or acted on, had they been reported, were the numerous sexual assaults on black women by Union soldiers.

Other abuses took the form of arbitrary, unjust and often unwarranted arrests. Although some 200 women were tried by military commissions as spies, smugglers, couriers and saboteurs, many others never had the benefit of trial. The slightest suspicious behavior was grounds to charge a man or woman with being a "notorious rebel" or "suspicious character." With nothing more substantial than these obscure charges, Union authorities forced hundreds of men and women from their homes, sending them "north of the Ohio River," where they would remain for the duration of the war. A number of women, accompanied by small children, made it no farther than Nashville or Louisville, where they found themselves confined in a military prison on various and frequently vague charges of disloyalty.[15]

Sherman reserved the harshest treatment for those suspected of guerrilla activities. In addition to troublesome raids in Kentucky by John Hunt Morgan and others, Confederate partisans posed a constant threat to Sherman's communications and his long and tenuous supply line, cutting telegraph wires, derailing cars and removing rails. Sherman wrote to General Stephen Burbridge, commanding the District of Kentucky, on June 21, demanding that he take "determined action" to put an end to these attacks. Sherman denounced guerrilla activity as nothing but "simple murder, horse stealing, arson and other well defined crimes." Guerrillas were "wild beasts unknown to the usages of war, and should be treated accordingly." Viewing those who gave aid and information to the guerrillas as no less guilty, Sherman believed they should be banished, not to the north, but out of the country. "Your military commanders, provost-marshals, and other agents may arrest all males and females who have encouraged or harbored guerrillas and robbers, and you may cause them to be collected in Louisville, and when you have enough, say 300 or 400, I will cause them to be sent down the Mississippi through their guerrilla gauntlet, and by a sailing ship send them to a land where they may take their negroes and make a colony with laws and a future of their own."[16]

Sherman then wrote to Secretary of War Edwin Stanton, again raising the question of banishment and requested Stanton's support. He doubted that Lincoln would sustain him and only hoped that Lincoln would not interfere. He proposed that those who "conspired against the state" might be deported to "Honduras, British or French Guyana, Santa Domingo, Madagascar, or Lower California." In closing he added that even harsher measures might be in order. "But one thing is certain, there is a class of people, men, women, and children, who must be killed or banished before you can hope for peace and order, even as far south as Tennessee." Nothing appears to have come out of his plan to deport civilians, but it clearly demonstrates his determination to punish and banish any man, woman or child who got in the way of his army.[17]

After two months of continuous fighting and a series of strategic moves on the parts of both commanders, Sherman reached the Chattahoochee River, which he later claimed was one, "if not the chief," object of the campaign. Atlanta lay before him, only eight or nine miles distant, and was "too important a place to be left undisturbed with its magazines, stores, arsenals, workshops, foundries, &c., and more especially the railroads, which converged there from the four great cardinal points." Brigadier General John W. Geary wrote to his wife, "Like Moses, we can find a high topped Pisgah, and from it view the Promised Land. *Geographically* speaking it is only eight miles from us, but *militarily* it may be much further." Now Sherman had to get his army across the river without heavy losses. His only solution was another flanking movement, but it would have to wait until they could cross the Chattahoochee River, still swollen from the June rains. It would be a short wait if the hot July weather continued. Meanwhile General George Stoneman's cavalry was already operating on the left flank of the Confederate army, some ten miles distant at Sweetwater. To cover the opposite flank, Sherman ordered General Kenner Garrard's division of cavalry, consisting of some 4500 men, to advance eighteen miles up the river to capture the important bridge and ford at Roswell.[18]

7

Hopeful to the Last

It is sad indeed to be driven from our homes by the vandals, but we must place our trust in the Lord, hoping for the best.
— Barrington King, June 4, 1864

Roswell was destined to play an important role in the contest for Atlanta. Her valuable factories manufactured large amounts of cloth and other goods necessary to clothe and supply the Confederate armies. More importantly she guarded one of the few approaches to the "promised land" that lay just across the river. Confederate military authorities posted guards to protect the bridge, factory owners took measures to safeguard the mills, and wealthy citizens made plans to leave. The mill workers could only watch and wait, uncertain as to what lay ahead.

Ever since the Union troops began threatening the Georgia border in December 1863, much time and energy had been spent in looking to the defense of Atlanta. Col. Marcus H. Wright, commanding the troops at Atlanta, complained that the numerous approaches to the city made it vulnerable to attack and "a difficult point to defend against large bodies of men." A massive line of fortifications circled the city with heavy rifle pits connecting the batteries. With no armies to defend the works, however, Rebel commanders were forced to rely on inexperienced and often unarmed local troops, comprised largely of men detailed to work in shops and factories.[1]

Making every effort to defend the approaches, Colonel Wright had written to the commanders at Marietta and Lawrenceville, expressing concern for the vulnerability of Atlanta and asking their cooperation in reporting any movement of the enemy. Wright issued instructions to Captain James King on the 7th of December, stressing the need for real vigilance on the part of the Roswell Battalion as the village of Roswell covered an important line of approach to Atlanta. The colonel hoped that the enemy would soon be driven from Georgia soil, "but it behooves us nevertheless to be very watchful." Wright instructed King to provide written reports of any enemy movement and to keep the neighborhood well picketed. The colonel sent another message to Captain King in February after General Johnston warned Wright to "be very careful" about the bridges over the Chattahoochee. King was ordered to maintain a sufficient guard at the Roswell bridge at all times and to take all necessary steps to ensure that his men were prepared and that their guns and ammunition were in good order.[2]

Although he planned to remain in Roswell until the very last moment, James King began making preparations in March to protect the property he would leave behind. Believing that the Union Army was sure to target the Ivy Woolen Mill, King devised a plan to save the factory. On March 9 he signed over a partial interest in the mill to one of his employees, Theophile Roche. Roche, a French national, had arrived in Roswell in January 1862 and immediately went to work in the mills, first as a weaver in the cotton factory and then in the woolen mill in the fall of 1863.[3]

James Roswell King (1827–1897), son of Barrington King. Owner of the Ivy Woolen Mill, James served the Confederate cause by manufacturing wool, which was desperately needed by the Confederate army. He hoped to save his mill by deeding a partial interest in the factory to a French national (courtesy the Roswell Historical Society).

By transferring an interest in the mill to the Frenchman, King believed the factory would be rendered neutral, thereby free from seizure or destruction. According to later testimony, the interest of fifty thousand dollars was given to Roche "on condition that he should remain and protect the property should it be at the risk of life." King explained, "This was upon the idea that when the Federal army came I would leave and on account of his nationality it was thought that he could protect the property."[4]

The mill owner later testified that there had been a disclaimer on the part of Roche of any future interest in the property unless he protected the property or gained it. "In other words, he relieved me of any liability to him in case the property was destroyed." King claimed that the interest was temporary and conditional while Roche later testified that it was an equitable interest for consideration of his services. If so, King must have considered Roche's services extremely valuable for the $50,000 interest reflected 50 percent of the value of the woolen mill.[5]

According to the certificate of interest dated March 9, 1864, Roche's interest was to date from the fifteenth day of March 1863. Many years later, in a suit filed over the destruction of the mill, Roche insisted that the transfer occurred in 1863, not 1864 when the document was signed. King was not able to remember or explain the discrepancy in the dates, but claimed that the transfer was executed in 1864 and effective as of that date. The certificate was written by James King, witnessed by his father, Barrington King, and notarized by H.W. Proudfoot, bookkeeper of the Roswell mills. "We do hereby certify that Theophile Roche is interested to the amount of $50,000 in the Ivy Woolen Mills of Roswell Cobb County Georgia — which interest dates from the fifteenth day of March 1863." The document was signed by J.R. King and Thomas E. King, even though Thomas had been dead for six months at the time the note was supposedly executed in 1864.[6]

The Confederate retreat from Cassville in May renewed fears of a possible attack on Atlanta. Captain King received another dispatch from Colonel Wright again urging him to exercise the greatest vigilance in view of enemy activity in their front. King's command consisted of 150 inexperienced soldiers, most detailed to work in the Roswell factories. The battalion of 100 armed infantry and 50 cavalry had four pieces of artillery. Colonel Wright was particularly concerned about the capture of the field guns by Union cavalry raiding parties not accompanied by artillery of their own. Wright urged King to offer all resistance possible if attacked by the enemy, but if the Yankee force was too large, the battalion was to fall back to the south side of the river and burn the bridge. Above all, Wright warned King to take every precaution necessary to prevent the capture of the artillery by the enemy, which would enable the Union forces to inflict great damage on the Confederates.[7]

On the 28th of May, Captain King reported the readiness of the battalion to Colonel Wright in Atlanta. The artillery was strategically placed with two cannon on the south side of the river commanding the bridge and fords and the other two at Roswell commanding the approaches to the village. The ammunition stores were across the river and held under guard. Pickets were well posted and couriers in place to keep King informed of any movement in the area. King informed Wright that he believed it was important for the battalion to hold its own at Roswell as long as possible as the presence of the men was inspiring the "feint hearted" with confidence and had turned back some fleeing refugees to their farms "where they should be."[8]

Despite King's assurances that the presence of the battalion had convinced some refugees to return to their homes, not everyone shared the same level of confidence in the local troops, and many of the wealthier families sought the safety of distant cities. Archibald Smith finally located a house to rent in Valdosta, a city in the southernmost part Georgia, where he believed they would be safe from enemy attack. Mrs. Smith had second thoughts about leaving, preferring to stay in Roswell "until driven off as fugitives" rather than flee to a log cabin with few comforts, but her husband was convinced that the move was necessary. It was not an easy decision for either of them since they would be leaving behind their youngest son, then enrolled at the Georgia Military Institute in Marietta. It was not the distance that troubled them as much as the fact that the famed military institute lay in the direct path of Sherman's army.[9]

The GMI cadets were already preparing for active duty and "yearning for the fray" when orders came for the battalion to prepare two companies for service. The number of drills increased and guns and accoutrements were issued to the young cadets, only sixteen to eighteen years of age. A few days later, restless and eager to do their part, the boys boarded the cars bound for the front line.[10]

The two companies numbering 150 cadets arrived in Resaca on May 14. Forming their lines behind a rail fence, the young boys in their dapper new uniforms took some teasing from some of the Confederate veterans nearby, but the young men would prove themselves in the moments to come. In their first encounter on the front line, the cadets fired on the enemy, killing and wounding a number of soldiers in the 9th Illinois Mounted Infantry directly in their front. A charge was made on the cadets by the mounted regiment, and the young men fell back to the safety of the woods, firing as they withdrew. Although under continual fire, the cadets suffered no casualties in the brief action. Earning praise from their officers for their conduct under fire, the cadets were withdrawn from the field and sent back to the military institute.[11]

The cadets served as provost guards in Marietta for the next few days, protecting government and private property until receiving orders to abandon the institute. With Union forces threatening Marietta, the decision was made to transfer the school to Milledgeville and to send the cadet corps to the field. At midnight on May 27, the 200 cadets took their last look at the campus and marched the mile to the rail station in Marietta where they boarded cars for West Point, Georgia, on the Chattahoochee River.[12]

Archibald and Anne Smith were packing and making final arrangements for the trip to Valdosta when they received the welcome news that the cadets were leaving GMI. With a sense of relief, the Smiths headed for the Atlanta train station on the 24th of May but found the city in a state of chaos. The mayor's call for troops only the day before had frightened Atlanta citizens and precipitated a mass exodus. Fortunately, with the help of Barrington King, Mr. and Mrs. Smith were able to get themselves and their possessions to the train depot. Archibald and Anne said their good-byes and boarded the train with only a small chair, some clothing and bedding, before heading for their new home in Valdosta, safe from the enemy at last.[13]

Despite Barrington King's vow to remain in Roswell until burned out of his home, the approach of the Union army appeared to weaken his resolve. Barrington purchased a home in Atlanta to store the furniture from Barrington Hall, and he and his wife packed their personal belongings in late May and moved to the new home which they occupied for a very short time. After receiving news that the Union forces had taken Marietta, Barrington decided that remaining in Atlanta posed too great a risk, and he and Catherine headed to Savannah to stay with one of their sons, Rev. Charles Barrington King, pastor of the White Bluff Congregational Church.[14]

Anticipating an imminent raid and unable to remove the machinery, Barrington resolved to keep the factories running as long as practicable. Before leaving he divided two months provisions among the hands, "it being safer with the people than our store in case of raid or capture." Barrington shipped hundreds of bales of cotton, large quantities of yarn, and a thousand yards of cloth to storage houses in Augusta, Newnan, Griffin and Macon and packed up all the factory books and papers to take with him to Savannah. To oversee the operation of the cotton mills in his absence, King called upon his superintendent, Olney Eldredge. Left in charge of the entire operation when Barrington left Roswell, Eldredge promised to run the mills as long as possible and to do his best to protect the property.[15]

Fearing that the Union forces would attempt to capture the bridges across the Chattahoochee River, General Gustavus W. Smith, commanding the Georgia militia, received orders on June 11 to burn the bridge at Roswell factory. Upon discovering that the local battalion had been posted at the bridge as guards, Johnston rescinded the order the following day, instructing Smith instead to make necessary preparations so that the bridge could be destroyed when it could no longer be defended. Johnston warned Smith that the enemy was threatening raids beyond the Chattahoochee and instructed him to use his entire force in watching and guarding the passages of the river as high up as Roswell.[16]

On June 16, a correspondent for the Atlanta *Southern Confederacy* visited Roswell and found it strange that although many of the citizens had fled at the approach of the enemy, the factories were running as if no enemy were within a hundred miles. Noting their immense value to the government, the correspondent predicted somewhat optimistically that the factories could be easily defended, the "natural advantages surrounding will enable our forces to hold it [Roswell] against overwhelming numbers, should the enemy attempt a raid upon the place. We have sufficient artillery to command every approach and the heights are well fortified."[17]

Nathaniel Pratt may also have believed that the village could be easily defended since he chose to stay in Roswell with his wife and daughter. The story is told that when Pratt's sons learned that Union forces were approaching the area, two of them rode home to make sure the family was safe. After they arrived, they loosened a board leading to the eaves on the south side of the house and called the space "Augusta." The same was done on the north and the space called "Macon." They hid everything of value in the spaces and then slipped the boards back into place. If questioned about the whereabouts of some article, the Reverend Pratt could respond, "it was sent to Macon or Augusta" without telling a lie. Although the property was occupied for nearly two weeks by Federal troops, the hiding places were allegedly never discovered.[18]

After receiving word that Marietta had been evacuated, the Roswell Battalion was ordered into the field. Believing that Roswell was in danger of an imminent attack,

Captain Will Clark, then commanding the battalion, sent a message to Ralph King, requesting an immediate consultation so that they could determine what had best be done. In the meantime, Clark instructed Ralph to evacuate the remaining members of the King family. "I would advise the ladies to be in readiness to leave immediately and Mrs. Tom King with her children especially." Tom's widow, Marie, had stayed in Roswell until the end, visiting Tom's grave every morning before breakfast. Now with the enemy so near, she was forced to take her children and flee to safety. With a pass from Will Clark, the women, children and servants were soon on their way.[19]

James King was the last of the "Royal Family" to leave, remaining until the last possible hour in order to oversee the operation of the woolen mill. Although he had been "hopeful to the last" that the enemy would be driven back, King knew it was only a matter of time before the Union forces arrived. Making final preparations, James sent the factory books to Atlanta but made no attempt to remove the machinery or stop production. Given the state of the railroads and the time constraints, it would have been extremely difficult to ship the machinery by train. He later testified that he would not have done so, even if he had the time and ability, not knowing any safer place to ship it. The truth of this would soon be painfully evident. In a last minute attempt to salvage what little he could, all finished goods were shipped to Atlanta, and then to Macon and finally to Columbia, South Carolina, for greater security. Much of his efforts would be in vain: $60,000 worth of finished goods would go up in flames in railroad cars outside of Columbia.[20]

After tending to his personal and business affairs, King gave last minute instructions to his overseer, Samuel Bonfoy, directing him to keep the machinery running until driven out by the enemy. Riding out of Roswell late on July 4, King left the fate of his factory in the hands of his new partner, Theophile Roche. Fearing the immediate arrival of Union forces and determined to protect his $50,000 interest in the Ivy Woolen Mill, Roche raised a French flag over the factory and another over Bulloch Hall, where he lived as a guest of the widowed Mrs. Thomas King. With the blue, white and red banner flying defiantly overhead, Roche prayed the Union army would recognize the sovereignty of France and spare the mill, in spite of the fact that the neutral factory was producing goods for the Confederate army.[21]

Reverend Pratt and Theophile Roche were not the only ones to remain in Roswell while others sought the safety of distant cities and towns. Several hundred defenseless women and children continued to labor in the mills. Amidst widely circulating stories of Yankee brutality, the women and children were left behind to face the enemy army that was even now on its way to Roswell. Perhaps the women took some solace in the presence of the 150 armed men guarding the approaches to the town, but even that measure of protection would prove to be short lived.

8

"The Women Will Howl"

*I repeat my orders that you arrest all people, male and female, connected with
those factories, no matter what the clamor, and let them foot it, under guard, to
Marietta, whence I will send them by cars to the North.... The poor women will
make a howl. Let them take along their children and clothing, providing they have
the means of hauling or you can spare them.*
— William T. Sherman, July 7, 1864

Shortly before sunrise on the 5th of July, a bell tolled in Roswell, beckoning the
spinners, the weavers, the carders and the dressers to the factories, which were running
at full capacity, no matter that the Union Army was only a short distance away. On
the other side of town, most of the grand homes near the square stood eerily silent. Of
the founding families, only Reverend Pratt, his wife, and his daughter, chose to remain
behind to face the advance of the Union army.

The women and children of the mills headed to the factories as they did every
other morning. With no means to leave and no place to go, they remained behind with
a few men, too young, too old or too sick to fight. Ordered to remain in the factories
and to run the machinery until the last minute, the operatives were instructed to protect the mill property as well as that of the mill owners.[1]

While the women and children tended their machines amid the deafening
din, Captain Will Clark, post commander, led the Roswell Battalion out of town
just three hours before the Federal troops arrived. Receiving orders late the night
before, the battalion abandoned the carefully constructed defenses and withdrew
from Roswell, having been ordered to report to Turner's Ferry on the left of the
Confederate line where General Johnston would use the men to strengthen what
he believed was his most vulnerable position. As Sherman had predicted, Johnston
expected the Union army to attempt another flanking maneuver against the
Confederate left, just as it had done time and time again throughout the campaign.
Clark and his troops crossed to the south side of the Chattahoochee River, leaving

behind only a small detachment of the 4th Tennessee Cavalry to patrol the Roswell Road.[2]

While Clark's men made their way across the covered bridge, General Kenner Garrard's troops prepared for their advance on the now defenseless mill village. Garrard, a 37-year-old West Point graduate, had been in command of the 2d Cavalry Corps since February 1864. Tall and sandy haired with a full beard and gray eyes, the reserved and retiring bachelor did not fit the role of the dashing cavalier. Sherman placed little confidence in Garrard's abilities and told Grant that he found the cavalry commander "slow" and "over-cautious."[3]

Regardless of any misgivings he may have had about Garrard, Sherman ordered him to capture the bridge and ford at Roswell. Garrard rode out from his camp on Rottenwood Creek promptly at 8 A.M., with the three brigades that made up the 2d Division Cavalry Corps. Colonel Robert Minty led the advance with his 1st Brigade composed of the 7th Pennsylvania, 4th Michigan and 4th U.S. Cavalry. Colonel Eli

Long followed with his 2d Brigade; the 1st, 3d and 4th Ohio, and Colonel Abram Miller, commanding the famed Lightning Brigade, brought up the rear with the 17th and 72d Indiana and the 98th and 123d Illinois. The six-gun battery of the Chicago Board of Trade accompanied the division.[4]

As the hot Georgia sun rose high overhead, Garrard's troopers rode toward Marietta, turned "when within two miles of it" and continued east for four miles before turning into the shade at Sope Creek. Garrard immediately ordered the 17th Indiana and the 7th Pennsylvania to move on toward Roswell. The 17th Indiana was to ride south down Sope Creek and burn the paper mills before making its way to Roswell, while the 7th Pennsylvania would head directly toward the village. The rest of the troops remained in camp, much to one soldier's relief, as "it was too fearfully hot to do anything."[5]

Major Jacob Vail's 17th Indiana troops, accompanied by a few companies of the 72d Indiana, rode down the west bank of Sope Creek until they arrived at

General Kenner Garrard (1827–1879). Commander of the Second Division Cavalry Corps at Roswell. Garrard ordered the destruction of the Roswell mills when he discovered they were manufacturing cloth for the Confederacy (courtesy the Library of Congress).

the Marietta Paper Mill. The mill was under the supervision of General William Phillips, one of the eight original stockholders. Phillips, a South Carolina native, had settled in Cobb County and served as a prominent member of the Marietta bar. At the outbreak of the war, Phillips received a commission as a Confederate colonel and organized the renowned Phillips' Legion, consisting of a six-company rifle battalion and a four-company cavalry battalion. While on active duty in Virginia in late 1861, Phillips became ill with typhoid fever. His health improved for a time, but a reoccurrence in August 1862 left him unfit for active service. He was forced to resign command of the legion, but it continued to bear his name until the end of the war. Phillips returned to Marietta and accepted a position in 1863 as a commander of the 9th Battalion of Cavalry, Georgia State Guards, but he still suffered from the effects of the original attack and was frequently confined to his bed. Phillips spent much of his time supervising the paper mill on Sope Creek.[6]

The waterpowered paper mill was incorporated in 1859 as the Marietta Paper Mill Company and was the first of its kind in the county, manufacturing paper products from cotton stalks, wood, and rags. In 1861 there were only fifteen paper mills operating in the seceding states and despite their average daily production of seventy-five thousand pounds, they could barely meet half the requirements Southern publishers placed on them each day. The Marietta Paper Mill supplied newsprint to local newspapers and was a major supplier to the Confederacy of foolscap, wrapping paper, letter paper, envelopes, and cartridge paper.[7]

The paper mill continued to operate until the arrival of Union forces on July 5. Although all of the stock on hand had been removed to Macon when the enemy troops drew near, General Phillips remained at the mill with a handful of employees. Witnessing the approach of Garrard's cavalry, the bitter and defiant general sent them a message informing the Union horsemen, "he had fought them [Yankees] from the beginning of the war and would continue to fight them to the end." He had been taught from childhood to "hate them as enemies" and he would "die hating them." Furthermore, he did not "seek any favor" from them, and "they might burn to their heart's content." In response, the Union cavalrymen completely dismantled the buildings and set the factory on fire. Phillips watched from the southern bank of the Chattahoochee as the mill went up in flames. Some of the Yankee cavalrymen torched the neighboring flour mills, and thick pillars of smoke soon darkened the noonday sky.[8]

While Vail's men destroyed the mills at Sope Creek, Major William H. Jenning's 7th Pennsylvania encountered troops of the 4th Tennessee two or three miles west of Roswell. After a brief skirmish, the Federals chased the outnumbered Rebels through the village and south toward the river where the Tennessee men attempted to make a stand. The Pennsylvanians drew sabers and charged. The Confederates could not hold the position but managed to drive the Yankees back long enough to make their way across the covered bridge. The Pennsylvania troopers tried to pursue, but the bridge burst into flames, stopping them in their tracks. In preparing for enemy raids, the Rebels had filled the bridge with dry straw and pine knots for quick destruction and it was immediately consumed by the blaze. Major Jennings quickly dispatched a courier to advise Garrard that while his men had driven the Rebels across the river and secured the crossing, they had lost the bridge.[9]

Disappointed that the bridge was gone, Garrard turned his attention to Roswell. Sending his 1st and 2d Brigades toward the village, Garrard ordered them to make camp two and one-half miles west of town at Willeo Creek. Colonel Miller remained behind with orders to concentrate the 3d Brigade on the east side of Sope Creek to guard against an approach of enemy troops.[10]

After establishing his headquarters, Garrard sent a message to Captain L.M. Dayton, Sherman's acting assistant adjutant general, to report his whereabouts as well as his intentions:

> I have to report for the information of the major general commanding that my command is camped on the Willeo Creek near Roswell Factory. My advance is at the Factory. I will destroy all buildings. The bridge at this point over the river is burnt by the rebels. The ford is passable; so reported by citizens. I sent a regiment to the paper-mills, burnt the paper-mills, flouring-mills and machine-shops.[11]

When the Pennsylvania troopers entered Roswell, someone sounded the factory bell, but no one was left to answer the call. Realizing they were at the mercy of the Yankee soldiers, Theophile Roche and several of the town's citizens rode out to Garrard's headquarters that evening and met Colonel Minty. Roche made known his French citizenship and demanded that the "rights of neutrals" be respected in themselves and their property. Minty sent Roche to Garrard who assured him that no order for the destruction of the mills in Roswell had been issued. Since Garrard had already stated his intention to "destroy all buildings," it appears that Garrard was giving some serious consideration to Roche's claim of neutrality; either that or he wanted the French flags in hand before making any move against the factories.[12]

At sunrise on July 6, Captain Darius Livermore, commanding the 3d Ohio Cavalry, was directed to report to General Garrard in person. Garrard ordered Livermore to move with his command on the road to Roswell and "capture that town, if possible." Garrard informed Livermore that he would find two factories at Roswell and another 1½ miles up the river "with French flags floating over the same, claiming the protection of the empire of France." Livermore was to "obtain the flags" in a "peaceable manner" if possible, but to obtain the flags, "under any circumstances," and then forward them to headquarters. Garrard warned Livermore about Roche: "You will find a superintendent running these factories in full force, who will no doubt claim protection under the flags."[13]

Livermore was ordered to take one squadron from his own regiment and one from the 4th Ohio Cavalry, with a section of the Chicago Board of Trade Battery to follow in support. The orders were remarkably specific, even instructing Livermore as to the pace of the advance. "Move out as rapidly as possible at a brisk walk and then at a trot and a gallop for about two miles and a fast gallop for about one mile, into the town."[14]

Livermore entered Roswell, deserted save for the hundreds of operatives inside the factory walls, with no opposition. He persuaded Roche to give him the French flags in exchange for a handwritten receipt. "This will certify that the bearer Mr. Theophile Roche has voluntarily given the undersigned two French flags. His property will receive the same protection as though the flags still remained on his premises." After capturing the town and the factories, Livermore forwarded the French banners to headquarters as instructed.[15]

With the flags safely in his possession, Garrard decided to make an inspection of the woolen mill. It is not clear what his reasons were for doing so, but he may, in all likelihood, have had some doubts about the alleged neutrality of the factory claiming protection under the French flag. Riding out to the mill at the mouth of Vickery Creek, Garrard and several other officers entered the factory, finding the operatives busy at work. A thorough investigation revealed that the factory was indeed supplying cloth to the Confederate government. Convinced that Roche's claim of neutrality was a farce, Garrard issued orders for the immediate destruction of the Roswell factories.[16]

At 4:30 P.M., Garrard's assistant adjutant general, Captain Robert Kennedy, accompanied by several members of his staff, delivered additional detailed instructions to Captain Livermore:

> General Garrard directs that you have carefully removed from the two factories (cotton and woolen) at Roswell and one factory 1½ miles up the creek, all goods suitable for Hospital and Army use, and after having satisfied yourself that no one is in either of the factories, you will set them on fire and burn them to the ground. The woolen factory near the river will be burned first, after which the cotton factory at the town will be burned. After these buildings are consumed, you will see that all is quiet, and then return to camp, bringing all of your men and all others you may find belonging to the command. In burning the factories, you will be very careful to see that none of the houses of the inhabitants are burned, and use all effort to save the property of the factory employees.[17]

Instructed to begin with the woolen factory, Livermore's troopers entered the mill and ordered the superintendent to turn off the machinery and evacuate the building. Enraged by the orders to destroy the mill, Roche warned of dire consequences if any one so much as laid a finger on property belonging to France. Ignoring the Frenchman and his idle threats, Livermore ordered a guard to clear the premises. The operatives left the building and the machinery was shut down. The remaining books and papers of the company were seized, placed under guard and forwarded to army headquarters. The Union soldiers "smashed the machinery and fired the buildings." In a few hours nothing remained but smoking ruins.[18]

Livermore then sent a detail into town under the command of Major J.C. McCoy, Sherman's aide-de-camp, to burn the two cotton mills. McCoy was accompanied by a considerable escort including a detachment of the 7th Pennsylvania and Silas Stevens of the Chicago Board of Trade Battery. Upon their arrival, McCoy asked the mill superintendent, Olney Eldredge, to show him around the factories, "to see the working of the machinery, the work that was turned out and the number of women, girls and children employed. In fact everything connected with the manufacture of rebel goods, and capacity of entire factory."[19]

After the inspection, "with the greatest politeness and civility on the part of the aide," McCoy informed Eldredge that they had orders to burn the mill. Eldredge was ordered to stop the machinery and to evacuate the operatives from the building. The machinery, which had been running at full capacity, was quickly brought to a full stop and the men, women and children filed out of the building and stood in wonder on the banks of the stream watching the preparations for the destruction of the mills.[20]

McCoy placed Stevens and two other soldiers in charge of the storehouse while McCoy reserved the "main factory" for himself. With painstaking detail, Stevens described his participation in the burning of the buildings:

> I caused to be placed on each floor, beginning at the top, saturated cotton with oil, in great quantities and carefully arranged everything ready to fire my building and waited with my men till the aide had started his fire, as a matter of courtesy. I did not wait long. I lighted the combustibles, which went off with a flash at the upper story first, then each successive floor from the top downward to the basement. So that I had a very interesting blaze at once while McCloud [McCoy] fired his machinery hall, from the basement or engine room, by this act the fire of the factory burned more slowly. My idea was not to endanger the buildings of the residents of the place whose houses were in the immediate vicinity, and if my fire was communicated by floors, from the top downward, there would possibly be less danger from flying sparks and each floor would fall quickly as burned, into the basement and the waters of the stream. The walls which were very stout would probably remain standing but the contents of the entire edifice would be consumed.... Long before the factory was well started, the contents of my building were entirely consumed.[21]

Stevens took great satisfaction in destroying the factories. "From this time on, till the end of the war, orders of this kind, I greatly enjoyed and many a bale of cotton and gin mills of every description my hand fired." Stevens believed that the burning of cotton produced more good, towards the ending of the cruel war, than did the deaths of so many soldiers. "A thousand bales of cotton belonging to the enemy burned by our forces, was better than a thousand lives destroyed in battle." With the buildings in flames and "beyond the point of rescue," Stevens was given permission to take one man and return to camp to report the success of the undertaking.[22]

Olney Eldredge and the mill workers stood helpless as the Yankee soldiers burned the factories, gristmill, cotton houses, storehouses, the president and the superintendent's offices. "All were consumed." Understanding that their fate now lay in the hands of Union soldiers, many of the women were moved to tears. Captain David Conyngham, Sherman's aide-de-camp, commented on the reaction of the mill workers: "it was feeling to witness how they wept, as this, their only means of support, was consigned to destruction." Not all of the women viewed the scene through tears. An unidentified mill worker later recalled that the operatives watched as the factory burned, "some weeping and crying, while others laughed with joy."[23]

Roswell Mill Ruins, sketched by Charles Holyland, Chicago Board of Trade Battery. "Ruins of the Roswell Manufacturing Co. Mills. Destroyed by a Detachment of the 7th Penn. Cavalry, 2 Div., Gen. Garrard comdg., and 1st Brigade Col. Minty who fired it by order of the War Department on the night of the 7th of July, 1864. During the Rebellion it was under the control and worked by the Confederate government being one of the most extensive in the South. It is situated in the village of Roswell, Cobb. Co. Geo — 9 miles South East of Marietta and 20 miles North West of Atlanta on the Chattahoochee River, and is known under the firm of Roswell King & Co. It was destroyed when the cavalry on the extreme left of the army attempted the crossing of the river. It employed near 700 operatives" (courtesy the Roswell History Society).

When the last of the flames was extinguished, all that remained were the thick brick walls. In a letter to the *Daily Toledo Blade*, an Ohio cavalryman, claiming "the honor of applying the torch to the celebrated cotton factories," likened the massive walls which now stood "in their nakedness" to the "remains of some antiquated and deserted castles." Private Charles Holyland of the Chicago Board of Trade Battery drew a meticulous sketch of the ruins detailing the size of the structures and extent of the destruction. The roofs are gone and the mill buildings are gutted; only the red brick walls remain.[24]

At 7 P.M. Garrard prepared a report to be forwarded to Sherman noting his occupation of the village now deserted by her "citizens of property." He described the Roswell factories, their importance to the Confederate war effort and the details of their destruction:

> There were some fine factories here, one woolen factory, capacity 30,000 yards a month, and has furnished up to within a few weeks 15,000 yards per month to the rebel Government, the Government furnishing men and material. Capacity of cotton factory 216 looms, 191,086 yards per month, and 51,666 pounds of thread, and 4,229 pounds of cotton rope. This was worked exclusively for the rebel Government.... There was six months' supply of cotton on hand. Over the woolen factory the French flag was flying, but seeing no Federal flag above it I had the building burnt. All are burnt. The cotton factory was worked up to the time of its destruction, some 400 women being employed. There was some cloth which had been made since yesterday morning, which I will save for our hospitals (several thousand yards of cotton cloth), also some rope and thread.... The machinery of the cotton factory cost before the war $400,000. The superintendent estimates that it alone was worth with its material, &c., when burnt over a million of our money.[25]

While the courier waited, Garrard finished his report and made a last minute change to a map he had drawn of the area on his arrival the day before. Garrard had written a note on the right hand side of the drawing: "Roswell is a very pretty factory town of about four thousand inhabitants. Mills & private property not injured by me." Apparently Garrard had given some initial consideration to Roche's claim of neutrality and had not intended to burn the mills, despite his pledge to destroy all buildings. Nevertheless, the situation had changed dramatically over the last 24 hours and before handing the map to the courier, Garrard took a pencil and crossed out the word "Mills."[26]

With their mission accomplished, Livermore and his troops returned to camp at 10:30 that evening, at which time Garrard complimented the command on its success. Like the iron works at Etowah and the paper mills on Sope Creek, these factories were part of the very industrial infrastructure that Sherman pledged to tear down. Years later Sherman would defend these policies as part of his plan to show Georgia "what war meant." Sherman claimed he "had a right to destroy" in order to "make them [Georgia] feel the consequences of war so fully they will never again invite an invading Army." Any establishment manufacturing goods for the Confederacy was doomed to destruction. Not everyone saw the wisdom in such practices, at least where the Roswell

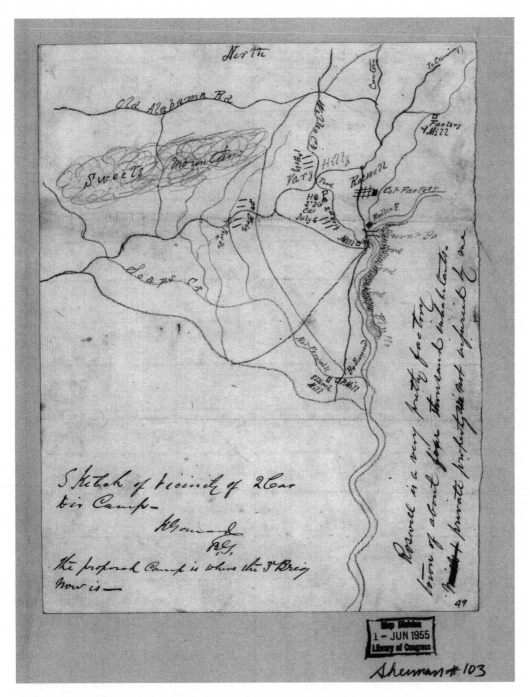

Garrard's map of Roswell and vicinity, July 1864, drawn by General Kenner Garrard on his arrival. Note that the word "mills" has been crossed out (courtesy the Library of Congress).

factories were concerned. A correspondent from the *Cincinnati Daily Commercial* wrote, "Their entire destruction by our authorities was, doubtless, determined by valid considerations of policy, but what these were is not so obvious." Another northern reporter from the *Hartford Courant* believed that the factories should not have been burned as they were "private property" and did not belong to the "Confederate authorities." He argued that the wanton destruction of private property would only "incense" the civilian population.[27]

The "wanton destruction" was not limited to the factories. Despite orders to the contrary, Roswell would not be spared the devastation that Federal troops had visited on other towns and villages on their march toward Atlanta. The spacious homes of the founding families, now abandoned, were soon overrun with Yankee soldiers. A correspondent to the *Cincinnati Daily Commercial* believed the Roswell aristocracy was only receiving its just reward. "The wealthy lords, who have domineered in this country for years, left their homes for ease and comfort and fled before the advancing foe. Their homes, filled with all the luxuries of wealth, were taken possession of and their effects given to the poor over whom they had lorded for time passed forever."[28]

Federal officers confiscated unoccupied homes for headquarters buildings and converted others into temporary hospitals. Houses not used for military purposes fell victim to the stragglers of the Union army. Acts of wanton pillaging and plundering increased and Garrard instructed the 2d Brigade's provost marshal, Lt. H.H. Siverd, to send out guards to "arrest and severely punish" all stragglers found out of camp without passes. Additionally, Garrard requested that Siverd personally see to the matter in order to prevent the "outrages" that were "almost hourly disgracing their commands."[29]

After receiving Garrard's report detailing the destruction of the Roswell mills, Sherman sent word of his approval by messenger. Captain Joseph C. Audenried of Sherman's staff arrived in Roswell at 5:30 P.M. and delivered a lengthy message from the Federal commander:

> I had no idea that the factories at Roswell remained in operation, but supposed the machinery had all been removed. Their utter destruction is right and meets my entire approval, and to make the matter complete you will arrest the owners and employees and send them, under guard, charged with treason, to Marietta, and I will see as to any man in America hoisting the French flag and then devoting his labor and capital in supplying armies in open hostility to our Government and claiming the benefit of his neutral flag. Should you, under the impulse of anger, natural at contemplating such perfidy, hang the wretch, I approve the act beforehand.

Then addressing himself to the military situation, Sherman instructed Garrard to attempt a crossing of the Chattahoochee, "I want a lodgment on the other bank as soon as possible anywhere from Roswell down to the vicinity of Sope Creek."[30]

Sherman continued on a more personal note with a vote of confidence and a word of warning:

I assure you, in spite of any little disappointment I may have expressed, I feel for you personally not only respect but affection, and wish for your unmeasured success and reputation, but I do wish to inspire all cavalry with my conviction that caution and prudence should be but a very small element in their characters.[31]

Sherman reserved his final words for the mill workers:

I repeat my orders that you arrest all people, male and female, connected with those factories, no matter what the clamor, and let them foot it, under guard, to Marietta, whence I will send them by cars to the North. Destroy and make the same disposition of all mills save small flouring mills manifestly for local use, but all saw-mills and factories dispose of effectually, and useful laborers, excused by reason of their skill as manufacturers from conscription, are as much prisoners as if armed. *The poor women will make a howl.* Let them take along their children and clothing, providing they have the means of hauling or you can spare them. We will retain them until they can reach a country where they can live in peace and security.[32]

Sherman sent a similar message to General Henry W. Halleck reporting Garrard's possession of Roswell and the destruction of the Roswell factories:

They had been for years engaged exclusively at work for the Confederate Government and the owner of the woolen factory displayed the French flag; but as he failed also to show the United States flag, General Garrard burned it also.... I have ordered General Garrard to arrest for treason all owners and employees, foreign and native, and send them under guard to Marietta, whence I will send them North. Being exempt from conscription, they are as much governed by the rules of war as if in the ranks. The women can find employment in Indiana. This whole region was devoted to manufactories, but I will destroy every one of them.[33]

The destruction of the Roswell mills was not unexpected, but no one had anticipated the arrest of the workers, especially when the firing of the factories would normally have ended the matter. Sherman's order to arrest and deport factory employees, particularly female employees, went far beyond the destruction of war resources. Whether indicative of the current hard war measures, or simply a changing perception of "military necessity," this was not the course Sherman had pursued under similar circumstances only one year earlier.

In May of 1863 Sherman and Grant entered Joshua and Thomas Green's cotton factory in Jackson, Mississippi. One of the largest in the state, the mill employed some 200 workers. Sherman and Grant stood for a time watching the tent cloth roll out of the looms with "C.S.A. woven into every bolt." After informing the owners that the factory would be destroyed, Sherman dismissed the operatives but allowed them to take as much cloth as they could carry. The Messrs. Green begged Sherman to spare the factory. While they admitted they had provided some cloth to the Confederacy, most of their cloth was woven for local use. More importantly, the factory was the sole source of employment for many women and poor families. Despite their appeals, Sherman believed the factory might prove too valuable to the Confederate war effort and ordered its destruction. Still, Sherman demonstrated some concern for the welfare of the workers and assured them that the Union army would provide food for their families until they could find employment or were able to find refuge elsewhere. There were no accusations of treason and no talk of arrests.[34]

But in July 1864, Sherman displayed little compassion for the women and children whose fate he held in his hands, the mill workers he claimed were "tainted with treason." It is not clear why he saw fit to treat these workers differently than he did those at the Jackson factory. These women and children, young boys, and old men were not spies or traitors. They simply worked in mills that supplied goods to the Confederate government — jobs that provided their only means of support. If the arrest of the Roswell mill workers can be justified by claiming that employment in Southern cotton and woolen mills constituted aiding and abetting the enemy, then why were the Jackson factory workers not arrested in 1863 under virtually identical circumstances?

While the Lieber Code did not specifically address factory workers providing services for an enemy government, it did maintain that unarmed citizens could be captured if "important" to the hostile government. Since the Lieber Code failed to define "important," it once again left much room for an ambiguous interpretation. It is doubtful that those arrested at Roswell could have played a significant role in the Confederacy in the months to come. Nor is it likely that the poor and uneducated mill workers would pose a serious threat, especially after the mills were gone.[35]

In general, the Lieber Code specified that unarmed citizens were to be spared "in person" and "in property." They were not to be "murdered, enslaved, or carried off to distant parts." A commander did have the power to expel, transfer, imprison or fine if unarmed citizens refused to take an oath of allegiance, but there is no indication that the Roswell workers were given that opportunity. Ultimately, "military necessity" overrode all other concerns and Sherman apparently deemed it necessary to send the unskilled women and children to the north. Writing some years after the war, Confederate colonel W.D. Pickett questioned the necessity of the expulsion: "Supposing the destruction of Roswell mills was within the usages of civilized warfare, can there be given one valid reason for the sudden deportation of these unfortunates from the comforts and protections of home?" Pickett believed that the decision to remove the women had its origin in a "bad heart" and predicted that these actions would forever be a "stain upon the character of the Federal commander."[36]

It is far easier to rationalize the earlier arrest of 44 skilled workmen at the Etowah Iron Works who might very well have found work in other manufacturing establishments aiding the Confederacy. Failing that, there was nothing to prevent them from donning uniforms and joining the gray-clad ranks. But justified or not, sending these men "across the Ohio River" was far less cruel since it was likely that all would find some kind of work up north. These same rationalizations, however, did not apply to the hundreds of unskilled women and children from the Roswell factories.

Sherman contended that the male factory workers were no different from soldiers and subject to the same treatment. It is true that many of the male employees in the Roswell factories were exempt from conscription by virtue of their skill, while others were soldiers detailed to work in the factories, just as at Etowah. What Sherman may or may not have known, however, was that all the detailed soldiers and able-bodied men had ridden out with the battalion. All who remained were young boys and aged or disabled men.[37]

Sherman attempted to justify the arrests in his official correspondence, although he makes no mention of the mill workers in letters to his wife or in his memoirs written ten years after the war. In his orders to Garrard on July 7 Sherman states that the men were subject to the same rules of warfare as if they were armed. He makes no similar argument for the women, only that that the women will be taken to a place "where they can live in peace and security." On the same day in a letter to General Halleck he wrote, "The women can find employment in Indiana." In another letter to Halleck on the 9th he added, "They were tainted with treason.... I will send all the owners, agents, and employees up to Indiana to get rid of them here." To General J.D. Webster at Nashville he directed, "When they arrive in Nashville, have them sent across the Ohio River and turned loose to earn a living where they won't do us any harm."[38]

While his correspondence seems to imply that he ordered the women sent north largely for humanitarian reasons rather than military necessity, Sherman had the women "arrested," "placed under guard," and "charged with treason," acts that seem strangely inconsistent with purely benevolent motives. Rather than the "military necessity" which Sherman never clearly establishes, his order for the arrest of the workers may have been motivated in no small part by his anger over Roche's fraudulent claim of neutrality. Indeed, Sherman was so outraged at the deception that he granted Garrard permission to "hang the wretch" if he so desired. In his message to Halleck on July 9, Sherman wrote that the factories had been transferred to the "English and French flags for safety," but states that he had not been deceived by "such nonsense." Sherman continued, "such fictitious transfer was an aggravation.... I take it a neutral is no better than one of our own citizens, and we would not respect the property of one of our own citizens engaged in supplying a hostile army." The women and children played no role in the deception staged by James King and Theophile Roche, but it was the innocent mill workers who would pay the greatest price.[39]

In accordance with Sherman's orders, Garrard conducted a thorough reconnaissance of the area seeking practicable fords across the Chattahoochee. Returning at 10 P.M., Garrard advised Audenried that he did not have enough time to prepare and could not effect a crossing the next morning as requested, but he assured the aide that he would have everything ready for the 9th.[40]

Although forced to delay the river crossing, Garrard wasted no time in ordering the arrest of the mill workers. Fortunately for those concerned, Garrard did not think much of Sherman's idea to let the mill workers "foot it" the sixteen miles to Marietta and decided to send them in empty supply wagons. The wagons could then pick up supplies and bring them back to Roswell on the return trip.[41]

At 4 P.M. on July 7, a staff officer arrived at Bulloch Hall and ordered Roche to report to the public square, as the "general commanding said forces" desired to speak

Chicopee, Nov. 21, 1866

My Dear Brother

Your favor of the 17th has come to hand, and I have written a statement of the facts, and hope you will be so kind as to arrange them as you see fit for print. I do not know how to write for the public. If what I have written is not what you wish, or if you wish anything else please let me know it. I am much oblige for the change to buy P.O. stamps with. All well as usual – Much love from all to all. Please let me know if you get this. Excuse this for I have written in great haste.
Ever your affectionate Brother
O. Eldredge

Olney Eldredge moved from Springfield, Mass to Milledgeville, Geo in 1846. He remained in midle Geo. manfg until 1861 – when he moved to Roswell Cobb County to superintend two large Cotton Factories owned by the Roswell Manfg Co. He had charge of the Manfg. Department until July 1864 – turning [illegible] about 5,000 lbs of cotton goods per day. In June 1864 the Confederate Army fell back to Marietta, and Genl Sherman's left wing of the Federal Army came within 12 miles of Roswell. At this time the President and Owners of the Factories went south leaving the whole in care of the Supt. On the 5th of July Genl Shermans Cavalry under the command of Genl Gerard came into Roswell. On the 6th just before sundown they fired the Factories, Machine Shop, Grist Mill, Cotton Houses, Store Houses, the President and the Superintendent's Offices, and all was consumed, together with the contents. On the 7th O. Eldredge was taken as a prisoner and carried to Gen Gerards Head Quarters and kept until the 8th. He was then sent home with orders to be ready to start for the Ohio River in three (3) hours. At the end of that time he together with his Family (consisting of three children) were put in a mule wagon and sent to Marietta – 13 miles. After remaining there two days he was put in a Baggage Car for Chattanooga. Without money except Confederate money which was of no use or Provisions and his property all left behind. To reach Mass he had 1600 miles to travel, on reaching Chattanooga he was oblige to get new papers to reach Nashville. At that place new papers must be had to reach Louisville. This place reached by riding in Baggage cars and begging. He could get no more transportation free. But by applying to the Presbyterian Church (of which he was a Nesting Elder for years) he was helped to Cincinnati, Ohio. There he applied to the Reffugee Aid Society, and with their aid found transportation to Boston, Mass where he arrived after thirteen days from the time of starting He was furnished with a certificate of loyalty, But was sent back because northern [Ohio?] helped the rebellion.

to him. On arriving, Roche and 44 other men, including Olney Eldredge, were met by four cavalrymen who placed them under arrest and marched them on to Garrard's headquarters. Reaching their destination at 9:30 that evening, the prisoners slept in the woods under guard and remained there until 4 P.M. the next day.[42]

Federal soldiers rounded up the women and children and placed the workers under arrest. Allowing them a short time to gather their belongings, the soldiers marched them out to the town square where they waited for supply wagons to transport them to Marietta. It is impossible to determine the number of women arrested nor can we rely on eyewitness accounts of Yankee soldiers whose estimates vary widely. Some simply mention several hundred women or female operatives, but others are far more specific with numbers ranging from 200 to as many as 1200. Lt. William Doyle of the 17th Indiana thought the number much higher, writing in 1897 that there were, in fact, 3000 hands. Most placed the number between 400 and 500, and since Garrard refers to 400 women in his official report that is the number most often cited. Often overlooked is the fact that Garrard was referring only to the number of female employees in one of the factories. The total number of women taken prisoner may easily have exceeded 500. Allowing for their children and aged parents, the number deported may have reached upwards of 1,000 or more.[43]

Roche and the other male prisoners returned to Roswell on the 8th. Given an hour to gather his possessions, Roche made a final protest against the order but to no avail. The Frenchman packed up what little he could carry in his carpetbag and headed for the square. Eldredge went home to get his three children, Mary, 19, Martha, 17, and Judson, 8, and what few possessions they could carry. After returning to the square, Eldredge and his family climbed into one of the wagons headed for Marietta. Eldredge was permitted to take along his Confederate money, money that would be of no use on his journey north.[44]

Soldiers loaded some of the women and children into the empty supply wagons heading for Marietta on the 8th along with Roche, Eldredge and the other men. Company H of the 3d Ohio and Company E of the 7th Pennsylvania had the "good fortune" to guard the train of some fifty wagons filled with factory workers and factory goods. Although an article in the *Nashville Dispatch* reported that all of the female operatives left Roswell in 110 supply wagons, the accounts of various soldiers indicate otherwise. Captain William Van Antwerp of the 4th Ohio wrote on July 10 that wagons had been busy transporting the operatives to Marietta for the previous two days, and a number of soldiers reported seeing many of the women and children in Roswell on the 10th and 11th still awaiting transportation.[45]

In a separate incident, Garrard's 2d Brigade arrested nine men on July 8. T.M. Boyd was listed as a wagoneer for the army at Roswell. George Eads, Thomas Quinn, Newton

Opposite: **Copy of Olney Eldredge Letter, November 21, 1866. One of the few firsthand accounts to survive, Eldredge's letter describes the destruction of the mills, his arrest, and the deportation of his family (courtesy the descendants of Olney Eldredge).**

Green, Elijah Smith, Andrew J. Whitington, Asel Hindman, Benjamin Smith and Peter Cobb appear on a list of "Rebel Citizens" detailed to work in the Roswell factories. Although they are listed as citizens, several of these men were members of the Roswell Battalion. Their service records do not indicate why they were absent from the battalion on the 8th of July. Additionally, it appears the nine men were arrested one day after the other 45 men had been taken prisoner. At some point, the Union authorities determined that at least three of the men, Eades, Hindman, and Green, were members of the Roswell Battalion and added their names to a list of "rebel deserters." Given the oath in Louisville, the "citizens-turned-deserters" would share the same fate as the others — all were sent north of the Ohio River.[46]

Many Union soldiers would describe the unusual events they witnessed at Roswell, some in letters home, some in makeshift diaries, and others for publication in newspapers. Some accounts, written years after the war, would find their way into memoirs, reminiscences and regimental histories. Whether the soldier wrote it the same day or many years later, each man seemed to have his own version. Virtually every account reported the burning of the mills, but accounts differed widely on such points as who led the details or what units participated. The women are mentioned less frequently. Some soldiers noted that the women were "sent" to Marietta or "sent" north, but never did they use the word "arrest." Other accounts suggested that the women chose to go north, and that the deportation was nothing more than a charitable deed carried out entirely for the benefit of the mill workers. A correspondent to the *Louisville Journal* reported that Sherman had in fact taken pity on the "poor creatures," and that the women had begged General Sherman to remove them "from the scenes of desolation." The writer added that in the "exercise of an enlarged and generous spirit of humanity, the General acceded to their request."[47]

Lieutenant Doyle also maintained that the journey north was a matter of choice as well as an act of mercy. Doyle's account, written some 33 years after the war, contained a number of errors, including his contention that some of the mill cottages were destroyed in the fire. Either his memory was severely impaired or he simply decided to

Mary Flagg Eldredge Torrey (1844–1923). The oldest daughter of Olney Eldredge, Mary was only 19 when forced from her home in Roswell (courtesy the descendants of Olney Eldredge).

embellish the facts in an attempt to cast the incident in a somewhat favorable and more merciful light.

> But in the terrible conflagration that ensued the sparks set fire to many of the working people's cottages and pitiful scenes occurred. Those women, girls and children rendered homeless had to take shelter with others, but they would all soon be homeless, for how could they earn a living when their source of subsistence was gone? A few days later Gen. Sherman gave orders to have such of these operatives as desired to be taken north on the empty trains constantly going back, and they nearly all availed themselves of the privilege and were taken care of by charitable people in Ohio, Indiana and Illinois.[48]

Regardless of what some believed to be charitable motives, the deportation was neither a choice nor a privilege. Sherman's directives were clear. He ordered their arrest, placed them under guard and "sent" them to Marietta to board trains that would take them hundreds of miles away from their homes and loved ones. The common soldier, however, may not have been privy to the specifics of the arrest order and may have believed that the deportation was in the best interests of the operatives. Nor would the soldiers have knowledge of the desperate conditions that awaited the mill workers north of the Ohio River.

Soldiers found the sight of so many women a novel one. Under the mistaken impression that most of the women had been sent to Roswell from northern factories, Sergeant Benjamin Magee of the 72d Indiana assumed most were northern born. He thought the "northern" women "were really good looking; most all the women we have seen for the past year have been fearfully homely." Magee would have been surprised to learn that there were few, if any, women from the north in the Roswell factories. Most of the female operatives were natives of Georgia or South Carolina. Other soldiers were not quite so taken with the young women from the mills. Private Charles Wills thought it difficult to find one who was "passably handsome." Captain George W. Pepper of the 80th Ohio found the women most disagreeable:

> They were not of the most handsomest features or pattern, looking at a distance more like walking corpses or painted cedar-posts, than the flowers of the South we were wont to read of. They were hoopless and bootless; nearly all used the weed, a respectable quid being within the lips of many. Their appearance confirmed the celibical determination of my boyhood.[49]

Pepper's unkind and unflattering comments were not far from the truth, a sad commentary on the hardships of factory life. Working inside the mills for twelve to fourteen hours a day, six days a week, these women rarely saw the light of day. Laboring under unhealthy conditions without adequate sunshine and fresh air, any woman would soon resemble a "walking corpse." Use of the "weed" or chewing tobacco was not at all unusual, even for young girls, then or for the years to come. Many believed that the tobacco kept the harmful lint out of their throats and prevented respiratory diseases like the dreaded brown lung. Where clothing was concerned, hoop skirts would hardly have been appropriate attire for factory work, and what little wages they received in company scrip barely provided for food and bare necessities. There was no money and no need for fancy clothes. Practicality and poverty determined their dress, not the desire to please the eye of an enemy soldier.

While the wagons headed for Marietta, the three brigades moved into Roswell, and Garrard made his headquarters at Barrington Hall. Colonel Long set up headquarters in the Mt. Carmel Methodist Church, a large brick building near town. The Roswell Presbyterian Church was converted into a hospital, as was Dunwody Hall, and the lawn of Great Oaks was full of men and equipment. Only the Smith house was spared and left unoccupied, probably due to its somewhat remote location.[50]

Roswell was teeming with horses and wagons and soldiers in blue. Hundreds of tents filled the town square. In the midst of this chaos, many of the women and children still remained under guard, lining the dusty roads, waiting for wagons to take them to Marietta. While the women waited, Garrard prepared to cross the swift-flowing Chattahoochee at Shallow Ford, a half mile downstream from the burned bridge.[51]

Although the river was deep and wide in most places and full of strong currents that made crossing dangerous, there were a few fords where the water was shallow enough for wading. Crossing at the ford presented its own challenges. Here, the river bottom was rocky and rough, full of trenches, pits, and holes. The steep, densely wooded bluffs on the opposite side of the river created naturally strong defensive positions, and a considerable force of Rebel cavalry was already in place. Getting his first look at the site, Sergeant Magee decided his brigade had been purposely camped in the dense woods and far from the river in order "that we might not know nothing of the dangers of the work before us."[52]

Just after dark, the 1st and 3d Brigades moved out and bivouacked a mile from the river. Called up at 3 A.M., the men fell into ranks and moved down to the river on foot under the cover of a dark moonless night. A blanket of fog along the riverbank helped to conceal their movements. The 3d Brigade got into position near the river with the 1st Brigade close behind. Four companies of skirmishers from the 3d Brigade hid in the brush along the edge of the water. Three additional companies, deployed as sharpshooters, formed their line on the bluffs and the Chicago Board of Trade battery posted its artillery on the high hill overlooking the river. Captain Chester Thompson, in charge of the skirmishers, rode to headquarters and informed Colonel Miller that his men were deployed and in position. Miller ordered Thompson to send the skirmishers across the river as soon as the artillery opened. Incredulous, Thomas replied, "You don't mean to say that we are expected to wade that river?" Miller answered, "Yes, that is what we have been sent here for, and we expect to do it."[53]

Thompson returned to his command just as the artillery sent forth a volley of shells that broke the silence of the night like "mighty thunder." Thompson gave the command "forward!" and the men plunged into the water without hesitation. General Garrard rode to the edge of the river and cheered them on shouting, "Bully boys! Bully boys! Whiskey in the morning!" The whole brigade urged them forward with cheer after

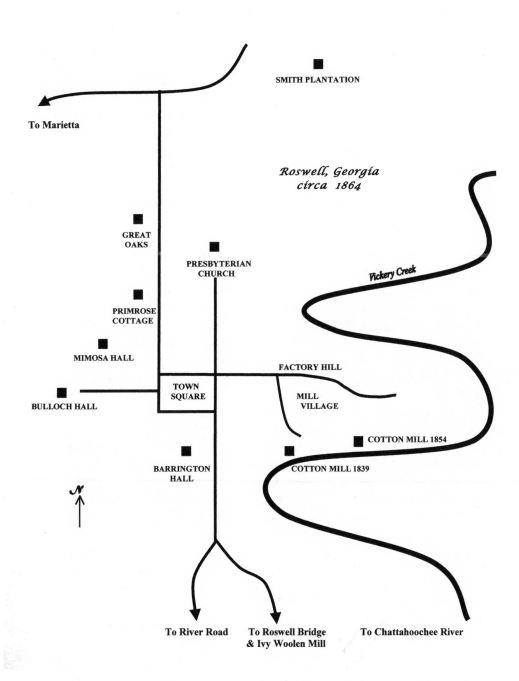

Map of Roswell — July 1864.

cheer. Although the current was strong, and the bottom rough and deep in places, the water coming up to their arms, the skirmishers moved steadily forward. Armed with Spencer repeating carbines, the cavalrymen were able to load their guns under water. Crouching low in the river, with only their heads exposed, the men loaded seven metallic cartridges into the magazine, then stood up, emptied the water from the muzzle and "blazed away at the astonished enemy." Joseph Vale claimed he could hear the Confederates yelling, "Look at the Yankee __ __ __ loading their guns under water!" Once the skirmishers reached the south bank of the river, the rest of the men in the 1st and 3d Brigades waded across, advanced "about a mile," and threw up strong defensive works, holding them until relieved later that afternoon.[54]

Marching to Garrard's aid, General John Newton's 2d Division of the IV Corps passed through Roswell on its way to the river, and the infantrymen witnessed a number of the women who still remained in town. Lt. John Tuttle noted in his diary that he saw 400 factory girls lining the sides of the road, "presenting quite a sad appearance." The IV Corps continued to the river and crossed over about seven in the evening, relieving Garrard's troopers who waded back across the river and returned to camp "wet, tired and hungry."[55]

The next morning, the church bell rang at 10:00 A.M., calling the Yankee soldiers to a "divine service" in the Roswell Presbyterian Church. The building had been converted into a Union hospital, much to the dismay of Reverend Pratt, who, according to the surgeon in charge, "was not at all pleased at our polluting his house with sick and wounded Yankee soldiers, notwithstanding the land of wooden nutmegs [Connecticut] was his early home." As there were few patients in the makeshift hospital, it was the perfect setting for Sunday services. William Records of the 72d Indiana noted that it was "quite novel to go to church at the sound of bell instead of bugle." The regimental chaplain for the 72d Indiana, Isaac de LaMatyr, preached to a full house, a service Benjamin Magee, also of the 72d, found "unusually impressive." Magee noted, "If the common people of the south had been permitted to look in upon our devotions, they must have been convinced that we Yankees were not the vandals their leaders had pictured us to be."[56]

On the other hand, the behavior of some of the Union soldiers shortly after the service might have persuaded the common people that the men were far worse than mere vandals. Fulfilling his promise of a reward for fording the river crossing, General Garrard sent around whiskey right after breakfast, only the second time the 72d Indiana had "drawn or ever had whiskey issued since entering the service." Sergeant Magee disapproved:

> We think this is a mistake, as the men never needed it, or asked for it, and always got along just as well without it. The whiskey ration was about a gill [4 oz.], and not enough to hurt anyone provided each one drank his own rations. But there was always some in each company who would never draw their rations at all, which would just leave that much more for somebody else, while among those who did draw their rations there were some who were not content to drink them alone, but had a way of gambling drink for drink till some would get a pint or even a quart and of course get foolishly drunk.[57]

To make matters worse, many of the women remained. James Zearing, regimental surgeon for the 57th Illinois, arrived at noon with the XIV Corps and wrote his wife the following day. "The operatives are still here, all very short of provisions." Explaining that his regiment had provided for the women by sending them on to Marietta, he added, "It was a very fine sight to see four hundred girls all at once, a sight we do not often see in the army."[58]

Whether or not 400 women remained is impossible to determine, but whatever the number, the sight of so many young women proved too great a temptation for some of the drunken soldiers. According to Magee, their "delirium" took form of "making love" to the women, and before night Colonel Miller found it necessary to move the brigade a mile north of the town. While the term "making love" is subject to interpretation, it is clear that Magee did not view the incident favorably. Would he have objected had it been only innocent, light-hearted flirting? Whatever the extent of the "delirium," it is not surprising that Magee was the only one to mention the shameful treatment of the women by the drunk and disorderly men. What is surprising is that Magee himself dared speak of it, even in the polite terms he used in his published history of the 72d Indiana. There is no other evidence to support Magee's recollection of the events, but the brigade was, indeed, moved north of town that same night. Sarah Blackwell Gober Temple, in her history of Cobb County, made vague mention of the alleged sexual assault. "It is not within my power, nor do I desire, either to prove or disprove the stories which are still told in Cobb County concerning the treatment of these women by Northern soldiers. The hideousness of war breeds atrocities and tales of atrocities. The strength with which these stories persist through the years in the county necessitates mention of them."[59]

On the same day, General Grenville Dodge arrived in Roswell with orders to construct a new bridge over the Chattahoochee as quickly as possible. The structure had to be in place, along with several other pontoon bridges, to enable the army to cross the river. Dodge made his headquarters near the river and immediately set to work. In order to save time, Dodge instructed Captain Armstrong, in charge of the 1500 men detailed to build the bridge, to tear down any buildings left from Garrard's fire. Dodge reported to Sherman that by using the material he expected to have the span completed in three days. Sherman sent his approval. "I know the bridge at Roswell is important, and you may destroy all Georgia to make it good and strong."[60]

In a strange twist of fate, some of the guards who had escorted the first of the mill workers out of Roswell soon found themselves prisoners. Having disposed of their "precious cargo," the empty wagons had been filled with supplies for Garrard's command. On July 10, Rebel scouts dressed in Federal uniforms surprised a detail of Ohio cavalrymen guarding the rear of the supply train as it returned to Roswell. The scouts captured four of the Ohio troopers without firing a shot and charged on the remainder of the guard, but the Yankees returned fire and drove them back. The Confederates sent the four captured cavalrymen to Andersonville. Privates John Lawrence, William Rogers and Alfred Stout survived the war, but Sergeant Thomas Stutesman met his death in the prison stockade just two months later. Although prison records list diarrhea as the cause of death, his military record indicates he died as a result of "inhumane treatment."[61]

Although there is little mention of the women after the 10th of July, there are some reports of soldiers seeing the women after that date. On July 11, Captain Tilmon Kyger entered in his diary, "There are still about four hundred women that have not been sent north." Charles Wills, a soldier with the 103rd Illinois, did not arrive until the 14th of July, but writes of seeing "several hundred" factory girls in Roswell. There is no record to indicate when the last wagon left or under what conditions the women were held.[62]

In writing of the events 50 years later, General Dodge made mention of the factory women, but never said that he saw them in Roswell, so it is not clear that he witnessed their fate. What he did say has raised a great deal of confusion. Dodge claimed that Garrard moved the operatives, "mostly women," to Marietta "by detailing a regiment of cavalry, each member of which took one of the operatives on his horse, and this way they were all taken to Marietta." While no other accounts have been found to substantiate this assertion and, indeed, there is much evidence to the contrary, this is often cited as a definitive source. Still it raises a possible scenario. If Garrard had been desperate to remove the women after the drunken debacle, it is conceivable that he ordered a detachment of cavalry to take the remaining women to Marietta sometime after the 10th.[63]

On July 12, Dodge sent word to Sherman that he had completed the bridge in only three days. According to his official report, "A foot bridge 710 feet long was thrown across the river, and from Monday [Sunday] July 10 until Wednesday [Tuesday] night, July 12, a good substantial, double track, trestle road bridge, 710 feet long and 14 feet high, was built by the Pioneer Corps from the command." This was a spectacular feat, and Sherman was amazed at how quickly Dodge had been able to erect the bridge. Rebel soldiers were quite impressed as well. According to a private with the 9th Kentucky Cavalry, "Sherman replaced the immense bridge across the Chattahoochee in so short a time that he was ever afterwards regarded by our boys as the champion bridge-builder of the world." With the new bridge in place, Federal troops began crossing the Chattahoochee for the final push to Atlanta.[64]

Roswell suffered dearly at the hands of the occupying troops. All but the mills were spared the torch, but Sherman's army had left its mark. The Presbyterian Church had been stripped of its pews to make room for the wounded. The hymnals and the pipe organ were destroyed. A large pine cabinet used for storing church books was still intact, but the left cabinet door had been removed and a checkerboard drawn on the flat service. Mt. Carmel Methodist Church fared no better. Soldiers had removed and destroyed the benches and pulpit and had broken the cornerstone and removed its contents. The Lebanon Baptist Church, a log building dating to 1837, was torn down in order to rebuild a bridge across Vickery Creek. Some claimed that cavalry troops desecrated graves in the cemetery. Bessie King told her husband, Barrington Simeral, that she heard that the Yankee soldiers "burst open" Roswell King's burial vault, and "rode round and round" the grave of Thomas King, while making "their horses paw it."[65]

Barrington Hall, Bulloch Hall, and Dunwody Hall still stood, but whatever contents had been left behind were gone or destroyed. Reverend Pratt's home had been relatively undisturbed, but the surrounding land was devastated. Writing to his nephew in December, Pratt described the occupation:

> My front and back yard were full of horses and tents and quarter-master stores up to my very doors. You may surmise that nothing was left on my premises. Thirty acres of promising corn, sixty or seventy bushels of wheat in the sheaf and seven acres of sorghum were utterly destroyed.... The outbuildings are here but without doors or shutters. Everything of mischief was done on the outside of my dwelling, which could be done, except burning. But God permitted us to dwell in safety, and on the whole we were treated with respect.[66]

The empty cottages and silent streets on Factory Hill marked Roswell's greatest loss. All that remained according to one soldier, were "old women" and a "very few aged citizens of African descent." Gone were hundreds of women and children. Among them, Lucinda, Molly and Easter Wood; Mary and Sarah Jane Kendley; recently widowed Georgiana Morgan; Adeline Buice, pregnant with her sixth child; and Mathilda and Elizabeth Smallwood. Hundreds of others remain nameless. Forced from their homes, separated from their families, all headed north on a journey that would take them far from Roswell, a journey from which many of them would never return.[67]

9

Sweetwater Factory

I have ordered the arrest of the operators at the Confederate manufactories at Roswell and Sweetwater, to be sent North. When they reach Nashville have them sent across the Ohio River and turned loose to earn a living where they won't do us any harm.

— W.T. Sherman, July 9, 1864

The Roswell workers would not be the only mill employees arrested and sent north. Having dealt with the situation at Roswell, Sherman turned his attention to a small manufacturing village in the heart of Campbell County, some 30 miles to the west. On July 9, Major Haviland Tompkins and a detail of eight men rode out to New Manchester with orders to destroy the large cotton factory on the banks of Sweetwater Creek and arrest the men, women and children employed by the mill.[1]

Only one week earlier, a detachment of Stoneman's cavalry commanded by Colonel Silas Adams had advanced to Sweetwater Creek on the extreme right of the Union Army. Arriving at the New Manchester Manufacturing Company, Adams and his troopers entered the factory, stopped production and ordered the employees out of the mill. The cavalrymen pulled the belting out of the machinery and removed the cloth and thread from the looms and spindles, but made no attempt to destroy the factory. The troops remained in New Manchester, patrolling the area and foraging for supplies for several days leaving the workers to wonder if the mill would be left unharmed.[2]

Making his headquarters at Maroney's farm on the old Tallapoosa Road on July 2, Adams sent out authorized foraging parties to seize food supplies for the troops, and it was not long before the countryside was nearly stripped bare. The *Atlanta Appeal* reported that the local citizens had been subjected to "every species of vandalism — such as only Yankee ingenuity can invent." Even the self-proclaimed Union men would not be spared.[3]

Miles Moseley, a local farmer and avowed Unionist, claimed, "Cavalry soldiers came every day to forage about 10 to 50 men at a time, until all was gone." After losing a mule, a two-horse wagon, corn, wheat, oats, 75 pounds of pork, 200 pounds of beef and 50 pounds of bacon, Moseley complained to Adams. The colonel responded, "Belongings and that kind of things he did not allow his men to take, but that they were allowed to take such things as forage and provisions."[4]

According to Isaiah Moseley, an abolitionist and "old line Whig," 1500 men came to his farm and took all of his stored food supplies on July 2. On the 5th and 6th, 600 troops "with three flags flying" cut nine acres of waist high oats. The field, "perfectly blue with soldiers" was soon relieved of its bountiful harvest. A like number of troops returned to cut eight acres of wheat over another two-day period. Moseley rode out to Maroney's farm on July 6 to see General Edward M. McCook who had also made his headquarters at the farm. Moseley hoped for a private interview with the general to seek compensation for the loss of his crops, but was met by one of the general's aides who simply told him to go home.[5]

Other men and women swearing loyalty to the Union filed similar claims after the

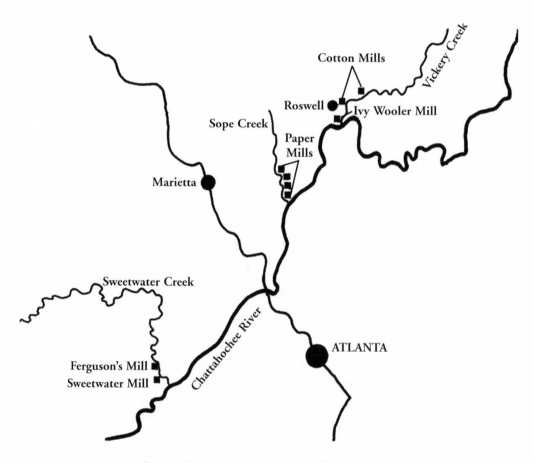

Map of Roswell, Sweetwater, Marietta and Atlanta — July 1864.

war, many testifying that the Union troops helped themselves to anything they wanted. Soldiers "freely appropriated" corn, wheat, bacon, horses, mules, oxen, cattle, hogs and wagons. When Frederick Aderhold begged the cavalrymen not to take all his stock, they told him they would leave an old mare, but an hour later, a dozen or more soldiers came back and took the mare as well.[6]

Union commanders enlisted the aid of free blacks to show them the roads and point out neighboring farms. Isaiah Love was virtually enslaved by the Yankees, albeit temporarily. Love spent nearly eight weeks with the Federal troops, first with Colonel Adams of Stoneman's command and then "waiting" on Lt. Colonel Fielder Jones, of Kilpatrick's command. In addition to acting as a guide and cook, Love was ordered to accompany the foragers to neighboring farms to slaughter confiscated chickens and hogs.[7]

Widespread foraging left little or nothing for the local citizens, but the loss of food and provisions would be the least of the injuries suffered by the families in Campbell County.

The New Manchester Manufacturing Company, known by locals as the Sweetwater Factory, stood on the banks of Sweetwater Creek, where the rushing waters made their final push to the Chattahoochee River, tumbling across shoals created by the hard rocks and quiet deep water. The land originally belonged to the Cherokee, but like Roswell had been divided into 40-acre land lots in 1833. Lot 929 was deeded to Phillip J. Crask who lost it to back taxes four years later. Sold on the courthouse steps to the highest bidder, the lot was purchased by John Boyle of Campbell County for $12.50 in 1837. Eight years later Boyle realized a substantial profit when he sold lot 929 for $500 to Colonel James Rogers of Milledgeville and Charles M. McDonald of Cobb County, a lawyer, legislator, co-founder of the Georgia Military Institute and 19th governor of Georgia, serving from 1839–1843.[8]

Inspired by the success of the Roswell factories and other textile mills throughout the state, Rogers and McDonald purchased the property with the idea of erecting their own cotton mill and began construction shortly thereafter. James Roswell King, owner of the Ivy Woolen Mill in Roswell, supervised the installation of the machinery and assisted the owners with operations through the years.[9]

The massive 48 by 120 foot five-story red brick factory was said to be taller than any building in Atlanta. Made up entirely of local materials, the bricks were formed on the site and burned on the banks of the creek, and the foundation stones quarried downstream. Designed to take advantage of the natural light, the mill's many windows flared outward on the inside of the factory walls to admit as much light as possible to the center of the wide floors, with the interior whitewashed to reflect the incoming light. By late 1849 the Sweetwater Manufacturing Company was in full operation.[10]

During the first year, with some two hundred people living within one mile of the factory, the mill employed sixty hands from among that small population. Customers traveled long distances on horseback and by ox-drawn wagons to bring their

cotton and wool to the mill to be exchanged for thread and yarn. Eventually the owners expanded the operation to produce cloth and soon enjoyed a reputation as manufacturers of quality yarn and fabric. Raw cotton delivered from the railhead in Atlanta
was converted into cotton yarns and osnaburg, a coarse, medium to heavyweight cotton cloth. Incorporated as the Sweetwater Factory in 1852, the newly formed corporation purchased the land from McDonald and Rogers. McDonald reorganized the
company in 1857 and changed the name, under the new charter, to the New Manchester Manufacturing Company.[11]

The small village of Sweetwater, or Factory Town as it was most often called, bore
little resemblance to Roswell some 30 miles away. Since the mill owners lived in Marietta several miles distant, day-to-day operations were left to the on-site superintendent. There were no palatial homes or plantations in Sweetwater, no fancy churches, and
no academies. It was a small farming community, and it was, for the most part, the
daughters and sons of the local farmers who went to work in the mill.

Although most of the New Manchester mill workers lived on nearby farms, some
of the employees resided in factory cottages built on the bluffs overlooking the mill. A
large bell in the factory tower called the workers to the factory early in the morning
and sent them home in the dark hours of the night. While working conditions were
probably much the same as at Roswell, the off-site owners exercised far less control over
the lives of their employees. Most workers lived in their own homes and attended local
churches and schools with friends and neighbors, not churches and schools built for
the benefit of the elite. There was a greater sense of camaraderie in this tight-knit community of mill workers and farmers. Nearly every factory employee, skilled or unskilled,
had lived in the area before the mill was built, and there is no evidence of the class
division so prevalent in Roswell.[12]

A local farmer, Angus Ferguson, operated a flour mill, a brick-making operation
and a sawmill one-half mile upstream from the New Manchester mill near a bridge that
spanned Sweetwater Creek. Ferguson's house and farm buildings rested on a hilltop overlooking his mills, which supplied the Sweetwater Factory with a substantial amount of
brick and lumber. Although Ferguson professed Union loyalties, he was first and fore-
most an enterprising businessman and later expanded his operation to meet wartime
demands and manufactured barrels and buckets for the Confederate army.[13]

In 1860, an ailing McDonald leased his interest in the New Manchester mill to
minority partners Colonel Arnoldus Brumby, co-founder of the Georgia Military Institute and a classmate of Sherman's at West Point, and William James Russell, son of a
large landowner and slaveholder in coastal Georgia. The lease of McDonald's interest
did not allow Brumby and Russell to exercise increased stockholder's rights, but it did
entitle them to receive the profits on McDonald's stock. The lease specified that the
interest would revert back to McDonald at the end of the five-year term. McDonald
had, in fact, offered to sell his interest shortly before 1860, but Brumby and Russell
declined, later agreeing to the terms of the lease. They could not have known at the

time what a wise decision that would be. McDonald died on the 16th of December 1860, the eve of the Civil War, his interest in the mill passing to his heirs.[14]

With Brumby acting as president and Russell as agent, the partners immediately invested an additional $14,600 in new machinery to increase the profitability of the mill and made other improvements including three houses for operatives. The new partners purchased thirty-five thousand feet of lumber from Angus Ferguson's sawmill over the next three years to construct the improvements. James King was called on once again to lend his expertise, reviewing and approving expenses. With the new machinery in place by the fall of 1860, the mill doubled its production, and the company paid its first cash dividend shortly thereafter.[15]

Although Brumby kept an office at the mill, both he and Russell lived in Marietta. Joshua Welch, the local superintendent, was in charge of the repair and maintenance of the machinery as well as the general supervision of the operation. Welch did not have a permanent home in New Manchester, but he was usually at the factory unless away on company business. When away, Welch left the factory in the hands of Henry Lovern, overseer of the card room, and Cicero Tippins, overseer of the spinning room.[16]

Tippins had been known to drink "to excess," but he was a superior spinner and Welch had retained him, knowing he would be difficult to replace. When Welch first arrived at the factory in 1861, there had been a grocery store nearby and "Tippins would occasionally go there and drink too much." Not wanting to dismiss the skilled workman, Brumby and Russell decided to take matters into their own hands and bought and closed the grocery. The rather extreme measure appeared to have worked. Henry Lovern claimed that Tippins "reformed" after liquor became difficult to obtain, and he seldom drank.[17]

The war would exact a heavy toll from the citizens of New Manchester. Although the flourishing village had doubled its population during the ten previous years, many lives would be lost in fighting on distant fields. Despite the fact that many of the citizens professed Unionist sympathies, large numbers of New Manchester men enlisted in local companies, determined to take their Confederrate loyalties to the battlefield.

In September 1861, Walter Washington Stewart, a farmer and mill boss, named his new son Jefferson Davis Stewart after the Confederate president. Six months later, in an even greater display of patriotism, 32-year-old Walter Stewart joined the Rebel ranks.[18]

Several volunteer companies were organized in Campbell County in 1861 and 1862. Some of the local men joined the Campbell County Guards or the Campbell Volunteers, but most of the New Manchester men enlisted in two units made up almost exclusively of men from the Sweetwater area.[19]

The Campbell Sharpshooters became Company F of the 30th Georgia Volunteers in September of 1861. The company suffered heavy casualties, losing nearly a third of the men from New Manchester. John Causey, a factory worker, enlisted in the

Campbell Sharpshooters but returned home two years later after being wounded in Mississippi. Charles Wilson also served with the unit but surrendered early in 1864 to Federal forces. Released on taking the oath of loyalty to the Union, Wilson also returned home. Neither Causey nor Wilson had seen the last of the enemy.[20]

In March 1862, a number of men, not yet serving, enlisted in the Campbell Salt Spring Guards, later Company K, 41st Georgia Infantry, some to pursue what they believed was their duty, others simply to avoid conscription. Walter Stewart was one of the first to enlist in the company along with a number of other men from the New Manchester area. For many it would prove to be a short term of service. In the fall of 1862, heavy fighting at the Battle of Perryville claimed many casualties. Joel Aycock, Charles Moseley, Wiley Humphries and Lloyd Blair were wounded, but many others lost their lives. Among the dead from Campbell County were Augustus Brown, James Abbott, John Cochran, Edward Hines, William McClarty, Jesse Renfroe, George Robbins, Edward Wood and P. L. Yawn. The devastating news of the dead and wounded saddened the residents in the little village that lay so far from the bloodstained fields of Kentucky.[21]

Members of the Salt Spring Guards who survived Perryville went on to Vicksburg where the company surrendered at the end of the siege on July 4, 1863. Paroled a few days later, some returned to the army, but many made their way home. One New Manchester soldier, Robert Joiner, was sick and remained behind in Vicksburg, only to die of disease two months later. Nelson Tucker's son, Burdine, was struck in the back by a "falling tree" at Vicksburg, permanently injuring his spine. After being treated at a hospital in Chattanooga, Tucker was sent home and detailed to work in the Sweetwater factory, as he was "unfit for further service." His disability would not keep him home much longer.[22]

Although a number of Campbell County men and women continued to support the Union cause, their sons did not always share the same sentiments. Many cast their lot with the Confederacy and joined the Rebel army despite the heartfelt pleadings of their parents. Disappointed that his sons, Burdine and William, joined the Confederate army in early 1862, Nelson Tucker forbade his wife to help them in any way. Tucker believed his sons should have taken their chances and hid in the woods, rather than join the Rebel forces. Three of Isaiah Moseley's sons enlisted in the Campbell Salt Spring Guards in the spring of 1862 against the wishes of their father. Consequently, James, William and Pike (Pinkney) Moseley received no aid or support from their family during the war. Miles Moseley tried to keep his two sons out of the army as long as he could, but William and Charles also enlisted in the Salt Spring Guards in March 1862. Professing no love for the Confederacy, Miles admitted to sending provisions, "out of sympathy for his own children." Likewise, Nancy Stewart would not let her Union sentiments prevent her from seeing to the needs and comfort of her three sons, and she admitted to sending money and clothing to Francis, George and James. Four of Frederick Aderhold's sons, William, Frederick, John, and James, also joined the

Confederate ranks. Bitterly opposed to the war, Frederick Aderhold turned his back on his sons, and he later testified that he contributed nothing to aid or support them while they were in the Rebel service.[23]

While some were willing to sever family ties in their determination to enlist in the Rebel army, a number of Campbell County men, usually citing Union sentiments, deserted from the Rebel army or tried to avoid service all together. Many of them chose to "lay out" in the woods, hoping they would not be discovered by the Rebel scouts who frequently scoured the area looking for shirkers and deserters. The loyal men and women of Campbell County frequently aided the "lay outs" and continued to proclaim Union sentiments, but not nearly so loudly or boldly as they had once done. Those attempting to assist the lay-outs did so secretly and often under the cover of darkness. Rebel sympathizers frequently threatened the known Unionists, and while acts of violence rarely occurred, many loyal citizens believed their lives were in constant danger. One resident claimed that a man was hanged and another "rode on rails" and whipped near Powder Springs for expressing Union sentiments. Rebels allegedly chased several men with dogs, and it was rumored that a pursuing pack killed a man named Bullock after it caught him near Campbellton. Eliza Tucker claimed that her husband had been threatened on several occasions and that only his good name and personal reputation prevented his being killed.[24]

Despite their fears of reprisals, perhaps no one did more for the Union cause in Campbell County than Nelson and Eliza Tucker whose

Nelson Tucker (circa 1811–1865). Avowed Unionist and New Manchester farmer Nelson Tucker told his wife he was "trying to make crops for the Yankees to subsist on while they whipped the rebels" (courtesy Deborah Howard).

allegiance lay with the Stars and Stripes. Many of the Union men had slaves to help work their farms, but Nelson never owned slaves; he and his sons worked their large farm on their own. Eliza later recalled that her husband had been urging their sons to work "almost incessantly" in 1864. She chided him for working the boys so hard when it was only a matter of time before either the Rebels or the Yankees came and took all the crops. Nelson explained that he was trying to make a crop for the Yankees to subsist upon while they "whipped the rebels" and did not expect to save it.[25]

Many local men testified to Eliza's constant efforts to feed and harbor the deserters and young men trying to avoid the conscription officers. Working tirelessly to "keep the boys out of the war," Eliza rode out at the hour of midnight on many occasions to carry news and provisions to the "lay-outs" at the crossroads, some five miles from her home. To provide shelter from the bad weather, Eliza had a hole dug under her kitchen floor so that the boys could hide when necessary. Pete Turner, Merrell Humphries, Joe Walker and Elisha Rodgers frequently availed themselves of Tucker's "haven of refuge."[26]

Nancy Stewart also did what she could to help the deserters and other men hiding out in the woods. Her cousin-in-law, Perry Stewart, testified that Nancy brought him food and provisions after he deserted from the Rebel army. William Strickland, a farmer and factory worker, was with the "boys" more or less every day, notwithstanding the fact that Strickland belonged to a local home guard unit. By virtue of his Confederate service, Strickland kept his friends informed as to the whereabouts of the guard and Confederate cavalry and could warn them of any imminent danger.[27]

Rather than enlist in the Rebel army or hide in the woods, other men looked for work in the local mills. William Strickland, William Causey and Columbus Blair, all sworn Unionists, found work in the New Manchester Manufacturing Company. Although preferring not to join in the rebellion, they had no qualms about working for a factory manufacturing goods for the Confederate army in order to be exempted from the draft.[28]

Like the mill at Roswell, New Manchester became a major contractor for the Confederacy during the war, supplying an excellent grade of yarn and cotton cloth. The Sweetwater factory purchased the best Sea Island cotton and manufactured quality goods widely praised throughout the South. The editor of the *Savannah News* believed the Sweetwater thread superior to that manufactured in the north and suggested that ladies would find the locally produced thread preferable to the "cheating Yankees spools with which they have heretofore been supplied, as a consequence of our unnecessary dependence on the north."[29]

Government authorities controlled production and profits with both the state and Confederate government purchasing goods at a fixed price. William Russell claimed that in order to keep his hands at the factory and out of the army, he had to supply ⅔ of their production to the government, a very large part for which he received no consideration.[30]

As part of the Georgia State Guard raised in 1863, a local company had been organized to "serve as infantry in Campbell County and especially in defence of the

New Manchester Cotton Mills and of the Flouring Mills on Sweetwater Creek in said county." Alexander's Infantry, commanded by James Alexander, was mustered into service in August 1863 for six months. The company of 79 men, composed mainly of mill workers, was never armed and never saw field duty. With the exception of Burdine Tucker, John Causey, and Charles Wilson, who joined Alexander's company after returning from their respective units, none of the soldiers had ever been in battle. In fact, the only enemy the unit faced during its term of service was roving bands of desperate civilians.[31]

Wartime privations brought a complete breakdown of law and order in Campbell County. Inflated prices and widespread food shortages drove some of the locals to take matters into their own hands, stealing what they could not obtain otherwise. Roads, such as they were, were always difficult for travel, but they became even more dangerous as instances of highway robbery increased. On several occasions armed citizens attacked and robbed the factory wagons loaded with goods for Atlanta.

On the 27th of January 1864, a "mob" estimated at fifteen or twenty men and twenty-five or thirty women arrived at the factory in wagons, buggies, and on horseback, and assembled at the door of the factory. Armed with guns, pistols, knives, and other weapons, the men and women intended to force their way into the factory, and to seize yarn and cloth, along with the stores of provisions meant for the mill workers. The factory doors were immediately closed and the unarmed state guard made "a show of defense" as best they could. The mob finally gave up after three hours but threatened to renew the attack at some future day.[32]

Three days later, superintendent Welch described the incident in a deposition, adding that it was "dangerous to continue operations of said factory unless some aid is rendered from some source to prevent further aggression." Brumby wrote to Governor Brown on January 30, enclosed the affidavit from Welch, and pleaded for protection, stating it was impossible to carry on with any security "even of life" unless the state took immediate action to protect the factory goods and the factory workers. Brumby believed that the operatives could protect the mill with arms and ammunition, but still needed additional troops to protect the wagons on the way to market. Brumby closed his letter "hoping that utter lawlessness and highway robbing is not to triumph yet in Georgia." Brown was apparently unable or unwilling to send aid. The state guards disbanded at the expiration of their service without ever having received any arms.[33]

Walter and Lizzie Stewart suffered a devastating loss on the 21st of April 1864 with the death of their youngest son, two and one-half-year-old Jefferson Davis Stewart. Even as the Stewarts mourned the passing of their son, Sherman's armies prepared for the campaign that would sound the death knell of the Confederacy.[34]

The townspeople of New Manchester had little doubt that Union forces would destroy the mill if the Confederate army could not stop their advance. With the two armies at Kennesaw Mountain and raiding parties even closer, local citizens grew increasingly concerned for their safety and the protection of their personal property. On the

8th of June in a letter to her husband, Margaret White mentioned that Federal soldiers had been in the area, and she expressed concern about the possibility of raids in New Manchester. "They are seizing all the cattle, sheep, hogs and some say mules this side of the river. They have been in this settlement but have not been here yet." Margaret informed her husband that his father was preparing to leave, adding, "and then I will be by myself. I will try to do the best I can and try to bear it as well as I can possibly can." She continued, "The children say howdy. Pa'pa, you must do the best you can for yourself. I will try to do the best I can for myself and children. Whatever our fate may be, I hope the Lord will provide for us.... Write often as you can and every opportunity you have to send a letter." She closed with a prophetic goodbye: "No more at present but remain your affectionate wife until death." Andrew White was captured by Union forces in Atlanta and sent north. He survived the war, but could not win the battle against smallpox, and died before he could return home to his family.[35]

In early July, with enemy forces drawing nearer, factory superintendent Joshua Welch made final preparations to save what little property he could. After arranging for ox wagons to deliver the finished goods to him at Baker's Ferry, four miles from the mill, Welch left New Manchester, riding out of town just one week before the Yankee cavalrymen arrived. Welch took the cashbook, shipping book, journal and ledger with him for safekeeping, along with all the money from the factory, some ninety to one hundred thousand dollars, in Confederate money, and Confederate certificates. Cicero Tippins, chief spinner and "reformed drunk," was left in charge with instructions to work the mill to "the last extremity."[36]

As in Roswell, the workers faced the advancing enemy alone. No effort had been made to close the factory or remove the machinery. Russell later claimed he simply did not have the time or manpower necessary to do so, estimating that it would have taken 90 thousand feet of lumber to box the machinery, three months to do the work, and 40 army wagons and two weeks to ship the machinery once it was boxed. More importantly, he did not know of any safe place to send it. The mill continued at full capacity until Adams's men arrived on the 2d of July and brought the entire operation to a halt.[37]

On July 7, a Southern newspaper correspondent mistakenly reported the destruction of the Sweetwater Factory, a full week before it took place:

> On Saturday afternoon [2 July] the Yankees burned the Sweetwater Cotton Mills and Ferguson's grist and flouring mills in Campbell County besides the dwellings along the road by which they advanced in that section. Their progress could be distinguished by the columns of rising smoke as the happy home of some families were destroyed by the flames.

Evidently the "columns of rising smoke" signaled the destruction of some other ill-fated structure meeting its end by the Yankee torch.[38]

There was, of course, no mistaking the source of the smoke-filled skies just two days later. Upon his arrival in New Manchester, Major Tompkins informed Henry

Lovern, the boss of the carding room, that he had instructions from General Sherman to burn this factory and "that he should do it in fifteen minutes." An employee of the factory, seventeen-year-old Sherrod Causey, witnessed the preparations for burning the mill. "Large cans of kerosene were carried to each of the five floors of the building, and each was thoroughly saturated. The mill was then torched. The warehouse-store received the same treatment." According to Causey, the troops poured water over the adjacent buildings to prevent the fire from spreading. With the factory in flames, the Union troops set fire to the two-story brick building that housed the company store as well as the superintendent's office, destroying any papers and property that had been left inside.[39]

Unionist Angus Ferguson was unable to protect his mills from a similar fate. The cavalrymen burned his sawmill, which was manufacturing goods for the Confederacy, and destroyed his flour mills as well, despite Sherman's previous orders forbidding the destruction of small mills that supplied the needs of the local population.[40]

After all the fires had been set, and the destruction well underway, Tompkins ordered the arrest of the New Manchester mill workers, giving them fifteen minutes to gather whatever personal belongings they could carry in their arms. Of those arrested, 43 men were listed as "political prisoners." Most of these men worked in the cotton mill in 1863 and early 1864 including Thomas and William Bell, John Causey, Gideon Jennings, Elijah Rodgers, Burdine Tucker, and avowed Unionists James Stone and Aaron Turner. Others were local farmers who may have found work in the factory just prior to the arrival of the Union army. The list also included Thomas Tolbert, the local postmaster, whose office was at the factory; Nathaniel Humphries, who ran the factory store; and Nathaniel's brother and nephew, John and Merrell Humphries.[41]

Several of the men in the Humphries family were shoemakers by trade, including John Humphries, and his three sons, Merrell, William and Joseph. It is believed that the Humphries owned or operated a shoe factory that was manufacturing shoes for the Confederate army. This may have been part of a leather-making operation at the Sweetwater mill. There are no surviving records that document the existence of a shoemaking business, but John and his son were arrested along with the other mill workers.[42]

Merrell Humphries may not have been working at the factory in any capacity in July 1864. Merrell enlisted early in the war and did not seem to share his parents' Union sympathies. However, there is no record of his military service after April of 1863, and he was clearly not with his regiment at the time of the Union occupation. Eliza Tucker later claimed that he was one of the boys she helped hide from the Confederate authorites. Perhaps he had a change of heart and sympathies. It appears that Merrell deserted from the Rebel army only to find himself captured by Federal troops. Listed as a political prisoner, Merrell must have passed himself off as a factory employee to avoid arrest as a prisoner of war.[43]

Merrell's younger brother, William Henry Humphries, who would have been about 16 or 17 at the time of the arrests, may have been the only Humphries son to avoid capture. Although he was employed by the Sweetwater mill, and served in the local defense unit, his name does not appear on the list of political prisoners. One possible explanation can be found in the *History of Douglas County*. The local history includes the story of a teenaged Humphries boy who was saved from arrest by hiding in a large baby cradle piled high with quilts. Since William was the only Humphries son known to be of the right age, he was very likely the one that got away. If true, William escaped the attention of Union soldiers and remained behind in New Manchester, while the rest of his family was sent north.[44]

Like Roswell, we have little information as to the number of women and children sent north, but most accounts place the number at 150 to 200. Whether or not they actually worked in the mill, many of the wives and children of the men arrested as political prisoners were also sent north, including Charlotte Elizabeth Stewart and her four children, Catherine Scarborough and her three sons, Mariah Bell and her nine children, Tabby Mauldin and her five children, and Amanda Maroney Humphries and at least four of her children. Sherrod and John Causey, their mother and sisters also made the journey north. Home on furlough from the Rebel army, John was captured while in his sick bed and passed off as one of the factory hands to avoid a Federal prisoner of war camp. Tompkins sent John Causey north with the others, including him on the list of political prisoners.[45]

Sixteen-year-old factory worker Martha Tolbert, daughter of the postmaster, claimed that she was arrested and sent north with the other mill workers, but her recollections are inconsistent with some of the known facts. Martha said that she was sent alone and that her parents stayed behind, but her father's name appeared on the arrest list, and was clearly one of the men sent first to Louisville and then north of the Ohio River.[46]

Tompkins assembled the factory workers at Ferguson's bridge just upstream from the factory. Separating the men from the women, Tompkins loaded them into empty supply wagons, but there was not enough room for everyone and many began the sixteen-mile journey to Marietta on foot. Lieutenant Isaac Brown with the 6th Indiana Cavalry passed the smoking ruins of the "celebrated Sweetwater" cotton mills, and found the site "a lonesome looking place." At some point, Brown saw the women heading north on the Marietta Road and described the scene in a letter to the Terre Haute (Indiana) *Daily Express*. "It was a sad looking picture to see the women sitting in groups, along the road, with their little bundles in their hands." On July 10, Captain Thomas Robertson camped in the vicinity of Stoneman's headquarters at Sweetwater Town, saw the women as they were about to ford the Buttermilk Creek. He wrote in his diary, "The boys were very clever in assisting them to cross."[47]

The arrest and exile of the New Manchester workers was chronicled in an article, which found its way into several northern newspapers. The story entitled "Exile of Sweetwater Operatives" appeared in the *Nashville Daily Times and True Union* on the 20th of July:

Monday night, over two hundred men and women were sent to this place from Sweetwater Cotton Factory, and its vicinity, by order of General Sherman. The factory is, or was before General Sherman destroyed it, located in Campbell County, on this side of the Chattahoochee or Sweetwater Creek, some fifteen miles from Atlanta. It employed over one hundred and fifty hands who manufactured osnaburgs, yarns, etc. mostly for the rebel army. The men were exempt from military service, on account of their skill. They are to be sent north of the Ohio River to earn their living during the existence of the war. If they are honest, well-disposed people they can readily find employment at excellent wages.... The destruction of these factories is a severe loss to the rebels as a large portion of their military clothing came from Campbell County.[48]

Such were the optimistic ramblings of an uninformed journalist. Predictions of abundant jobs and high wages would prove completely untrue.

10

Precious Cargo:
Marietta to Louisville

If you could look upon their young faces, and see the appeal for sympathy written there, you would involuntarily think, how little the women of Northern America know of the real concomitant evils of this war.
—*Atlanta Daily Intelligencer*, 3 August 1864

Marietta

On July 3, Benjamin Nourse rode through Marietta as part of Garrard's command, took the road to Roswell and helped drive the rebel cavalry as far as the Rottenwood Creek. That night, recording the day's events in his diary, he reflected, "Marietta, I think, is one of the prettiest towns in Georgia—fine houses, clean streets and shade everywhere." Within a few days time, Marietta's clean streets were overflowing with soldiers in blue. Garrisoned by Union troops and fortified for defense, the town quickly took on the appearance of a "conquered military city." The famous Kennesaw House was converted into a Soldier's Home, the courthouse into a temporary prison, and the "fine houses" into army hospitals. Signs on local shops had been replaced with those announcing temporary locations of the United States Christian Commission, the Army Post Office, and the Medical Purveyor of the Department of the Tennessee.[1]

Southern ministers no longer proclaimed the word of God from the pulpits. The only preacher remaining in Marietta had been arrested and confined to his premises. Reverend S. Benedict, an "avowed rebel," had requested permission to continue his church services, but his petition was denied, as he was unwilling to offer prayer for the president of the United States. To ensure that the religious needs of the Union soldiers were not neglected, however, the Western Sanitary Commission held a series of public services every night in the Presbyterian chapel and the Christian Commission sponsored a soldiers' prayer meeting every afternoon.[2]

As the grand depot for Sherman's armies, Marietta had become the most important point south of Chattanooga. One correspondent for the *Cincinnati Daily Commercial* counted nine trains arriving and departing each day, bringing stores of supplies to provision the three armies as they continued their advance toward Atlanta. The correspondent noted that by July 27 an entire block of buildings, "as large as any in Cincinnati," was packed full and overflowing with all kinds of rations. To protect the depot and prevent a raid on his rear, Sherman established a strong military force at Marietta and ordered the soldiers to fortify the town. "A few hours' work will convert any good brick or stone house into a citadel." Buildings on the square and houses by the depot were confiscated, their doors and windows barricaded and loop-holed, to provide shelter for infantry. Suspicious citizens were to be sent north, "no matter the seeming hardships." The "pleasure and convenience" of citizens was not to interfere with the safety of the depot, and severe punishment awaited those who posed any kind of threat. "Should any one be caught molesting our road, telegraph wires, or our stores, he should be disposed of finally and summarily, especially if disguised in the garb of a citizen." To carry out these instructions, Sherman looked to Colonel Newell Gleason, commanding a brigade of the XIV Army Corps.[3]

Sent to Marietta on July 4 with instructions to garrison the town, Gleason received additional orders from General George H. Thomas the following day. Desiring to prevent outrages against the local citizens, Gleason was instructed to "preserve public and private property in Marietta as nearly as possible in the state in which you found it, and prevent plundering and pillaging," arresting all deserters and stragglers. In addition to guard and picket duty, some of the brigade was placed on provost duty and was responsible, according to Gleason, for "receiving and sending north, a large number of factory employees from Roswell and other places."[4]

The first of the wagons filled with the operatives rolled into Marietta on July 9, the same day Colonel Gleason received orders to send the operatives to Nashville by train. Until arrangements could be made for the journey north, Gleason had the workers taken to the Georgia Military Institute, then serving as headquarters for Major General Thomas and the Army of the Cumberland. The famed academy that once trained young Southerners in the school of war was now in the hands of the Union Army; the beautiful grounds covered with Federal tents, the flower gardens and lawns trampled and destroyed. Unloaded from the supply wagons, the workers were turned over to the provost guard and confined in the empty classrooms at the military academy.[5]

On foot and in wagons, more civilian prisoners arrived the following day. The New Manchester mill workers and their families joined the operatives from Roswell. There was not enough room for all of the women at the academy, and some of the "factory girls" were quartered in vacated houses. Provost guards stood watch over the next few days while the women and children waited for the trains that would carry them far from home.[6]

On July 10, Thomas sent a message to Sherman, advising him of the arrival of the mill workers and expressing some concern about their welfare:

> The Roswell factory hands, 400 or 500 hundred in number, have arrived in Marietta. The most of them are women. I can only order them transportation to Nashville where it seems hard to turn them adrift. What had best be done with them?

Sherman promptly responded, "I have ordered General Webster at Nashville to dispose of them. They will be sent to Indiana."[7]

Although most of the arrivals were women, they weren't all factory workers. A correspondent to the *Louisville Journal* reported that family members arrived with some of the mill workers. "It was really a sad spectacle to witness these young women accompanied by their parents and smaller brothers and sister come into Marietta to get transportation to the *land of plenty* beyond the confines of the so-called Southern Confederacy."[8]

For his part, Thomas did not believe that the Southern civilians should be sent north. Nor was he alone in this opinion, although the reasons generally had more to do with practical rather than humanitarian concerns. Andrew Johnson, the military governor of Tennessee, explained his feelings on the subject to Thomas on July 29, suggesting that the prisoners being sent to Nashville should instead be "pressed back with the rebel army." He continued, "Let them [Rebels] hear the cries of suffering, and supply their stomachs and backs with food and raiment." Johnson believed that by sending the prisoners north, Sherman was relieving the Confederate government and only adding to the Rebel sentiment. "Let them fall back with the army." Thomas shared similar views and said as much in his letter to Johnson on July 30. "I have always held the same opinion about sending rebels south instead of north that you do, and have had frequent conversations on that subject with General Sherman." However, the prisoners would have to be sent through the lines under a "flag of truce," which Sherman "does not like to do at this time." Thomas concluded, "They will probably all be sent south after the campaign is over."[9]

Despite an unfortunate encounter with army stragglers and Union guards on the 3d of July, Barrington King's brother, William King, then living at Marietta, became quite friendly with some of the Union officers stationed in and around Marietta who "afforded him much agreeable society." One such captain, William Rankin, assistant quartermaster for the 1st Cavalry Division, spoke frequently with William King. Although he had heard rumors the day before, it was Captain Rankin who confirmed that the factories in Roswell had been destroyed. Rankin told King that he had talked with many of the operatives who had arrived in town, and found that they spoke in very bitter terms of his brother, Barrington, and Barrington's assistant, George Camp. "They seemed to hate them both with a bitter hatred." Rankin remarked that William King was another matter. When asked if they knew William, the workers responded favorably, speaking of him in the "kindest of terms."[10]

On July 10, William King went into town and met Olney Eldredge and Samuel Bonfoy, overseers of the Roswell cotton and woolen factories. Eldredge and Bonfoy described the sad conditions at Roswell, stating that the factories had been "utterly destroyed" and that they and all of the operatives, men and women, had been arrested and were now in Marietta on their way north. They alleged that "every one of the houses of the resp [sic] settlers of Roswell had been broken open and plundered and everything of value had either been taken away or destroyed and done almost entirely by the operatives, that the soldiers had committed few depredations."[11]

Some of the female operatives found employment in Marietta, and avoided the long journey north, thanks to the kindness and generosity of Major General Grenville Dodge. Passing through Marietta on his way to Roswell, the commander of the XVI Corps noticed the large number of factory women and tried to assist them in finding work in a field hospital. Dodge told Assistant Surgeon John Ashton of the 7th Iowa Infantry to hire as many of the girls as he could use as nurses. Sergeant James Snell saw Dodge draw a $100 bill out of his pocket and gave it to the hospital steward, saying, "Take this, and use it in paying for the washing of clothes, etc. of the sick and wounded of our command."[12]

Wagonloads of women and children continued to arrive, prompting one correspondent to write on the 15th of July, "Marietta, for three days has been overrunning with men, women and children from Roswell." The presence of so many young women did not escape the attention of Federal soldiers, particularly those assigned to guard them. The 100th Indiana had been sent to Marietta on detached duty to guard the stores of supplies arriving daily, but several of the men were detailed to guard the female mill workers. One of the soldiers, Theodore Upson, described some of the "400 women" as "tough" and found it was a "hard job to keep them straight and to keep the men away from them." He added, "General Sherman says he would rather try to guard the whole Confederate Army, and I guess he is right about it."[13]

While the mill workers awaited transportation, Major Haviland Tompkins, responsible for burning the mills at New Manchester, was now charged with the care of "these multitudes of homeless people" and was "looking after their comfort" and issuing "rations for ample sustenance." It was only a few days before they began to board the trains that would take them north, first to Chattanooga, then to Nashville, and finally to Louisville, Kentucky, where other arrangements would be made for their transportation across the Ohio River.[14]

Furnished with nine days' rations, the operatives crowded into the boxcars as space on the trains became available. Olney Eldredge was among the first to leave Marietta, claiming he remained there only two days before being placed in a baggage car for Chattanooga. Writing only two years later, Eldredge recalled that he and his family were sent on their way without provisions or money, except for his own, then useless, Confederate money.[15]

Newspapers, north and south, carried the story of the arrest and deportation of the female workers. An article in the *Richmond Sentinel* declared that the "Autocrat of Russia or Sultan of Turkey" would never have perpetuated a more inhuman act than

Sherman did by tearing the helpless women away from their homes and sending them north. "What is most remarkable, the Poles, whose countrywomen have been torn from their homes, and whose villages transported to Siberia, are found in the Yankee army, sustaining the perpetrators of such outrages."[16]

Not surprisingly, an article in the anti–Lincoln *Harrisburg* (Pa.) *Patriot and Union* held a similar view of the events:

> A newspaper correspondent published a story, which we trust, for the sake of the officer implicated, as well as our own national good name, may prove to be unfounded. It is to the effect that General Sherman, finding at Roswell, in Georgia, four hundred factory girls, employed in a large cotton factory at that point, ordered the whole of the unfortunate creatures to be sent north of the Ohio. Gen. Sherman has shown on two or three occasions that his ability as a military commander is quite compatible with something not far removed from imbecility in respect to civil matters. He writes stupendously foolish orders on things political, and is evidently incapable of administering a village on practical principle. But it is hardly conceivable that an officer bearing a United States commission of Major General should have so far forgotten the commonest dictates of decency and humanity, (Christianity apart) as to drive four hundred penniless girls hundreds of miles away from their homes and friends to seek their livelihood amid strange and hostile people. We repeat our earnest hope that further information may redeem the name of General Sherman and our own from the frightful disgrace which this story as it now comes to us must else inflect upon one and the other.[17]

Another northern correspondent expressed a slightly more objective view of the "novel" events. His article made its way into several newspapers, and it appeared in the *Cincinnati Daily Commercial* on July 19:

> Having marched rapidly, the day before, upon the large cotton factory at that point [Roswell] he [Garrard] took it altogether by surprise, destroying a vast quantity of army canvas, which was extensively manufactured there, and taking captive four hundred factory girls. The latter capture was certainly a novel one in the history of wars, and excited not a little discussion as to the disposition, which was proper to be made of the fair captives.

Martha Louise Eldredge (1846–1926). Martha was 17 when Union soldiers arrested her father. Martha later married Thomas J. Minhinnett, whose father had been employed by the Roswell factories for many years (courtesy the descendants of Olney Eldredge).

The writer acknowledged that the solution was complicated since the prisoner of war cartel made no provision for exchanging prisoners "of this sort." He believed that the women were in fact guilty of giving aid and comfort to the enemy, along with a large amount of tent-cloth, but argued that it was an involuntary service for many of them. Sherman solved the hopeless entanglement with "crinoline, tent-cloth, and cartels" by loading the women into wagons and sending them to Marietta, to be sent north of the Ohio and set at liberty[18]:

> Only think of it; Four hundred weeping and terrified Ellens, Susans, and Maggies transported in springless and seatless army wagons, away from their lovers and brothers of the sunny South, and all for the offense of weaving tent-cloth and spinning stocking yarn.... I leave the whole business to be adjudged according to its merits, by your readers.[19]

Nashville

> *Precious Haul — Four hundred factory girls were captured by the Federal forces below Marietta, and are expected here to-day or tomorrow, on their way north.*
> *—Nashville Dispatch— July 23, 1864*

Notifying his chief of staff, General J. D. Webster, then at Nashville, of the imminent arrival of the mill workers, Sherman ordered them sent "across the Ohio River," but added that Webster could imprison any whom he thought dangerous. Sherman's orders did not authorize the release of any of the captives, but Webster apparently had some discretion and freed Theophile Roche and Olney Eldredge in Nashville. Ironically, of all those arrested, Roche was most responsible for the deception at the woolen mill, yet Webster chose to set him free, while the women and children continued on their journey to Louisville.[20]

Most of the mill workers had passed through Nashville by the end of July, but a number of them still remained in Marietta. On July 29, Captain S. A. Stockdale, provost marshal general at Nashville, wrote to the provost marshal at Chattanooga, asking to be notified when the factory operatives left that place for Nashville. It is not known when the last of the mill workers left Marietta, but it appears that some remained at the institute for more than three weeks awaiting transportation to the "land of plenty."[21]

Louisville

> *The train which arrived from Nashville last evening, brought up from the south 249 women and children, who are sent by order of Gen. Sherman to be transferred north of the Ohio River, there to remain during the war. We understand there are now at Nashville 1500 women and children who are in destitute condition, and who are to be sent to this place to be sent north. A number of them were engaged in the manufactories at Sweetwater at the time that place was captured by our forces. These people are mostly in a destitute condition and have no means to provide for themselves a support. Why they should be sent here to be transferred North is more than we can understand.*
> *—Louisville Democrat— 21 July 1864*

The trains from Nashville, filled with their human cargo, began arriving in Louisville in mid–July. Uncertain as to what lay ahead, the mill workers found themselves without food or money in a city already overrun with refugees. In 1864 Kentucky's largest metropolis and most important trade center was a crowded, dirty, river town on the banks of the Ohio, where hogs ran free and beggars filled the streets. While refugees had been arriving in the city for months, the numbers increased dramatically with Sherman's invasion of Georgia, and Louisville was fast becoming the "asylum of the poor of all sections."[22]

Many Southern refugees flocked to the city on their own, seeking an escape from the horrors of war. They came seeking safety when their towns became battlefields. They came seeking food and employment when they were hungry and could find no work. They came seeking protection from roving bands of guerrillas, jayhawkers, bushwhackers, army stragglers, deserters, and sometimes their own neighbors. And others came seeking shelter when their homes were confiscated for officers' quarters and hospitals or maliciously torched in retaliation for real or imagined offenses. Louisville offered the safety of numbers and at least some semblance of law and order. Opportunities for employment and economic assistance were better in Federally held cities for those willing to take the oath of allegiance to the Federal government. For those acting out of sheer desperation, the oath was often a small price to pay for some sense of security.

The overwhelming number of refugees were women, children, and aged or sick men who were left behind when younger men marched off to war; they were those least able to protect themselves or their property from the stragglers who preyed on defenseless citizens. Wagons and horses were hard to come by, and many were forced to travel on foot, taking only those belongings they could carry in their arms. Hundreds more arrived by train from Nashville, among them the women and children from Roswell and New Manchester.[23]

Although Sherman ordered the arrest of the women, formal charges were never issued, and no evidence has been found to indicate that any official record was made of their transportation or of their confinement at any point from Marietta to Louisville. According to the director of the military railroads, "No record was kept of the contrabands, refugees, and rebel deserters that poured back from the front during the period of active operations." The women and children were confined against their will and held under guard but appear to have been treated much the same as refugees in all other respects.[24]

An article in the *Louisville Democrat* of July 21 reported the arrival of 249 women and children in Louisville the day previous. The article noted, "A number of them were engaged in manufactories at Sweetwater at the time that place was captured by our forces." Although there is no mention of male prisoners, the men from New Manchester arrived at the Louisville Military Prison that same day. The prison register contains the names of the 43 male "political prisoners" arrested in Campbell County. Burdine Tucker, John Causey and Charles Wilson, along with 40 others, were paroled and discharged the following day by Captain Stephen E. Jones, commissary general for rebel prisoners in the state of Kentucky, who ordered them sent north of the Ohio River where they were to stay for the remainder of the war.[25]

Until transportation could be arranged to take them across the river, the workers and their families were housed in a large hospital building at 10th and Broadway, newly built to serve the military prison across the street, and not yet supplied with gas or water. Synthia Stewart, nine years old at the time of her arrival in Louisville, recalled many years later that they "were called prisoners" and "turned loose in a big old hospital house — which had an enclosure around the house so that nobody could come in or go on."[26]

Synthia's mother, sisters and brothers, along with her uncle, James Scarborough, and his family had been sent to Louisville with the mill workers from New Manchester. A family reunion of sorts ensued shortly after they arrived when Synthia and her uncle happened to see Synthia's father, Walter Stewart, coming down the street in front of the refugee house. Captured near Atlanta on August 3, Walter Stewart was just one of a large number of Southern prisoners on their way to the prison barracks just across the road. Scarborough was able to obtain permission for a brief visit and he and Synthia's mother, Charlotte Elizabeth Stewart, met with Walter in the prison yard under the watchful eyes of the guards. Walter told his wife that he was to be sent to the prison at Camp Chase, Ohio, the following day but assured her that he would find some way to stay in touch and promised to return to Louisville after the war. Upon taking the oath of allegiance, Charlotte was released in Louisville, found employment working "for the government," and remained in the city with her children.[27]

The journey to Louisville was particularly difficult for three young sisters from Roswell, eighteen-year-old Lucinda Elizabeth Wood, her fifteen-year-old sister Molly, and eleven-year-old sister Easter. Their father, Robert Wood, had enlisted in the Confederate Army at the outbreak of the war and moved his family to Roswell so that the children could find work in the mill while he was away. Serving with the 36th Georgia, Wood was sent home on furlough in late 1863 but died before he was able to return to his regiment. Six months later, Garrard's forces arrested his widow and sent her and the children north.[28]

In recalling the events many years later, Lucinda told her son that she and her family arrived in Louisville by boat. While all other known accounts indicate that the operatives reached the city by train, it is possible that some of the workers were sent by rail to Chattanooga or Nashville and then to Louisville by river to relieve the crowded conditions on the trains. Although Lucinda and her sisters left Roswell with their mother and grandmother, only the three young women survived the ordeal. Their mother, Marguerite, took sick on the trip and died just before reaching Louisville. Their grandmother, Polly Sumner, was also ill and allegedly died "while sitting in her chair as they carried her off the boat."[29]

For many years it was rumored that military authorities imprisoned the women and children from the Roswell and Sweetwater mills in the Female Military Prison at Louisville and placed them in the care of the famous, or infamous, Dr. Mary Walker, but prison registers indicate otherwise. The Female Military Prison, located some distance from the refugee house, did not open its doors until August and held only 25 to 30 women at that time. Furthermore, the names of the mill workers do not appear on any of the prison registers. Although the mill women were confined at the refugee house, a number of other Georgia women, arrested during Sherman's Atlanta campaign, spent many long, difficult months behind the walls of the female facility.[30]

The last of the women were released from the Female Military Prison on April 21, 1865, in accordance with Special Orders No. 48. "The following named female prisoners now confined in the female military prison are unconditionally released from arrest and allowed to return to their homes." The seven women, Susan Burchfield, Jane Call, Eliza Freeman, Mollie Goelet, Mary and Suze McCraw and Sallie Thompson had spent nine months behind bars for crimes of disloyalty. Finally they were free to return home.[31]

Conditions in the refugee house grew steadily worse. Confined in a building without heat or water, the women were in desperate need of food, medical attention and care. A few women, like Charlotte Stewart, were fortunate to find work in Louisville, some taking positions once filled by slaves:

> From the *Louisville Daily Journal* we learn that when these women and children arrived at Louisville, they were detained there, advertised to be hired out as servants, to take the place of a large number of Negroes who have been liberated by the military authorities and are now gathered in large camps throughout Kentucky where they are fed and supported in idleness and viciousness at the expense of loyal taxpayers. Thus while these Negro women are rioting and luxuriating in the Federal camps on the bounty of the government, the white women and children of the south are arrested at their homes and sent off as prisoners to a distant country to be sold into bondage, as the following advertisement fully attests: NOTICE — Families residing in the city or country wishing seamstresses or servants can be suited by applying at the refugee quarters on Broadway, between 9th and 10th. This is sanctioned by Capt. Jones, Provost Marshall.[32]

Much has been made of this article, citing it as evidence that the military authorities "sold" the women into slavery. A similar article submitted by an agent of the Refugee Commission on the 13th of September, however, provides some additional insight:

> Employment for Refugees; The undersigned, agent of the refugee commission, has charge of men, women, girls and boys who are healthy and capable and whose services can be obtained on very reasonable terms. Application may be made to him at the Refugee Home on the southeast corner of Broadway and Tenth Streets, from 9 A.M. to 12 P.M. every day.

The refugee commission had no intention of selling the refugees into slavery; rather they were attempting to find work for the desperate men, women and children who ended up in Louisville without any means to care for themselves or their families.[33]

Nancy Ann Bryant Pilgrim was fortunate to find work in the "fields" of Kentucky with other "prisoners." According to one unidentified account, both Nancy and her husband, Green Amos Pilgrim, had been employed by the Sweetwater Factory and were sent to Louisville with her brother and sister. Green was not well, and may not have been working in the mill at the time it was destroyed. With an invalid husband and small child, Nancy had to take any available work to help provide for her family, and often went out in the woods to cut wood.[34]

Many children remained with their mothers in the refugee hospital. One account, however, claims that the sisters from the Sisterhood of Nuns of Nazareth in Bardstown, Kentucky, came to Louisville and took many of the children, while others were distributed throughout the country wherever homes could be found.[35]

Living conditions for refugees remaining in Louisville worsened day by day. On August 13, the *Louisville Daily Journal* called attention to the suffering Southern refugees, noting that more arrived on every train in a city unprepared to care for them. Old men, women and children huddled together in barracks with no provision for comfort. While many were sick and filled with despair, large numbers were dying and hurried to "rude unknown graves." The writer begged the citizens of the city to visit the refugee barracks to see the "sorrow, destitution, and suffering" for themselves. "The need is pressing, the case is urgent; the suffering is great; and relief in some shape must be speedily obtained." All were asked to do their Christian duty in supplying clothing, linens, homes and kind, cheering words.[36]

The Louisville Refugee Commission worked diligently to help the hundreds of refugees that continued to pour into Louisville from all over the South. Organized in April 1864, in response to the rapidly increasing number of refugees, the commission was dedicated to helping the refugees find opportunities for "remunerative industry and the means of self-support." Dependent on private donations of money and clothing, the commission published a number of notices in the local newspapers pleading for assistance. An article on the 24th of August noted that many of the refugees were sick, destitute and in immediate need of proper food, medical attention, medicines, and care. "There are children of every age — some so attenuated as to be living skeletons — perishing for the want of proper care.... Men, women and children — a vast majority being women and children — all lie together, dozens of families in one room, many of them utterly destitute." The commission appealed for funds, "whereby the sick and needy may receive proper care and support; but more especially whereby these refugees may all be collected for transportation to other points, where they can obtain permanent employment."[37]

An article the following month made another plea for assistance, reporting that although several hundred refugees had been provided for and sent from the city, more than one hundred and fifty women and children remained at the refugee house on

Broadway, and nine-tenths of them were prostrate with disease. There had been a number of recent deaths from what appeared to be a form of typhoid, and doctors claimed that all would die if immediate relief was not forthcoming. It is likely that some of the mill women and children were among the number still held at the refugee house in September. An unnamed mill worker informed a correspondent in late August that while many had been sent to Indiana, "many still remained."[38]

11

Land of Plenty

Why they should be sent North to be supported by the charities of loyal people, will strike every one as singular. The people of Indiana, in which State most of these people will stop, already have their charities taxed to their utmost limit in support of their own widows and orphans, made by this war.
— New Albany *Daily Ledger*, July 21, 1864

History has recorded but few of the names of the women and children who arrived in Indiana from Roswell and New Manchester. Since it appears that no records were kept of the Southern "refugees," it is impossible to identify the individual mill workers or to ascertain when they arrived or in what number. Even so, it is important to understand the conditions they faced in this "land of plenty." Contrary to Sherman's assurances that the operatives would "live in peace and security" and "find employment," a very different fate lay in store for those sent across the Ohio River.[1]

Put ashore at Evansville, New Albany and Jeffersonville without food, money or provisions, the mill workers found themselves at the mercy of the local citizens who were ill equipped to handle the arrival of hundreds of impoverished refugees. There were no private or public agencies in the river towns in July of that year to offer any assistance. Many of Indiana's own citizens were suffering, and any relief efforts were directed towards the soldiers and their needy families.[2]

The state was very active in its commitment to care for Indiana soldiers at home and on the battlefront. After Indiana troops suffered heavy casualties at Fort Donelson in February 1862, the state created its own sanitary commission to care for soldiers in the field. While most of the goods and funds spent by the Indiana Sanitary Commission came from voluntary contributions, military agents, paid by the state, were responsible for most of the distribution work.[3]

The state agency believed they were better able to care for their own and refused to unite with the United States Sanitary Commission. The national organization, in turn, criticized the Indiana agency for its "indiscreet zeal which was willing to recognize State lines even in its ministrations of mercy on the battlefield" and found its efforts indicative of "that obnoxious heresy of State sovereignty, against which the whole war was directed." Indiana's adjutant general came to the defense of the state agency, claiming there was nothing to gain by changing the State Commission to an auxiliary of the United States Commission. Rather, he believed there was much to lose, including "the home interest, the State pride and the liberality impelled or increased by them."[4]

The efforts of the Indiana Sanitary Commission were not limited to soldiers in the field. The agency operated a soldiers' home in Indianapolis for all soldiers passing through the city. It originally accommodated only 100 men but was eventually expanded to lodge 1800 and became the largest of its kind in the midwest. Wives, mothers and children of soldiers who came to Indianapolis looking for loved ones could find food and shelter at the Ladies Home located near the railway station and operated by the Sanitary Commission. However, little was done for the women and children at home.[5]

Concerned for the welfare of the needy families who were deprived of their normal income while the men were in the army, the state authorized county commissioners and incorporated cities and towns to levy special taxes to raise money, but the measure met with little success and was often altogether ignored. At the governor's urging the state legislature finally provided for a special state tax in 1865 to benefit soldiers' families, but the measure came too late to be of any significant help.[6]

For the most part it was the charity of local citizens that provided whatever assistance the families received. In November 1862 Indiana governor Oliver P. Morton appealed to the people of the state for aid, and he made similar appeals in 1863 and 1864. After receiving letters from needy people all over the state, Morton recommended the creation of local citizen committees to ascertain needs and solicit funds. In response, many communities organized Soldier's Aid Societies, while local sanitary societies performed similar duties in other places. Churches helped raise additional funds, as did various other organizations through fairs, balls and other events specially designed for that purpose. Citizens responded generously, but the contributions were sporadic and insufficient for the thousands of families that suffered while their loved ones risked their lives in the service of their country.[7]

With so much time, energy, and money going to the care of their own, there was nothing left to provide for the exiles and refugees who began pouring into Indiana several weeks before the mill workers arrived. Evansville's township trustee, J.P. Elliott, set up a temporary shelter and erected tents at Blackford's Grove to provide for 100 women and children who landed at the town wharf on July 7. Elliott then published an article in the *Evansville Times* pleading for assistance for the refugees who had been driven from their homes and thrown among strangers, most of whom were sick and dying.[8]

Representatives from the *Evansville Daily Journal* called on the camp of refugees at Blackford's Grove a few days later and published their findings in the newspaper on July 12. The visitors found 97 persons in the camp, 91 were women and children, and all but five or six were sick and unable to care for themselves. "It is indeed a sad sight to see a mother and four or five children all lying sick in the same tent, neither able to help the other." A 25-year-old man had died the day before and others would soon follow. The article stated that much had been done to "relieve the distress and ameliorate the condition of these wretched people," particularly noting the efforts of two "angels of mercy" who had entered the camp the day after it was formed and devoted themselves to this "Samaritan work." Mrs. Dr. Mills and Mrs. Captain Coyle worked from morning to night to care for the suffering refugees and had achieved great success, but much more help was needed. The *Journal* pleaded for clothes, provisions, and money, "for it is impossible to get along without money." The article closed with a suggestion that "an appeal should be made to the Government to make some provisions for this class of people, of whom we may expect large numbers to be landed here during the summer." The writer had no way of knowing that hundreds of women and children were already making their way north from Georgia that very day.[9]

On July 14 a notice in the *Evansville Daily Journal* announced that Elliott was closing the refugee camp. Making an appeal to "save the lives of these unfortunate people," Elliott called upon "all persons who can take one or more of the little children into their families, temporarily or permanently" to call at the camp immediately adding that it would be "impossible for them to recover while exposed to the many disadvantages of camp life." Elliott sent the refugees to the fairgrounds where they would find water and temporary shelter. On the 19th, he once again made a plea on behalf of the refugees, asking for contributions, and urging readers to consider taking some of the refugees into their homes.[10]

The editor of the New Albany newspaper was far less sympathetic to the predicament of the Southern refugees. On July 21 the New Albany *Daily Ledger* noted a "small detachment of the Southern Confederacy in the shape of two hundred and nineteen men, women and children" were en route to Indiana and expressed concern for the burden this "undesirable population" would be to the people of the state:

> On what plea of public policy these disloyal citizens of Georgia and other Southern States are sent North we cannot imagine. Indiana, as the Journal remarks, is getting the great majority of these exiles, on account of its continuity to the northern terminus of the Nashville railroad. If they are not fit to live in the South on account of their disloyalty, are they fit to live in the North? Is it right to throw upon Indiana, because she happens to be North of the Ohio, the burden of supporting this class of people?

While the writer expressed confidence in General Sherman, he suggested that the general had acted unwisely. "We fear he has not, in this instance, sufficiently considered the injustice he is likely to do to the people of Indiana in thus throwing upon them an undesirable population, and one which cannot, at least for some months to come, earn their own livelihood."[11]

The small towns were soon full of strangers. Crime was on the increase and the *New Albany Ledger* was quick to associate the evils with the Southern refugees arriving from Louisville. Desperation forced a number of women into prostitution. The New Albany newspaper noted an alarming increase of the "shameful evil.... The war has thrown among us hundreds of abandoned women, who were banished beyond the lines of our armies." Noting there were "several hundred such characters" in the city at the present time, they called upon the authorities to get rid of them. "Is it intended to make our city a sort of Botany Bay for the refuse and criminals of the rebel States and Louisville?"[12]

The intolerable situation finally received some attention in early August when the Louisville provost marshal, Captain Stephen E. Jones, wrote to Sherman about the growing problem of refugees on the shores of Indiana. Jones informed Sherman that the large number of refugees and paroled prisoners sent north of the Ohio River "to remain during the war" was inflicting serious injury upon the border of Indiana, and especially on the city of Jeffersonville. Under existing orders, Jones had no choice but to release all prisoners on the north bank of the Ohio River. He was not authorized to furnish them transportation to the interior portion of the state. Consequently a large number were left without employment or any means by which they could gain support. Jobs were scarce, and the refugees and prisoners were destitute and unable to pay their passage by rail or steamboat to points where employment might be obtained. Jones believed the problem could best be solved by furnishing transportation for the refugees, at the government's expense, to interior points where they might find employment.[13]

In reply to Jones's request, Sherman issued General Orders No. 22 on the 12th of August. Refugees, male and female, would be "forwarded at the expense of the United States, if unable to pay their own way, to Cincinnati or St. Louis by water or to any point not over 100 miles by railroad." Additionally, commanding officers at Cairo or Louisville should "endeavor to put this class of people in the way of honest employment as much as possible" by working with agents of the Christian Commission or labor agencies.[14]

The citizens of New Albany welcomed the news, believing the order would benefit all parties concerned. The New Albany *Daily Ledger* set forth its position in an article on August 16. "Hitherto it has been the practice to land these persons on the Indiana shore without means or subsistence, leaving them to shift for themselves." Now, the writer asserted, by sending them further into the interior, "they will better be able to procure employment and earn a livelihood, and the border counties be relieved of a superabundance of this class of persons."[15]

General Orders No. 22 did not put an end to all shipments of refugees to the border towns. Expressing an uncharacteristic and surprisingly compassionate opinion, on December 1, the *Daily Ledger* reported another arrival of thinly clad refugees in "very distressed circumstances" with no money to "procure the necessities of life." Describing a "squalid scene of want," the article noted that something must be done for the "poor, destitute people," or they would soon be dying of starvation and exposure.[16]

With the onset of winter, the homeless refugees desperately sought shelter from the bitter cold. A newspaper article in late December reported the desperate conditions in the Jeffersonville area. "The New Albany Ledger learns that there are a large number of refugees in and around Jeffersonville, some of whom seem to have no homes or habitations but old stables, barns, log houses &c., in the woods back of the city." Closing with a sentence that underscored the horrors facing these homeless refugees, the article continued, "In one or two instances, children have been found dead in the woods — actually starved or frozen to death."[17]

Conditions in New Albany were no better. The *Daily Ledger* called attention to the plight of the suffering refugees in their city:

> Many refugee families in this vicinity are passing the cold weather now upon us in miserable hovels built by placing boards against fences to afford temporary shelter. Their sufferings may be imagined when it is known that they are thinly and poorly clad and most of them dependent upon charity for the food which keeps them alive.[18]

On December 29, the New Albany paper reported another tragic death:

> Two refugees, a man and his little daughter, were found dead on Tuesday, in a miserable hovel, near the river, between this city and Jeffersonville. Their names were unknown, and it is supposed they either starved or froze to death. The sufferings of the poor destitute refugees during this pinching cold weather are terrible. No one should refuse to aid them.[19]

Even those sent into the interior of the state often found themselves without work or shelter. The report of the state's adjutant general acknowledged the hopeless conditions that awaited Southern refugees in Indianapolis, noting that most arrived in a "state of deplorable destitution," with no means to maintain themselves. Strangers in an unfamiliar land, the refugees did not know where to go or what to do and were generally left in the depot at Indianapolis without "direction or assistance." The cold, the rain, and the wind forced homeless refugees to shelter themselves "as best they could in out-houses or any accessible place till the charity of the neighbors provided them with something better."[20]

Desperate for help, Governor Morton wrote to Secretary of War Edwin Stanton on December 28, 1864, requesting assistance. Morton noted that large numbers of Southern refugees, particularly women and children, "entirely destitute," were filling the depots and streets. The citizens were doing their best to help the homeless refugees, but much more help was needed. Morton told Stanton that he had been informed that rations were issued to such refugees at other points and wanted to know if there was any order or regulation by which such rations could be issued in Indiana, explaining that it would relieve a great deal of suffering.[21]

Stanton promptly responded that he was unable to send aid. "I cannot find that any issues of supplies have been made to destitute persons or refugees except in the rebel States under the pressure of an immediate military necessity." Stanton claimed that he would be glad to "afford relief" to the distressed and needy persons, but that he had no power under the existing laws. He told Morton that he had been urging the

adoption of some legislative measure, "either organizing a bureau or granting authority," but nothing had yet been accomplished.[22]

There was, in fact, no congressional authorization for relief to the suffering refugees
in Indiana. It appears that no such legislation was considered or even proposed in 1864
or 1865. Indeed, the only record of Congress that even refers to the plight of Southern
refugees in the North was one in which Senator John Sherman of Ohio, ironically, the
brother of the man most responsible for the crisis, presented a petition from the Refugee
Relief Commission of Ohio seeking funds for "furnishing poor white refugees of the
south with seed and farming implements, and tools to such as are mechanics." This
modest petition was referred first to the Committee on Public Lands, and then to the
Committee on Finance. No bill was ever offered, and the idea died in committee. The
only other legislative activity remotely related was a bill offered in the Senate to "provide a fund for indigent loyal refugees from the state of Texas." That measure was also
referred to committee and died without action. In the end, Congress did nothing to
alleviate the human suffering caused by its own armies and its own war policies.[23]

Many would question Sherman's rationale for sending so many Southern women
and children to Indiana, perhaps none more so than Indiana newspaper editors. It is
impossible to determine how much Sherman knew about the desperate conditions that
existed in Indiana. On the other hand, there was little reason for him to expect that
the hundreds of women and children would find work, food, or shelter in the river
towns north of the Ohio River. The vast number of refugees flooding the streets of
Louisville had created an enormous burden for the refugee aid societies in that city,
and there were no such organizations in the small towns across the river. Sherman
seemed to be motivated more by the "military necessity" of removing these women and
children far to the rear of his army than by any sense of concern for their welfare.
Whatever his reasons, Sherman elected to send the women north with empty promises
of peace and security.

Women from Roswell and Sweetwater hoping to find work in Indiana mills faced
bitter disappointment. The northern textile industry was suffering from a shortage of
cotton, and there was no work for the great number of women desperate to provide
for themselves and their families.

The only cotton mill of any size in Indiana was a huge industrial complex at Cannelton. The mill, which opened in 1851, was an impressive four-story building with
walls of variegated sandstone blocks, and twin 106-foot-high towers on either side of
the entrance. Louisville lawyer Hamilton Smith and his business partners built the mill
in the hopes of creating industrial development in the Midwest to rival the textile industry of New England. The mill relied on the South for cotton and the cities of Cincinnati and Louisville for commercial goods. Originally known as the Cannelton Cotton
Mill, the name was changed to the Indiana Cotton Mill when the company was sold
to a newly formed corporation in 1853, but the new name never seemed to catch on.[24]

Although the Civil War brought prosperity to southern cotton mills, the war dealt devastating blows to the northern factories and forced many to suspend operations. The Indiana Cotton Mill was particularly hard hit. The mill had done well in the months just prior to the war, leading the owners to invest an additional $3000 in company owned housing, but the prosperity would be short-lived. Blockades and Federal restrictions on obtaining cotton from the South brought the northern cotton markets to a standstill, and the Cannelton mill was faced with a severe shortage of cotton. The prospects were so bleak by September 1861 that management cut the workday in half in an effort to keep the factory operating. Finally the directors resorted to closing the mill for various lengths of time, from March to June 1862, from April to November 1863, and again in 1864.[25]

The closings were especially hard on the women and children, always the first to lose their jobs each time the mill closed and the last to be rehired when it re-opened. Workers struggled to make ends meet even when the mill was operating, as management continually reduced wages and hours in an effort to keep the machines running. Wages fluctuated from month to month, sometimes by as much as 25 percent, and hours worked per day varied from full to three-quarters to half-time throughout the war. Facing severe shortages of cotton and the inability to sell their finished goods, the mill owners announced in September of 1864 that they would soon be suspending operations. Various notices appeared in the *Louisville Democrat* expressing concern for the operatives who were "unfitted to earn a comfortable living at any other occupation." Finally in October, the "heart of Cannelton" ceased to beat and many persons were thrown out of employment. The *Cannelton Reporter* noted sarcastically, "It is one of the few trifling inconveniences of the war. Only a few hundred women and children will be made destitute. One of the items by which we purchase glory on the tented field." This time the mill remained closed for eight months.[26]

In 1864 the women and children of Roswell and New Manchester could not find work at the Cannelton Cotton Mill. The company could not provide for its own employees, let alone offer employment to hundreds of women from southern mills. Nevertheless, many of the operatives survived the hardships of the first winter, and in the face of great adversity made their way to Cannelton and found employment in the mill after it reopened in May 1865. Some would stay a few years; others remained in Indiana for the rest of their lives.[27]

12

News from the Home Front

Dear Old Roswell I am afraid we never will meet in a home there again. Oh what a war, a cruel war, and how little the Yankees feel it.
— Barrington Simeral King, July 25, 1864

While the Roswell elite waited anxiously for news from home, rumors of the town's destruction spread like wildfire. Barrington King feared that all was lost. More than a month had passed since the Yankee occupation, and he had still received no word from Nathaniel Pratt in Roswell. He heard vague reports that his beloved "Barrington Hall" had been destroyed as well as the cotton and woolen mills. It was the loss of his home that troubled him the most. The mills were of less concern. Even if the factories had been destroyed, King was certain something would be left of the "wreck," and since he had well prepared for that possibility, storing cotton in warehouses throughout the state of Georgia, the stockholders would have the financial means to rebuild with very little additional investment.[1]

Barrington's fifth son, Barrington Simeral, stationed near Stoney Creek Depot, Virginia, received conflicting reports from men returning from Atlanta. On July 20, Barrington wrote his mother that he was doubly anxious to hear the truth, as he had heard so many rumors. One soldier reported that the Yankees had destroyed the factories and burned most of the buildings in the village. Another said that the enemy had burned the woolen mill and was running the cotton mill for their own benefit. Someone else claimed the factory was burned under a British flag. The younger Barrington confessed, "He didn't know what to believe." A few days later a report reached him that the factory and every home had been burned. "It is impossible for me to realize it." Passing on the news in another letter to his mother, Barrington explains his "soul felt desire" to drive the Yankees from the "soil they now pollute, and to recover the homes they have made desolate."[2]

The Smith family received word from George Camp in July that that the Yankees had entered Roswell, but they had received no reports of the actual damage. Contradictory newspaper accounts led to the confusion, and filled them with a sense of dread.

"We [see] in one paper that the Roswell factory had been burned & in another that it had not but now that part of the country is given up it is only a question of time."[3]

Barrington Sr. heard in July that two of the mill managers had been sent to Marietta. He mentions their arrest in a letter to his son-in-law, but makes no mention of the other workers. In fact, in the many letters from that period that survive, none of the families, not the Kings, the Smiths, nor the Pratts, express one word of concern or sympathy for the fate of the hundreds of women and children who were arrested and deported. The factory owners, safe in their places of refuge, seemed indifferent to the plight of those they left behind. On September 7, William Smith, writing to his mother, described a conversation with family friends in Montgomery, Georgia, "They saw the train that had the factory girls from Roswell being carried north." No further comment was made.[4]

Letters written in September would frequently mention the factory hands, but never out of concern for their safety and well-being. The Kings and Smiths finally heard from Nathaniel Pratt in September, the first real news from the home front. On September 9, Anne Smith wrote to her son with good news. According to Reverend Pratt, the mills had been destroyed, but the houses still stood, although they had been "ransacked from top to bottom & every thing carried off mostly by the factory & Parkertown people." Anne Smith confessed she was not surprised by the actions of those she believed responsible for much of the vandalism: "It is nothing more than I expected of those people when they had things in their power."[5]

Reverend Pratt and Anne Smith were not alone in their determination to blame the factory workers, or "those people" as they were frequently called, for much of the damage that occurred to the homes left vacant by their wealthy owners. After receiving a letter from his sister informing him that the "home people" had done all they could to make the Union soldiers search their houses for hidden goods, Barrington King relayed the information to Archibald Smith, adding, "We have done much for that class of people, but they have no gratitude & now shew what we had to manage."[6]

Although the preponderance of evidence suggests that it was the soldiers who bore the greatest responsibility for the theft and property damage, it is clear that the some of the workers were involved. After their arrest, the two mill managers, Olney Eldredge and Samuel Bonfoy, confided to William King in Marietta that the workers had participated in much of the vandalism in town. Even if this was true, it should have not have surprised anyone given the animosity between the mill workers and mill owners. When questioned by Captain Rankin in Marietta, the operatives spoke of Barrington King and George Camp in "very bitter terms" and "seemed to hate them both with a bitter hatred."[7]

Although the factory people and the Roswell nobility lived within the same geographic confines of the town, they lived in two very different worlds. King's prewar correspondence reveals little about his relationship with the workers. In fact, the only time they are mentioned is in connection with some illness making its way through the factory. Even then he seems less concerned for the health of the employees than he is for the effect that the outbreak will have on the factory's production.[8]

King never appeared to be particularly sympathetic in his dealings with his employees or his "possessions." In 1861 he sold a young slave woman while retaining possession of her 2-year-old daughter. King's ledgers do not indicate why Sarah-Ann was sold without her daughter, but they do reveal that the proceeds of the sale were used to buy another slave named Margaret. Such actions, while not entirely uncommon, were generally something more compassionate men tried to avoid. King's attitude towards the mill workers after July 1864 highlighted a similar lack of charity to his former employees.[9]

It is unreasonable to expect a close bond between the mill employees who labored in the factories and the men who made their fortunes at their expense. And even the best relationships would no doubt be severely strained if workers were left behind to protect the property of their wealthy employers. It is true that some of the mill managers stayed behind to oversee the work of the factories, but they were educated, skilled workers who would be better able to fend for themselves if the mills were destroyed, unlike the hundreds of women and children who would be left on their own. Whatever the reasons for the animosity between the two classes, the chasm would grow even wider during the days and months that followed the destruction of the Roswell mills.

Roswell's upper crust seemed to forget that Union soldiers bore some responsibility for the pillaging and plundering of their homes and possessions. The abuses had been so widespread by July 6 that the provost marshal had been ordered to take immediate action to prevent the "outrages disgracing their commands." Union officers and northern newspaper correspondents had no hesitation in laying blame at the feet of the Yankee soldiers.[10]

And there would be others to share the blame. Reverend Pratt informed the Smiths in November that people were coming from miles around to look for iron and other things that could be salvaged from the factories. According to Helen Smith, Pratt said that the "crackers did more harm to the place than the Yankees." The next month Pratt wrote his nephew that the worst problem he then faced was from Confederate soldiers at home without leave. He claimed there were "40 to 50 soldiers, some who were stealing horses and mules, taking the few hogs left from the already robbed and almost starving soldier's wives — poor widows." Pratt asked Barrington if there was not some way to get these men returned to their regiments.[11]

Despite the reports of destruction and depredations committed by the Union forces, as well as Confederate deserters, a number of Roswell citizens insisted on holding the mill workers at least partially responsible. At a meeting of the stockholders of the Roswell Manufacturing Company in June 1865, details of the destruction were noted. In their version of the events, the U.S. Army entered the village on the 6th of July and destroyed both cotton factories and cotton houses the following evening, but did little injury to the store building and dwelling houses for the operatives. According to Barrington King, it was the workers who bore much of the blame:

> "We regret much to report the conduct of a few men in our employment for years with the women and children from whom we *expected protection* [author's italics] to our property. They plundered and destroyed to a large amount, tearing down the shelves in the store to burn, breaking glasses and otherwise injuring the houses, hauling off iron and copper to sell, and putting the wheel in motion and seriously injuring it by throwing down rocks."[12]

What isn't clear is when the factory workers had time to wreak such havoc. The factories were in operation when Garrard's men arrived, and the workers were rounded up the next day. It is quite likely that some of the workers participated in acts of vandalism during the night before their arrest, but most of the vacant homes had already been confiscated by the Federals and were being used for hospitals or headquarters buildings. Particularly troublesome is the details of how and when the workers were supposed to have hauled off the missing iron and copper when most, if not all, of the able bodied men had ridden off with the Roswell Battalion.

Quick to condemn the workers for real or imagined offenses, the Roswell elite showed little consideration for the exiled workers. Not one expression of concern or compassionate sentiment can be found in their letters. No one even seemed curious as to the fate of so many displaced women and children.

13

Return to Roswell

Thank God on arrival here I was astonished to find the old mansion so little injured.... In walking the street to Brother Pratt's no one would imagine the place had been occupied by the army; but going towards the creek to see the destruction of our fine mills "all destroyed," the loss of two sons, another wounded and one with a broken wrist, all caused by the late unnatural war, made me sad indeed.
— Barrington King on his return to Roswell, July 22, 1865

Citizens and soldiers returning to Roswell found their town had escaped without serious injury, but there was much work to be done. The entire Army of the Tennessee had followed Garrard's cavalry through Roswell but the only structures completely destroyed were the mill buildings. The stately mansions and churches were in need of repair but still stood, and the foundations of the mills were good. But neither the town nor its people would ever be the same. Every person had been touched by the war, from mill worker to the "Royal Family," and many lost something much more precious than buildings. What price the lives of so many young men who would never return?[1]

Those who survived the war began the long journey home. The founding families, the Kings, Dunwodys, Smiths, Pratts, and Bullochs had been well represented in the long bloody war, their sons serving in various units and numerous capacities. Many made the ultimate sacrifice.

The King family lost two sons in the war. The beloved Captain Tom met his untimely death at Chickamauga. His brother Barrington Simeral was killed near the close of the war in a courageous charge on a line of dismounted cavalry near Fayetteville, North Carolina. Barrington was mortally wounded, the artery of his thigh being severed. Lt. Wiley Howard, commanding Company C of Cobb's legion, and Howard's brother grasped King, wheeled him about, and removed him from his horse under a terrific fire. He was buried nearby and Howard later directed one of Barrington's brothers to the place. Barrington's remains were removed and re-interred at Roswell.[2]

The inscription on Barrington's headstone incorrectly states that he was killed at

Bentonville. According to Howard, Bentonville was "some forty or fifty miles distant from where he so gallantly fell leading the charge, about a month before that last great battle was fought." Writing of King's death, Howard added, "Epitaphs do not always speak the truth; but King died as gloriously as he could have possibly done on the bloody field of Bentonville."[3]

James Roswell King continued to serve as a captain with the Roswell Battalion for some months after the evacuation of Roswell but was detailed to work in Macon in March 1865 after inventing a machine to straighten railroad iron, something that would be extremely beneficial to the Confederacy considering Sherman's fondness for heating and twisting railroad ties as to render them useless. At the end of the war, James and his family returned to Roswell.[4]

Ralph Browne King first enlisted under General William Hardee in Savannah and served as a member of the Chatham Artillery. Released from active service on account of his health, he was sent to Roswell and detailed to work at the Roswell Manufacturing Company. While there he served as a first lieutenant in Company B of the Roswell Battalion. After the factories were destroyed, he was ordered to Savannah and was later seriously injured in the evacuation of that city.[5]

Joseph Henry King originally enlisted in the 8th Georgia Infantry but was forced to resign after he was wounded at First Manassas. He later served as a first lieutenant in Company A of the Roswell Battalion and remained with the unit though the end of the war. The youngest brother, Clifford A. King, who ended the war as an acting assistant aide-de-camp to Lt. General William Hardee, was fortunate to survive the war without injury.[6]

John and Jane Dunwody's four sons served in various positions during the war, and one of them would not return. Henry Macon Dunwody received a commission as captain in the 51st Georgia Infantry in March 1862. He was promoted to major in May 1863 but lost his life at Gettysburg a few months later when he was mortally wounded in the fighting at the Wheat Field on July 2. Henry's brother John served as an infantry disbursing agent and James, a Presbyterian clergyman, served briefly as a chaplain. Henry's youngest brother, Charles Archibald Alexander Dunwody, was commissioned first lieutenant of the Roswell Guards but was wounded at First Manassas and forced to resign in September 1861. In the spring of 1862 Charles was appointed major and assigned to command the Camp of Instruction in Calhoun, Georgia. After the war ended, Major Dunwody returned to Roswell, farmed land he owned and founded the town of Dunwoody. Charles Dunwody built the first postwar bridge to span the Chattahoochee River near Roswell.[7]

Archibald and Anne Smith returned to Roswell from Valdosta in April 1866, still grieving over the loss of their oldest son. After enlisting in the Savannah Volunteer Guards in April 1862, William Seagrove Smith was detailed to the Signal Corps in Savannah and remained there until the city fell to Sherman in December 1864. Smith participated in General Hardees's retreat through the Carolinas to Raleigh where he suffered a severe attack of typhoid fever in May. Taken in by kind and compassionate strangers, Willie died a few weeks later. Willie's father purchased a print of the famous painting by William D. Washington, *The Burial of Latane*, depicting the burial of a Confederate captain on a southern plantation far from home. No doubt they found the similarities in the death of Captain Latane and the loss of their son. A copy of the painting hangs in the Smith home as of this writing.[8]

The Smiths' youngest son, Archibald Smith, served as quartermaster sergeant with the Georgia Military Institute Battalion of Cadets under the command of Major Francis Withers Capers. Archie returned to Roswell after the war but moved to LaGrange, Georgia, after the death of his father in 1886 and his mother and aunt in 1887. His sisters, Lizzie and Helen, never married, lived alone in the Smith house until their deaths.[9]

James Stephens Bulloch died in 1849, his wife and children moving north prior to the outbreak of hostilities. Two of his sons returned to fight for the Confederacy. James Dunwody Bulloch, veteran of fifteen years in the U.S. Navy, served as a Confederate naval agent with the rank of commander. Since Bulloch's primary duty was to secure ships for the Confederacy, he was dispatched to Europe on June 4, 1861, and authorized to buy, build and arm ships. He supervised the construction of 24 vessels in European shipyards, including *Enterprise, Alabama, Alexandria, Florida, Shenandoah* and the ironclad *Stonewall*. His most famous purchase was *Alabama*, the most successful commerce raider in history. Bulloch had hoped to captain *Alabama*, but command went instead to Raphael Semmes. *Alabama* met her fate at the hands of *Kearsarge* in the historic engagement off Cherbourg, France, in 1864.[10]

James Bulloch became a British citizen and remained in England with his wife until his death. In 1883 he wrote a substantive two-volume work, *The Secret Service of the Confederate States; or How the Confederate Cruisers were Equipped in London*. Bulloch died on January 7, 1901, the same year his nephew, Theodore Roosevelt, became president of the United States.[11]

The United Daughters of the Confederacy added an inscription to Bulloch's Liverpool grave marker in 1968 to honor his service. It reads in part "Strong ties of common ancestry existed between the Confederate States and the Mother country, England. Warm ties of friendship developed between Bulloch and the English people, and at the end of the war he chose to remain in Liverpool."[12]

Bulloch's younger half-brother, Irvine Bulloch, served as a midshipman on *Alabama's* final voyage. President Theodore Roosevelt boasted that his Uncle Irvine fired the last two shots from the ship. Rescued by a civilian ship after the *Alabama* went down, Irvine returned to Liverpool and was posted to CSS *Shenandoah*. Irvine, like his brother, chose to remain in England and Wales where he worked as a cotton merchant until his death on July 14, 1898.[13]

Both James and Irvine were honored in 2001. On January 7, 2001, 100 years after James' death, a Virginia contingent of the UDC returned to Liverpool, England, to place black wrought iron Southern crosses on the grave of James Bulloch and that of his brother Irvine.[14]

The Pratt family was the only one of the original Roswell colony left in the town when the Federal forces arrived. All of Reverend Pratt's sons, with the exception of thirteen-year-old William, went off to fight for the Confederacy and each of them returned home. Bayard Hand Pratt and Horace Pratt served with the Georgia State Troops, Horace commissioned as a captain. Henry Barrington Pratt served as a chaplain. Nathaniel Alpheus Pratt, a professor of chemistry and geology at Oglethorpe University, organized his own company, the Jordan Grays, but was made assistant chief of the Confederate States Niter and Mining Bureau with the grade of captain before the unit saw active duty. Charles Jones Pratt, appointed drill master at the Camp of Instruction at Macon, resigned in early 1863 to work as an engineer on the projected Atlanta and Roswell Railroad, which never materialized. He then served as a junior first lieutenant in the Roswell Battalion.[15]

Barrington King returned to Roswell in July 1865. Surveying the damage to the mill with his former agent, George Camp, King noted that the foundations of the 1854 mill were good, the operatives' houses were standing and the machine shop, cotton house and office could be repaired. King believed the mill was worth rebuilding and felt some obligation to the local residents to do so. "The country around feel the loss they have sustained by the destruction of our mills and anxious that we rebuild." On the 19th of July, the Roswell Manufacturing Company held a meeting of its stockholders and resolved to rebuild as soon as possible. While the company's losses had been heavy, there was enough cotton on hand to fill one mill with machinery and put it in motion without calling on the stockholders for a dollar, despite the high prices for materials.[16]

The 1854 factory was rebuilt and was back in operation by early 1867, but Barrington King would not be there for the reopening. Kicked in the chest by a horse, King died in January 1866 and was buried in the Presbyterian Church Cemetery with a marker that read, "To the Memory of Barrington King First Settler of Roswell and President of the Roswell Factories." With the deaths of Roswell King and his son and co-founder, Barrington, the King dynasty which had reigned for more than 30 years began to crumble.[17]

The "Royal Family" gradually lost control of the Roswell Manufacturing Company after Barrington's death. His estate was divided among all the children, their heirs, and Barrington's widow, Catherine Nephew King. In order to meet the heavy reconstruction taxes, Catherine was forced to sell most of her stock to General Andrew Jackson Hansell who took over as president. James King assisted with the management of the mill, but poor health prevented his taking a more active role in company operations.[18]

The mill continued to operate despite an 1881 flood that damaged all the company's dams. In 1882, the corporation constructed a new mill on the hill above the earlier mill complex. The old factory was struck by lightning in 1926, and the ensuing fire destroyed the mill, picker house, and warehouse. Instead of rebuilding, the directors decided to expand the 1882 structure on the hill.[19]

The cotton mill refused to die. During the years of the Great Depression, the new mill operated only sporadically. In the 1940s the mill turned to the manufacture of laundry netting and carpet backing as a means of survival, although it continued to produce cotton yard and cotton cloth. The Roswell Manufacturing Company finally closed its doors in 1975 and sold the machinery for scrap iron.[20]

The Ivy Woolen Mill was also rebuilt after the war, but the ownership changed hands several times in the mid–1870s. It was sold to the Laurel Mills Manufacturing Company in 1881 and remained in operation until 1917. According to local lore, the Woolen mill once again manufactured Roswell Grey wool for uniforms during World War I.[21]

14

The Mystery of
the Lost Mill Workers

*My widowed daughter, Eliza Ray, was sent north by General Sherman in his raid
through Georgia from her home near Marietta with her 5 children. Information
on her whereabouts will be thankfully received.*
— Columbus (GA) *Daily Sun* December 12, 1867

While the wealthy and privileged returned home to the open arms of friends and
family, no such homecoming awaited the brothers, husbands and fathers of the mill
workers. Only the empty houses and deserted streets on Factory Hill greeted returning soldiers searching for families, now gone without a trace. No one knew exactly where
the women had been sent, and there was no place to turn for assistance. Newspapers
provided few clues. Louisville papers had lost track or lost interest in the plight of the
mill workers by August 1864. While Indiana papers published numerous articles about
Southern refugees, they published no lists of names, and neither was there any specific
mention of the workers from Roswell and Sweetwater. With no word from his daughter in three years, Elijah Roberts placed an advertisement in a Georgia newspaper hoping to find some news of Eliza and her children.[1]

The frustrating search for the names of the mill workers remains a challenging
task for those attempting to tell the story. Years of exhaustive research have failed to
turn up a list of the women arrested and sent north. Provost marshal and prisoner
records are incomplete, and many records have been lost or destroyed. More important, there is no credible evidence that such a list ever existed.

Apart from oral histories and a few personal accounts, we are left with population
and militia census records to provide clues to the names and identities of possible mill
workers. While the 1860 population census provides a list of those who worked in the
mill at the time of the census, there is no way to know if they were still employed by
the factory in 1864. Indeed by 1864, many of the men had gone to war, and many more

women had come to the mills to support their families. The names of hundreds of women remain unknown.[2]

Although some writers suggest that most of the workers returned to Roswell, such theories have never been substantiated, and primary sources tell a different story. In truth, very few mill workers returned to their former homes, although a fair number were found living in other cities and towns throughout the state of Georgia by 1870. Given the inadequacy of available documentation, it is impossible to determine if these individuals were part of the deportation, or if they simply left Roswell on their own. We do know that of the hundreds of men, women and children sent north, many never made the journey back home.

That being said there is little mystery about their failure to return. Indeed, there are a number of reasons why returning may not have been a viable option. Perhaps most important, the women were very young. According to the 1860 Roswell census, 40 percent of the female workers over fifteen years of age were seventeen or younger, and another 40 percent were in their twenties. It is probable that a number of the women, like Lucinda and Molly Wood and Mary and Sarah Jane Kendley, married men in Kentucky or Indiana and settled there.[3]

Some eventually found employment in the north. Although there was no work to be found in 1864 in the Cannelton Cotton Mill, the factory was up and running in 1865 and some of the operatives did obtain work during that year. In fact, a number of Roswell families appear on the Perry County census of 1870.[4]

It is also important to keep in mind that the journey back to Georgia would have been very difficult to manage, especially for a young woman or a single mother. Even if she managed to scrape together the means to arrange for the long and arduous trip back to Roswell, she could not be sure what awaited her there. Since she had no way of knowing if the mills had been rebuilt, there were no guarantees that she could find work or shelter in the place she once called home.

There would be few jobs in Roswell for the returning mill workers if Barrington King had his way. King believed the operatives, "whom we had entrusted with the protection of our property," were at least partially responsible for the destruction at Roswell. Writing to his son in July 1865, King mentioned that some of the families sent north had returned looking for work. King, however, had no intention of hiring them: "We are determined to have a new sett with very few exceptions, no difficulty about labourers, the returned soldiers anxious for work at 60 [cents] per day and appear very orderly." Perhaps more revealing was Barrington's letter to another son two days earlier: "Hands in abundance, work at old prices 60/100 per day, *they boarding themselves*" [italics authors']. King added that all the workers were on their best behavior; "employ none but those with clean hands!"[5]

In truth, there was very little waiting for those who managed to return to Roswell. After making the long, hard journey back to the village, most found that home as they knew it no longer existed. The cottages on Factory Hill housed a new set of workers. Without prospects of employment in the mill, circumstances forced the returning workers to move on in hopes of finding work elsewhere. One only need look at the grave stones in the old cemeteries to see how few of "those people" spent the rest of their lives in Roswell.

Finally there is the question of survival. Large numbers of southern refugees died of disease, starvation and exposure. Even though we cannot determine just how many were Georgia mill workers, we do know that at least five of the women died before they could return home and several still lie buried beneath northern soil. Many of the women who succumbed to sickness and hunger left young children, innocent boys and girls who would suffer most of all. The orphaned children now found themselves all alone in an unfamiliar land, hundreds of miles from their childhood homes. Poor and penniless, they had to depend on the charity of strangers, who took many of them into their homes. No doubt many were welcomed into the families, but a number of the orphans were taken in as domestic servants. While there are no known accounts documenting such stories, a large number of young Georgia children could be found living with Indiana families throughout the state in 1870.[6]

Tragically, there are few personal accounts. Most of the women from the Roswell mills, unable to read and write, lacked the ability to leave behind a written record. Instead of their own words, we must turn to census records, newspaper articles, battle reports, and the letters, diaries and reminiscences of Union soldiers. A few accounts survive by those arrested and deported, but most were written, and in one case recorded, many years after the war and much of the information is vague and confused. In a few instances, too few, information and insight have been provided by oral family histories, but it is clear that we will never know many of the names and experiences.

One of the most recent accounts to surface was written by Olney Eldredge, superintendent of the Roswell cotton mill. Writing to his brother in 1866, Eldredge briefly described the details of his arrest and the journey north with his three children. Released in Nashville, Eldredge persuaded the authorities to allow him to continue on to Louisville where members of a local Presbyterian Church assisted him in getting to Cincinnati. From there, with the aid of the local Refugee Aid Society, he was able to make his way back to Boston. Returning to Roswell after the war, Eldredge was one of the favored few rehired by Barrington King to work in the new cotton mill.[7]

Some interesting and insightful information is found in several depositions taken in the 1880s. Theophile Roche filed a lawsuit against the United States government for $70,000 over the burning of the woolen mill. His testimony includes an account of the destruction of the mills as well as details of his arrest. Although other depositions made in support of the government's case attempted to discredit Roche's testimony, Eldredge's letter validates much of Roche's deposition and in fact, casts a great deal of doubt on the integrity of the government witnesses. Like Eldredge, Roche took the oath of allegiance and was released on his arrival in Nashville. Roche traveled to New York and then on to France. His lawsuit was dismissed in 1883 for want of prosecution.[8]

Lucinda Wood never forgot her journey north. She and her sisters were orphaned by the time they arrived in Louisville. Losing their father in Roswell a few months prior to their arrest, their mother and grandmother died on the way to Kentucky. Lucinda and her sisters remained at the refugee hospital until they could find employment and a place to stay.

Lucinda's brothers Joseph and William either accompanied them on the trip north, or found them later in Kentucky. After leaving the refugee house, Lucinda lived with her brothers and sisters until she married James Shelly in 1866. Her sister Molly married John Tarrant from Illinois about the same time and when they moved to Illinois in 1871, James and Lucinda followed. Lucinda became seriously ill in 1886 and her doctor warned that she might not survive another cold winter. She and her husband decided to take their family and relocate to the more healthful climate of North Georgia.[9]

Lucinda's account of the difficult trip back to Georgia reveals why most women would not have attempted such a journey on their own. Loading the wagon with only a few belongings and eight children, James and Lucinda, then five months pregnant, headed south in October. They traveled by day and slept on the ground at night and under the wagon when it rained. It took twelve days to reach the southern Kentucky border, but the Tennessee roads were "hillier" and travel became slower. After four weeks, the team was "fagged down" and the family managed to travel only fifteen miles a day. James and Lucinda arrived at Lucinda's uncle's house near Jasper, Georgia, early in November after a journey of thirty-two days at a cost of $33. The Shelly family settled nearby, and Lucinda gave birth to her ninth child two months later. Apparently the Georgia climate was just what the doctor ordered, for Lucinda lived another 34 years.[10]

While the details are sketchy, Adeline Bagley Buice and her four children were also among those sent north. Her fifth child was born a month later in Chicago. It is not clear how or why Adeline ended up in Illinois when most of the others were sent to the river towns of Indiana. Somehow Adeline met up with her husband, who had been arrested in March 1864, and like Adeline sent north of the Ohio River. Joshua and Adeline remained in Illinois for a few years where their sixth child was born in 1866. They returned to Georgia shortly thereafter and were living in Milton County by 1870. Adeline died in 1910 and was buried in Sharon Cemetery in Forsyth County. Her descendents placed a headstone on her grave in the early 1990s: "Adeline Bagley, wife of Pvt. J. Buice, 1825–1910, Roswell mill worker caught up and exiled to Chicago by Yankee army —1864 — returned on foot 1869."[11]

Indiana census records list a number of Roswell factory workers and their families as residents of Perry County in 1870. Six years after Sherman ordered them sent "north of the Ohio River," more than three dozen men, women and children from Roswell lived in Cannelton, Indiana, eighteen employed by the Indiana Cotton Mill. The Kendleys, Morgans, Bryants, Fretwells, Moores, and Jameses were among those who settled in Perry County.

John Kendley was serving in the Roswell Battalion when his brothers and sisters were arrested and sent to Indiana. He remained in Cobb County and was living in Smyrna, Georgia, in 1870. His brothers Thomas and George found work in the Indiana Cotton Mill and lived with their sister, Mary, and her husband, Albert May, whom she married in July 1865. Sarah Jane Kendley married Andrew Nichols from Kentucky in 1870, and George eventually married a woman from Ohio. Only Thomas appears to have remained single. Mary visited Georgia twice, once in 1870 and again in 1919, the only one of the family known to have made the journey back home.[12]

Nineteen-year-old Georgiana Morgan, her four-year-old son, William, and two-year-old daughter, Lula, were sent north with the workers from Roswell. Georgiana had gone to work in the Roswell factories after her husband, Alexander, enlisted in the 42d Georgia Infantry. Alexander died in Mississippi in July 1863, one year before her arrest. Widowed with two young children and no means of support, Georgiana made her way to Cannelton and found work in the Indiana Cotton Mill.[13]

Eleven members of the Pleasant Bryant family resided in Perry County in 1870. Pleasant and his son Augustus were both employed by the Roswell mills in 1863.

Left: Thomas Hugh Kendley (1846–1915). Roswell Mill worker Thomas Kendley found work at the Indiana Cotton Mill in Perry County, Indiana. He never returned to Georgia (courtesy George and Elizabeth Kendley). *Right*: Mary Kendley (1843–1924). Sent to Indiana with her brothers and sisters, Mary married Albert May and settled in Perry County. She visited Georgia on a couple of occasions, but Indiana remained her home (courtesy George and Elizabeth Kendley).

Ten years later, all eleven family members were employees of the Indiana Cotton Mill including the youngest Bryant, nine-year-old William.[14]

Lively Moore arrived in Indiana with her three children, John, Robert and Cora. John married Mary Hopkins in 1869. Both Mary and her mother were Georgia natives, but the circumstances of their arrival in Indiana are not known. John and his sister, Cora, were both employed by the Cannelton mill in 1870.[15]

Elizabeth James and her seventeen-year-old daughter, Sarah, also settled in Indiana. Sarah eventually obtained work in the Indiana Cotton Mill and married a young man from Tennessee in December 1869. According to the 1870 census, Sarah and her husband, Noah Swallow, were living with her mother and two other female factory workers from Georgia, Lucenia Moore and Charlotte Brown.[16]

Littlejohn Fretwell, along with two sons and two daughters, worked in the Roswell mills before the war. By 1870 ten members of the Fretwell family were living in Indiana, and Littlejohn, his son Isaac and daughter Louise, were all employed by the mill at Cannelton.[17]

A Farr descendant claims that Samuel Farr and his family spent some time in Cannelton but returned to Roswell after the war. On his arrival in Kentucky, Farr was given a choice of going to prison or working at the Indiana Cotton Mill. Not surprisingly he chose the mill. Even though the Cannelton mill was facing great difficulties in July and August 1864, there may have been an opening for an experienced overseer. The Farrs returned to Roswell sometime before 1870, and both Samuel and his wife are buried in the Roswell Methodist Church Cemetery.[18]

Benjamin Reeves, his mother, Mary, and younger brother and sister were living in Perry County in 1870, and Benjamin was working at the Cannelton Cotton Mill. Although he did not appear on the 1860 Cobb County Census, Benjamin was a member of the Roswell Battalion, and very likely employed by one of the Roswell factories.[19]

Mathilda and her daughter Elizabeth Smallwood settled in Jeffersonville, Indiana. Elizabeth and her sister, Sarah, were employees of the Roswell factory in 1860, and Elizabeth found work at a woolen mill in Clark County. Sarah's whereabouts have not been determined. There is no record of the women returning to Georgia.[20]

Factory worker, Margaret Smith Duffey and her two-year-old daughter were among those sent to Indiana. Her husband, Vestal M. Duffey, a sergeant in the 56th Georgia, either accompanied her or was able to locate her after the war. A son was born in Indiana in 1866, but they were back in Georgia by 1868 when their second son was born. Perhaps unable to find work in Roswell, the Duffeys settled in Forsyth County.[21]

Two Roswell mill families ended up at the Laurel Hill Mill in Lawrence County, Tennessee. George Eads was arrested in Roswell on the 8th of July and sent north of the Ohio River after taking the oath in Louisville. The family spent some time in Indiana, and a son was born there in 1866. In 1870 George and his family were in Tennessee, and both George and his daughter were employees of the Laurel Hill Mill.[22]

Ead's neighbor Jesse Williams was arrested in Roswell and also lived in Indiana some years before moving to Lawrence County, Tennessee. By 1870 Jesse and his three sons had found work in the Laurel Hill Mill, one of the largest and most profitable in Lawrence County. The mill closed at the turn of the century and the community died shortly thereafter. The two-story brick building was reduced to a pile of scattered brick, and the cemetery where Jesse Williams is buried is the only reminder of the once-prosperous 19th century mill village.[23]

Stories of New Manchester's tragic end have painted vivid pictures of mass destruction with both homes and factories in flames. An eyewitness to the burning, however, claimed that Union soldiers took every precaution to protect the other buildings and no physical evidence has been found to support theories that the mill homes were burned. Whether or not the entire village was destroyed, the destruction of the mill did mark the end of the small mill town. The factory was never rebuilt, and the workers simply returned to their farms or moved away to seek work elsewhere, abandoning the houses and buildings near the mills. All that remains is the Old Factory Town Cemetery, where graves are marked with rocks in place of headstones, and the silent, haunting, vine-covered ruins of the towering mill, a monument to the once thriving village of New Manchester.

An 1867 lawsuit filed by Charles McDonald's heirs alleged that Russell and Brumby violated the terms of the lease by abandoning the factory to its fate in the face of the enemy, since the lease specified that the New Manchester mill was to be returned in good condition. After years of litigation, the claim was eventually dismissed, but depositions from the 1867 lawsuit provide virtually the only written record, albeit sketchy, of the events that took place in July 1864.[24]

The abandoned village became part of the newly created Douglas County in 1870. Eight years later, the superior court ordered the factory site sold on the courthouse steps to settle the affairs of the corporation. The property changed hands several more times before being acquired by the State of Georgia in 1972 as part of the Sweetwater Creek State Conservation Park. Committed to preserving the mill ruins and sharing the history of New Manchester, Sweetwater Creek State Park opened a visitor and interpretive center in October 2006 to better tell the story of the destruction of the mill and the exile of her people.[25]

The history of New Manchester has long been marked by myth and speculation. In addition to rumors of total destruction, a tale of mass executions surfaced in 1987, when a Marietta newspaper cited a local historian's contention that Union soldiers sent the women north as ordered, but took the men out some distance, shot them in cold blood and then buried them in a mass grave near Marietta. The newly discovered list of Sweetwater employees arrested as political prisoners and received at the Louisville Military Prison has finally put that theory to rest. Additionally, further research proved that a large number of the men and their families returned to the area following the war. Some of the workers returned to their own farms while others simply moved to nearby towns.[26]

Sweetwater Mill Ruins. The vine-covered ruins of the Sweetwater mill, and the Old Factory Town Cemetery, are all that remain of the once thriving village of New Manchester (courtesy Dan Emsweller).

Few details are known about their experiences, but more than half of the men arrested in New Manchester have been traced back to the Sweetwater area. John C. Alexander, John H. Alexander, Thomas and William Bell, John Busby, John Causey, John, Merrell and Nathaniel Humphries, Gideon and Joseph Jennings, William Mauldin, Miles Moseley, Elijah Rodgers, James Scarborough, James Stone, Thomas Tolbert, Burdine Tucker, Aaron and Robert Turner, Thomas White, Charles Wilson, and John Wright all returned to Georgia after the war.[27]

Unionists Nelson and Eliza Tucker and six of their children made the decision to leave Campbell County about the same time their son Burdine was arrested. They remained in Marietta for a couple of months, where Eliza and her daughter Elizabeth helped nurse Union wounded. In October the Tuckers headed for Louisville where they stayed until after Nelson's death on April 16, 1865. It is not known when or where their paths first crossed, but somewhere along the way, Elizabeth Tucker met James Carroll, a Union soldier. It is possible they met when Carroll's unit, the 25th Illinois Volunteer Infantry, marched into Georgia in the spring of 1864 with the Army of the Cumberland. He was wounded in North Georgia and may have been one of the soldiers Elizabeth nursed back to health in Marietta. Carroll returned to Illinois in September 1864 when the unit disbanded, but was back in Georgia as a sergeant with the 150th Illinois Volunteer Infantry in May 1865. Three months later the Union soldier married the Southern mill worker in Marietta. Carroll made Georgia his home and remained in the county for the rest of his life.[28]

Although Henry Lovern was present at the destruction of the mills, his name does not appear on the list of men arrested

Elizabeth Tucker (1847–1938). Daughter of Union sympathizers Nelson and Eliza Tucker, Elizabeth married a Yankee soldier in August 1865. Elizabeth's family voluntarily relocated to Louisville but returned to Georgia after the war (from History Files of the Sweetwater Creek State Conservation Park).

in New Manchester. Henry was still in Georgia and working for Princeton Manufacturing in 1866 when he was requested to testify in the lawsuit filed by the executors of the McDonald estate.[29]

Thomas Bell and his oldest son, William, were both employees of the New Manchester Manufacturing Company when Union cavalrymen destroyed the Sweetwater mill. Thomas, his wife, Mariah, and their nine children headed back to Georgia soon after the war. Pregnant with their tenth child, Mariah gave birth to a baby boy in Villa Rica, Georgia, soon after their return. Raford Pinkney Bell was born on August 22, 1865. Mariah died three weeks later. The cause of her death remains unknown.[30]

James Carroll (1842–1912). Union soldier James Carroll married Elizabeth Tucker, a New Manchester mill worker, in August 1865 (from History Files of the Sweetwater Creek State Conservation Park).

William Mauldin, one of the 43 men arrested in New Manchester, was sent to Indiana, along with his wife, Tabby, and their five children. A sixth child was born in Indiana in 1865, but the Mauldins were back in Georgia by 1868.[31]

Captured by Union forces at Decatur, Alabama, in October 1864, while serving with the 41st Georgia, John Humphries was sent to a federal prison at Camp Douglas, Ohio. Paroled seven months later, Humphries headed south and found his father and mother, John W. and Amanda Humphries, and their younger children at Jeffersonville, Indiana, where they settled after being sent north with the other mill families from New Manchester. John found work in a government stable until he earned enough money to bring his family home. By 1870 all of the Humphrieses had returned to Campbell County.[32]

Sherrod Causey claimed

Bell Family. Left to right seated: Elizabeth Jane Bell, William Henderson Bell, Elizabeth Bell (William's wife). Left to right, standing: James Winfield Bell, Raford Pinkney Bell, and Sarah Agnes Bell. William and his father, Thomas Bell, worked in the New Manchester Cotton Mill. All of William's family was sent north, including his brothers and sisters pictured here, with the exception of Raford, who was born after they returned to Campbell County in 1865 (from History Files of the Sweetwater Creek State Conservation Park).

that his family was sent to Jeffersonville and turned loose to fend for themselves. Eventually making their way to Indianapolis, the family remained there until 1865 when they returned to Georgia. Causey's version of the events at New Manchester was written many years after the fact when he was 86 years old. It suffers from some faulty recollections, but it is significant as one of the few eyewitness accounts.[33]

The Summerlins, a prominent Campbell County family, were among those caught up in the chaotic events of July 1864. Joseph Summerlin, nearly seventy, died during the early years of the war, leaving his widow to care for their children. Although there is no evidence that thirty-four-year-old Susan Summerlin worked in the mill, Union forces sent Susan and her sons Homer Milton and Eugenius Napoleon north with the other workers. Years later, Homer told stories of traveling on the trains and being called "refugees." Susan and her sons were among those who managed to make their way back to Georgia after the war.[34]

Sent north of the Ohio River with the mill workers, Thomas Tolbert, the New

Manchester postmaster, returned to Georgia shortly after the Confederate surrender and settled in Carroll County, Georgia, where he found work in a local cotton factory.[35]

Factory worker Martha Ann Freeman Wright and her two young children were sent north. The details are not known, but Martha Ann died a short time later in Indiana. Her husband, Isaac Wright, apparently found the children and was back in Campbell County by 1870.[36]

Elizabeth Jennings Young, daughter of factor worker Gideon Jennings, was only five at the time of the arrest but often talked about the trip north. Her family was sent to Indiana where they remained until after the war. Elizabeth, her father and six brothers returned to Georgia two years later when she was seven. Elizabeth's mother was not so fortunate. A Jennings descendant believes that Jane Jennings died in Evanston, Indiana. Her burial place remains unknown.[37]

Nancy and Green Amos Pilgrim returned to Atlanta by train in 1865. Unfortunately they came down with smallpox on their arrival and had to be cared for by charity until they were well enough to travel. The Pilgrims did not return to New Manchester since the factory had been destroyed, but headed back to their family home in Greene County on foot.[38]

"Uncle James" Scarborough and his wife and children ended up in Louisville where he helped take care of the Stewart family until his brother-in-law, Walter Stewart, was released from prison. Eager to return to Georgia, the Scarboroughs left Louisville immediately after the war, and eventually settled in Madison County were James found work as a blacksmith.[39]

One of the most detailed accounts of the journey north and life in Louisville comes from the recollections of James Scarborough's niece, Synthia Stewart Boyd. Only nine years old in July 1864, Synthia related her version of the events in an oral history recorded in 1947 when she was 92. Synthia, her mother and brothers and sisters were all sent to Louisville and held in the refuge house until her mother was able to find employment. After Synthia's father was released from the prison at Camp Chase, Ohio, in May 1865,

Synthia Catherine Stewart (1854–1951), from a tintype made when she was about 17 years of age. Synthia's father, Walter Stewart, was serving in the Confederate army when the rest of the family was sent to Louisville. Synthia recorded her version of the events when she was 92 (from History Files of the Sweetwater Creek State Conservation Park).

Walter (1828–1904) and Charlotte Elizabeth Russell Stewart (1835–1887). Formerly a mill boss at the New Manchester mill, Walter joined the Confederate army, but he was captured and sent north as a prisoner of war. After his release, he found his wife and children in Louisville, Kentucky, and worked in a local tannery until he could earn enough money to return to Georgia (courtesy Mary Stewart Newton).

he traveled to Louisville to find his family. Stewart found work in a local tannery, and finally saved enough to bring the family back to Georgia.[40]

Not all of the Stewart family would return. A family letter written in 1876 stated that Walter's younger sister, Sarah Stewart Reeves, had lived as a refugee and died in Louisville, Kentucky. Sarah's husband, John Reeves, was a mill worker at the Sweetwater factory, but his name does not appear on the list of men arrested in New Manchester.[41]

As for the mystery of the women still not accounted for, perhaps Synthia Stewart Boyd summed it up best in 1947: "Some mill women died, some remarried, others were able to save enough to return home. But most were not as fortunate as we were."[42]

Epilogue

The years have wrought inevitable change, but the beauty and quiet dignity of antebellum Roswell has survived. The majestic homes of the founding families have been restored to their original beauty and they still stand, memorials to an era long past. Barrington Hall, Bulloch Hall, Primrose Cottage, Great Oaks, Mimosa Hall, the Smith Plantation: each one a tribute to those who dreamed of castles in the middle of a wilderness, and through sheer determination, perseverance, and sacrifice, made those dreams come true.

Most of the original homes and churches are within the Roswell Historic District, which closely follows the boundaries of the town as laid out by Roswell and Barrington King in the 1830s. The entire historic district was added to the National Register of Historic Places in 1973. Barrington Hall, Bulloch Hall, and the Smith Plantation have been purchased by the City of Roswell and are open to the public. Great Oaks and Primrose Cottage currently operate as event facilities, and Mimosa Hall remains in private hands.[1]

The Roswell Presbyterian Church has been in continuous operation since 1840 and looks much as it did when it was built. Although new buildings have been added to meet the needs of the growing congregation, early morning services are still held in the original sanctuary with its raised pulpit and slave gallery.[2]

The town square remains the focal center for many social activities. A memorial to Roswell King was unveiled at the head of the square in October 1939, and the Roswell Chapter of the United Daughters of the Confederacy placed historical markers in the center of the square in 1940 to commemorate the six founding families of Roswell.[3]

Many of the mill workers' cottages still stand on Factory Hill. Although most have undergone major updating or remodeling, at least fifteen of the original dwellings are similar in age, style and material and can be easily identified. Five of the homes still have the central chimneys common to New England cottages.[4]

The Old Bricks, constructed in 1840 to house employees of the Roswell Mills, are said to be among the oldest buildings in the country in continuous use as apartments. For many years these buildings, once the humble dwellings of factory workers, were home to the Founders Club, an exclusive special event facility. Atlanta-based developers purchased the rare antebellum townhouses in 2004 and transformed them into luxury residential row homes.[5]

The old general store originally built in 1839 and then rebuilt in 1854 still stands on the town square. Here the mill workers made their purchases with company scrip issued by the Roswell Manufacturing Company. The building was converted into a restaurant in recent years. Diners looking out the front windows can see the gazebo built for President Theodore Roosevelt when he visited his mother's girlhood home in 1905. Locals claim that the old store is haunted by star-crossed lovers: Michael, a seventeen-year-old Union soldier, and Katherine, a young girl from Roswell who stole his heart.[6]

Little remains of the mills at Roswell, the old dam, a long raceway, remnants of stone walls, broken bricks, and fragments of foundations. Along the creek, near the site of the old mill, the machine shop stands, the only building with a link to the distant past. A path from the shop leads down to the stream; a remote and almost forgotten place, where the only sound is the roar of the rushing water as it flows over the dam and into the creek below, winding its way to the Chattahoochee.

* * *

Honoring the Memory of
The Four Hundred Women, Children, and Men
Millworkers of Roswell
Who Were Charged with Treason
and Deported by Train to the North
by Invading Federal Forces

A new landmark has been added to Roswell's historic landscape. In Old Mill Park on a ridge overlooking Vickery Creek, stands a monument to the Roswell Mill Workers.

In 1998, the Roswell Mills Camp of the Sons of Confederate Veterans resolved to erect a monument to ensure that these men, women, and children would not be forgotten.

For many years the only memorials in Roswell were the plaques in the town square that paid tribute to the founders. The mill workers are as much a part of the town's history as Roswell King, if not more so, yet many of Roswell's own citizens had never heard their tragic story.

The ten-foot-tall granite Corinthian column, unveiled in July 2000, stands in a small park in the heart of the mill village. The monument honors the mill workers, the men, women, and children of Roswell torn from their homes by military decree and sent away to a distant land, hauntingly reminiscent of another time, another people,

Roswell Monument. Photograph of the monument after unveiling on July 8, 2000 (courtesy Randal Holderfield).

and another trail of tears. While many of their names are unknown, the monument stands as a tribute to each and ensures their place in history.[7]

The memorial also serves as a poignant reminder that the horror of the Civil War, as with all wars, was not confined to the field of battle. It invaded cities, small towns and oftentimes the hearths and homes of innocent victims, leaving only sorrow and despair in its wake. The story of the North Georgia mill workers is just one more heart-breaking example.

Appendix:
List of Mill Workers Arrested

Sweetwater Arrests — July 1864

"Roll of Political Prisoners"

List of men from Campbell County received at Louisville Military Prison on July 20, 1864, and discharged July 21, 1864, with the notation that they were discharged by the order of Captain S.E. Jones, "paroled, to remain north of the Ohio River during the war." All the men were from Campbell County, with the exception of John Conn from Lumpkin County.

Alexander, John C.
Alexander, John H,
Abercrombie
Baker, Charles G.
Bell, Thomas
Bell, William
Brisindine, Leroy
Busby, John
Causey, John H.
Conn, John
Crooker, Charles
Dembrie, John
Humphries, John W.
Humphries, Merrell M.
Humphries, M.H.
Jennings, Gideon
Jennings, Joseph W.
Kirby, Ruben
Liles, Lafayette
Mauldin, William
Meeks, Sivern

Moseley, Miles
Rodgers, Elijah
Sanders, James
Scarborough, James B.
Simmons, James J.
South, John
Stone James D.
Stone, William
Tolbert, Thomas
Tucker, Burdine T.
Turner, Aaron
Turner, M.J.
Turner, Robert T.
Turner, Sivern
Washington, James W.
White, Thomas
Wilson, Charles F
Wright, John M.
Wrigley, Daniel
Wrigley, Pinckney

Names are spelled as they appear on the original roll.

Registers of Political Prisoners 1863–1865, Louisville, Kentucky, Military Prison (National Archives Microfilm Publication M598, roll 95), Selected Records of the War Department Relating to Confederate Prisoners of War, 1861–1865, Record Group 109, National Archives Building, Washington, D.C.

List of Rebel Citizens Arrested by 2nd Brigade Division Cavalry USA

"Exempted from the rebel draft
by being detailed in factory C.S.A. at Roswell"
Date of arrest: July 8, 1864

Cobb, Peter
Eads, George
Green, Newton
Hindman, Asel
Quinn, Thomas
Smith, Benjamin
Smith, Elijah
Whitington, Andrew J.

List of Rebel Citizens Arrested and Lists of Deserters, May–September 1864, Vol. 57/142, Cavalry Corps Military Division of the Mississippi, RG 393, Records of the U.S. Army Continental Commands, 1821–1920, National Archives Building, Washington, D.C.

Chapter Notes

1—Roswell King

1. Sarah Joyce King Cooper, *King and Allied Families* (Athens, 1992), pp. 1–4, 6–7; Darlene Walsh, ed., *Natalie Heath Merrill's Narrative History of Roswell, Georgia* (Roswell, GA: Roswell House, 1996), pp. 5–6; Meta Roswell King, *Some Family History*, August 29, 1929, unpublished manuscript, p. 1, Barrington King Papers, GDAH, hereinafter cited as BKP.

2. Ibid., Cooper, *King*, pp. 13, 17.

3. E. Merton Coulter, ed., *Georgia's Disputed Ruins* (Chapel Hill: University of North Carolina Press, 1937), pp. 77–78; Malcolm Bell, Jr., *Major Butler's Legacy: Five Generations of a Slaveholding Family* (Athens, GA: University of Georgia Press, 1987), p. 160; Medora Field Perkerson, *White Columns in Georgia* (New York: Bonanza Books, 1956), p. 145. Very few buildings survived the Civil War but Thomas Spalding's home on Sapelo Island was lovingly restored, preserving the original design. The home stands unique and impressive even now.

4. Cooper, *King*, p. 26; Margaret Davis Cate, *Our Todays and Yesterdays* (Spartanburg, S.C.: The Reprint Company, 1979), p. 231; Mrs. Howard H. McCall, comp., *Roster of Revolutionary Soldiers in Georgia* (Atlanta: Georgia Society, Daughters of the America Revolution, 1941), Vol. 3, p. 137.

5. King, *Family History*, pp. 2–3; Cooper, *King*, pp. 26–27, 74.

6. Bell, *Butler's Legacy*, pp. 154, 159–160.

7. Ibid., pp. 107, 139, 146, 151, 165; Frances A. Kemble and Frances A. Butler Leigh, *Principles & Privilege: Two Women's Lives on a Georgia Plantation* (Ann Arbor: University of Michigan Press, 1995), p. 199.

8. Bell, *Butler's Legacy*, pp. 131, 151–152.

9. Ibid., pp. 173, 176, 182.

10. Ibid., p. 177.

11. Ibid., pp. 182, 187, 223–224.

12. Cooper, *King*, pp. 35–37; King, *Family History*, p. 2; Darlene M. Walsh, ed., *Roswell: A Pictorial History* (Roswell, GA: Roswell Historical Society, 1994), p. 38; Walsh, *Narrative History*, pp. 9–10.

13. E. Merton Coulter, *Auraria* (Athens, GA: University of Georgia Press, 1956), p. 27.

2—The Colony

The quote introducing this chapter is from Archibald Smith, Jr., Personal Recollections, not dated, Smith Papers, (AC 88–012), GDAH. The Smith Family Papers were made available by James L. Skinner III and Arthur N. Skinner on behalf of the Skinner Family.

1. Indenture dated December 20, 1836, Mark Sims to Roswell King, Lot 384, Cobb County, Georgia, BKP; Walsh, *Narrative History*, pp. 12–13.

2. Ibid., p. 12.

3. Ibid., pp. 11–12

4. Ibid., pp. 13–14; Cooper, *King*, pp. 37, 40.

5. William R. Mitchell Jr., Roswell Historic District, National Register of Historic Places Nomination, 1973; Plan of the Roswell Property, 12 February 1909, GRHL.

6. Walsh, *Narrative History*, pp. 13–14; Mitchell, *Historic District*, entry 6.

7. *Atlanta Journal*, June 10, 1923; Cooper, *King*, p. 43; Walsh, *Narrative History*, p. 23; Frederick Doveton Nichols, *Early Architecture of Georgia* (Chapel Hill: University of North Carolina Press, 1957), p. 119; Mitchell, *Historic District*, entry 1; Annie Hornady Howard, ed., *Georgia Homes and Landmarks* (Atlanta: Southern Features Syndicate, 1929), Vol. I, pp. 29, 31.

8. Nichols, *Early Architecture*, p. 132; Walsh, *Narrative History*, p. 24; Mitchell, *Historic District*, entry 3; Lucian Lamar Knight, *Georgia's Landmarks, Memorials and Legends* (Atlanta: Byrd Printing Co., State Printers, 1914), Vol. II, pp. 217–218.

9. Nichols, *Early Architecture*, p. 132; Walsh, *Narrative History*, pp. 24–25; Mitchell, *Historic District*, entry 4; Howard, *Georgia Homes*, p. 91; Walsh, *Roswell*, p. 39. Military and cemetery records indicate that the surname is correctly spelled as Dunwody, but it has often been spelled Dunwoody as in the town of Dunwoody, which was named for Major John Dunwody.

10. Arthur N. Skinner and James L. Skinner, eds., *The Death of a Confederate, Selections from the Letters of the Archibald Smith Family of Roswell, Georgia, 1864–1956* (Athens, GA: University of Georgia Press, 1996),

pp. xv–xvi, xx; Smith, Personal Recollections, Smith Papers.

11. Walsh, *Narrative History*, pp. 18–19; Roswell Presbyterian Church, *A Historical Sketch of the Roswell Presbyterian Church*, church program, October 22, 1939, p. 3, BKP.

12. Ibid., p. 19; Clarence Martin, *A History of Roswell Presbyterian Church* (Dallas: Taylor, 1984), pp. 26–27; Mitchell, *Historic District*, entry 9; Oliver King to Kate Simpson, December 28, 1914, BKP.

13. Walsh, *Narrative History*, pp. 18, 25; Helen Magill, *History of Roswell Church Organization*, unpublished manuscript, BKP; Roswell Presbyterian Church, *Historical Sketch*, p. 3; Mitchell, *Historic District*, entry 8.

14. Martin, *Roswell Presbyterian*, p. 29; Walsh, *Roswell*, pp. 39–40.

15. Ibid., p. 39; Roswell Presbyterian Church, *Historical Sketch*, pp. 3–4; Martin, *Roswell Presbyterian*, p. 27; Mitchell, *Historic District*, entry 9.

3 — Roswell Mills

The quote introducing this chapter is from W.J. Cash, *The Mind of the South* (New York: Vintage Books, 1991), p. 200.

1. U.S. Census Office. Sixth Census, 1840. *Compendium of the enumeration of the inhabitants and statistics of the United States* (Washington, 1841), pp. 253ff; Broadus Mitchell, *William Gregg: Factory Master of the Old South* (Chapel Hill: University of North Carolina Press, 1928), pp. 49–51.

2. *The American Heritage Dictionary*. Third Edition. 2000, p. 1001.

3. Emory Q. Hawk, *Economic History of the South* (New York: Prentice-Hall, 1934), p. 291.

4. Frank Podmore, *Robert Owen: A Biography*. Reprint. London: George Allen & Unwin, 1923 [1906]), pp. 131–135, 162–165, 172.

5. Mitchell, *William Gregg*, pp. 16, 54–55, 60, 78.

6. James L. Skinner, III, ed. *The Autobiography of Henry Merrell, Industrial Missionary to the South* (Athens: University of Georgia Press), p. 141; Barrington King, "Expenses on and near Vickery Creek," n.d., BKP.

7. Richard Coleman, *A Short History of the Roswell Manufacturing Company of Roswell, Georgia* (Atlanta: Richard Coleman, 1982), p. 3.

8. Ibid.; George White, *Historical Collections of Georgia* (New York: Pudney & Russell, 1855), p. 402; Skinner, *Merrell*, pp. 130–131.

9. *Acts of the General Assembly of the State of Georgia, 1839* (Atlanta, 1870), pp. 116–117.

10. Skinner, *Merrell*, pp. 140, 142.

11. Ibid., 167, 174–175.

12. Ibid., 181–182.

13. Ibid., 172, 180–181, 195.

14. White, *Historical Collections*, p. 402; Roswell Manufacturing Company, Minutes of Stockholders' Meetings, 1840–1900, pp. 41, 44, GRHL. A photocopy of the minutes is in the custody of the Roswell Historical Society, but the original records are held by the Dekalb Historical Society Archives.

15. Walsh, *Roswell*, p. 258; Coleman, *Short History*, p. 5.

16. Skinner, *Merrell*, p. 131; J.D. DeBow quoted in Richard W. Griffin, "The Origins of the Industrial Revolution in Georgia: Cotton Textiles 1810–1865," *Georgia Historical Quarterly* 42 (1958), pp. 365–366, 368; United States. Census Office. 8th Census, 1860. *Manufactures of the United States in 1860* (Washington, 1865), pp. 715–18, 60–64.

17. Quoted in Judith A. Ranta, *Women and Children of the Mills* (Westport, CT: Greenwood Press, 1999), p. 68.

18. David Williams, *The Georgia Gold Rush* (Columbia: University of South Carolina Press, 1993), p. 17. This book is a good source for additional information on the Georgia gold rush and land lottery.

19. Skinner, *Merrell*, p. 155.

20. Brooke Hindle and Steven Lubar, *Engines of Change* (Washington, D.C.: Smithsonian Institution Press, 1986), pp. 186–187.

21. U.S. Census Office. Eighth Census, 1860, Population of the United States, Georgia, M-653, Records of the Bureau of the Census, RG 29, DNA; Hawk, *Economic History*, p. 290.

22. William Robert Shelly, *The Life Histories of James William Shelly and Lucinda Elizabeth Wood Shelly* (Rome, GA: n.p., 1928). According to this family history, Robert Wood moved his family to Roswell before enlisting in the Confederate Army so that every child who was old enough could find work in the cotton factory. A copy of *Life Histories* was provided by Carmel Boswell, wife of Dewey E. Boswell, great-grandson of James William and Lucinda Elizabeth Wood Shelly. Walter Stewart's granddaughter claimed that Walter Stewart bought a farm near the mill so that his wife could find work in the Sweetwater factory in order to support the family while he was in the army. See Mary Stewart Rawlinson, ed., *The Walter Stewart Family History* (Columbia, S.C.: State Printing, 1982), p. 340.

23. Hawk, *Economic History*, p. 290.

24. Hindle and Lubar, *Engines*, p. 192; Ruth Holland, *Mill Child: The Story of Child Labor in America* (New York: Crowell-Collier Press, 1970), pp. 16–17.

25. James Silk Buckingham, *The Slave States of America* (London: Fisher, Son, 1842), Vol. II, pp. 111–114.

26. Sir Charles Lyell, *A Second Visit to the United States of North America* (New York: Harper & Brothers, 1849) p. 36.

27. U.S. Census Office. Nonpopulation Census Schedules for Georgia, 1850–1880, T-1137, Records of the Bureau of the Census, RG 29, DNA; Hawk, *Economic History*, pp. 290–291.

28. Skinner, *Merrell*, pp. 149, 161, 165–166.

29. Ibid., p. 166.

30. Ibid., pp. 168–169; *Williams' Atlanta Georgia Directory, City Guide & Business Mirror* (Atlanta, 1859).

31. Skinner, *Merrell*, p. 169.

32. Eighth Census, 1860, Georgia. Overseers John Brown, Larkin Brown, Isaac Burney, John Owens, Samuel Farr, John Drake and John Medley were all native Georgians. Theodore Adams, George Camp and Samuel Bonfoy were from New York. Jason Wood and Olney Eldredge were from Massachusetts. Francis Minhinnett and Jonathan Kershaw were both from England,

although Kershaw had lived in Pennsylvania for a number of years before coming to Georgia.

33. Mitchell, *Historic District*, entry 16.

34. Ibid., entry 11; Walsh, *Roswell*, p. 53.

35. Skinner, *Merrell*, p. 243.

36. Fannie K. Pratt, *In Memory of Roswell King*, n.d., BKP.

37. Archibald Smith, Jr., Personal Recollections, Smith Papers; Jennings J. Rhyne, *Some Southern Cotton Mill Workers and Their Villages* (Chapel Hill: University of North Carolina Press, 1930), pp. 200–201; Martin, *Roswell Presbyterian*, pp. 28–29; Eighth Census, 1860, Georgia.

38. Mitchell, *Gregg*, p. 78.

39. Quoted in Philip S. Foner, ed., *The Factory Girls* (Urbana: University of Illinois Press, 1977), p. 221.

40. Rhyne, *Mill Workers*, p. 18.

41. Hawk, *Economic History*, p. 291; Holland, *Mill Child*, pp. 16–17.

42. Ibid.

43. Carolyn M. Ware, *The Early New England Cotton Manufacture: A Study in Industrial Beginnings* (New York: Russell & Russell, 1966), pp. 251–252; Victoria Byerly, *Hard Times Cotton Mill Girls; Personal Histories and Poverty in the South* (New York: ILR Press, 1986), p. 18; Foner, *Factory Girls*, pp. 236–242, 326, 342.

44. Barrington King to Eva King Baker, February 11, 1848, BKP.

45. Buckingham, *Slaves States*, p. 113.

46. Price Van Meter Fishback and Shawn Everett Kantor, *A Prelude to the Welfare State* (Chicago: University of Chicago Press, 2000), pp. 102–104.

4 — Roswell Grey

The quote introducing this chapter is from Thomas E. King, January 18, 1861, quoted in Joseph C. Stiles, *Capt. Thomas E. King, or a Word to the Army and the Country* (Charleston: South Carolina Tract Society, 1864), p. 15.

1. Allen D. Candler, ed., *The Confederate Records of the State of Georgia*, Vol. I, 206, 208, 211, 740–747; Joseph T. Derry, *Georgia*, in Clement A. Evans, *Confederate Military History*, 12 Vols. Reprint. (Harrisburg, PA: Archive Society, 1994 [1899]), 6:3–4.

2. Derry, *Georgia*, 6:5.

3. T. Conn Bryan, *Confederate Georgia* (Athens: University of Georgia Press, 1953), pp. 8–9; *Journal of the Public and Secret Proceedings of the Convention of the People of Georgia Held in Milledgeville, and Savannah, in 1861, Together with the Ordinances Adopted* (Milledgeville, GA: Boughton, Nisbet & Barnes, State Printers, 1861) pp. 32, 39.

4. Ibid., pp. 166–167, 182, 192–193.

5. Roswell Presbyterian Church, *Historical Sketch*, p. 5; Barrington King to W.E. Baker, October 12, 1861, BKP.

6. Compiled Service Records of Confederate Soldiers, War Department Collection of Confederate Records, RG 109, DNA.

7. Compiled Service Records, RG 109; Eighth Census, 1860, Georgia.

8. Virginia King Nirenstein, *With Kindly Voices* (Macon, GA: Tullous Books, 1984), p. 141.

9. Ibid., pp. 141–142.

10. Stiles, *Thomas E. King*, pp. 18–19; United States War Department, *War of the Rebellion: A Compilation of the Official Records of the Union and Confederate Armies*, 128 vols. (Washington, 1880–1901), Series 1, Vol. 2, pp. 470, 492, 495. Cited hereinafter as OR. (Unless noted, all citations are to Series 1).

11. Stiles, *Thomas E. King*, p. 46.

12. Compiled Service Records, RG 109; Eighth Census, 1860, Georgia.

13. Thomas E. King to His Excellency Jeff Davis, February 14, 1862, Letters Received by the Confederate Secretary of War, 1861–1865, M-437, reel 56, War Department Collection of Confederate Records, RG 109, DNA; Bryan, *Confederate Georgia*, pp. 38–39; Stiles, *Thomas E. King*, p. 12.

14. Thomas E. King to Honorable J.P. Benjamin, Compiled Service Records, M-266, reel 218, War Department Collection of Confederate Records, RG 109, DNA; Thomas E. King to W.H.S. Taylor, ibid.

15. Thomas E. King to Eva King Baker, July 1, 1862, BKP.

16. Candler, *Confederate Records*, Vol. 2, pp. 103, 191.

17. Ibid., p. 192.

18. Compiled Service Records, RG 109; Eighth Census, 1860, Georgia.

19. Sarah Blackwell Gober Temple, *The First Hundred Years* (Atlanta: Walter W. Brown, 1935), p. 254; Candler, *Confederate Records*, Vol. 3, p. 168; Lynwood M. Holland, "Georgia Military Institute, The West Point of Georgia: 1851–1864", *Georgia Historical Quarterly* 43, no. 3 (September 1959), p. 244; Gary Livingston, *Cradled in Glory* (Cooperstown, NY: Caisson Press, 1997), "Foreword."

20. Livingston, *Cradled in Glory*, pp. 10–11, 13.

21. Ibid., 69; Holland, *Military Institute*, p. 244; Temple, *First Hundred Years*, p. 197; Compiled Service Records, RG 109; Ralph King to Fannie King Pratt, April 6, 1918, BKP.

22. Mary A. DeCredico, *Patriotism for Profit: Georgia's Urban Entrepreneurs and the Confederate War Effort* (Chapel Hill: University of North Carolina Press), p. 35.

23. Record of Ordnance Stores Passing Through Atlanta, March 1863–July 1864; Ch. 4, Vol. 87, RG 109, War Department Collection of Confederate Records, DNA; Bryan, *Confederate Georgia*, 107–108; Marietta Paper Mills, Invoices, 1862–1864, Confederate Papers Relating to Citizens and Businesses, M-346, reels 122, 655, War Department Collection of Confederate Records, RG 109, DNA, hereinafter cited as Confederate Papers.

24. George Camp to N.I. Bayard, April 25 and May 7, 1861, BKP.

25. Barrington King to W.E. Baker, May 4, 1861, BKP.

26. Roswell Manufacturing Company, Invoices 1861–1864, Confederate Papers, M-347, reels 136, 186.

27. Olney Eldredge, *Memorial Resolution*, Roswell Presbyterian Church, n.d.; Olney Eldredge to My Dear Brother, November 21, 1866. Copies of both documents provided by Olney Eldredge's great-great-

grandson Michael Eldredge, on behalf of the descendants of Olney Eldredge. Michael Eldredge and Mattie Lisenby, Olney's great-grand-daughter, were extremely helpful in providing photographs and information on Olney and the Eldredge family; U.S. Census Office. Seventh Census, 1850, Population of the United States, Georgia, M-432, Records of the Bureau of the Census, RG 29, DNA; Eighth Census, 1860, Georgia.

28. Barrington King to W.E. Baker, May 23, 1862, BKP.

29. Ibid.

30. *Southern Confederacy*, September 16, 1862; *Mobile Register and Advertiser*, September 29, 1862.

31. *Athens [GA] Southern Banner*, November 4, 1863.

32. Barrington King to W.E. Baker, November 14, 1863, BKP.

33. *Southern Confederacy*, December 13, 1861.

34. James R. King to George W. Randolph, May 6, 1862, Confederate Papers, M-346, reel 540. King requested exemptions for J.S. Wood, J.N. Brown, R.J. Groover, S. Mackey, T.L. Bridges, S. Low, J. Cronan, John Burnett and two unnamed spinners.

35. Deposition of James Roswell King in *Theophile Roche vs. the United States*, Case Number 466, French and American Claims Commission, Records of the Department of State, RG 76, DNA; OR 23, 2:767.

36. OR 23, 2:767

37. Archibald Smith to William Smith, May 14, 1863, Smith Papers; Barrington King to Col. R.H. Chilton, December 28, 1863, King Family Papers, MSS 753, Kenan Research Center, GAHC, hereinafter cited as KFP.

38. Helen Zubly Magill to Anne Smith, August 13, 1863, and Anne Smith to William Smith, August 24, 1863, Smith Papers; Compiled Service Records, RG 109.

39. OR 30, 4:643; Catherine Nephew to Eva King Baker, September 24, 1863, BKP; Barrington King to W.E. Baker, September 15, 1863, BKP; Stiles, *Thomas E. King*, pp. 23–24, 26.

40. Stiles, *Thomas E. King*, pp. 7–8, 28; Charles Quintard to My Darling (Eliza Catherine Quintard), September 21, 1863, BKP.

41. OR 30, 2:79, 108; *King*, unpublished manuscript, n.d., pp. 1–2, BKP.

42. Quintard to My Darling, BKP; Caroline Nephew to Eva King Baker, September 24, 1863, BKP; *King*, unpublished manuscript, n.d., p. 2, BKP.

43. Livingston, *Cradled in Glory*, p. 104.

44. *Mobile Register and Advertiser*, September 16, 1863; Barrington King to W.E. Baker, Dec. 14, 1863, BKP; Anne Smith to William Smith, August 24, 1863, and September 14, 1863, Smith Papers.

45. *Augusta Daily Chronicle and Sentinel*, January 20, 1864.

46. Walsh, *Roswell*, p.48.

5 — Sherman Takes Command

The quote introducing this chapter is taken from OR 17, 2:260.

Unless otherwise noted information on Sherman's life and military career before the Atlanta Campaign is drawn from John F. Marszalek, *Sherman: A Soldier's Passion for Order* (New York: Vintage Books, 1994 [1993]); Richard M. McMurry, *Atlanta 1864* (Lincoln and London: University of Nebraska Press, 2000), pp. 19–20; Ezra J. Warner, *Generals in Blue* (Baton Rouge: Louisiana State University Press, 1964), pp. 441–444; William T. Sherman, *Memoirs of General William T. Sherman* (New York: The Great Commanders, 1994 [1875]).

1. Warner, *Generals in Blue*, p. 442; W.T. Sherman to Prof. Henry Coppee, June 13, 1864, in Brooks D. Simpson and Jean V. Berlin, eds., *Sherman's Civil War* (Chapel Hill: University of North Carolina Press, 1999,) pp. 651–652; Sherman, *Memoirs*, p. 6.

2. Sherman, *Memoirs*, pp. 115–116, 124, 129, 132.

3. Ibid., pp. 148, 150, 156; *Cincinnati Daily Commercial*, December 11, 1861.

4. Marszalek, *Sherman*, pp. 177–178; Sherman, *Memoirs*, pp. 184–185.

5. T. Harry Williams, *McClellan, Sherman and Grant* (New Brunswick, NJ: Rutgers University Press, 1962), p. 46.

6. OR 17, 1:608–609; Marszalek, *Sherman*, p. 245.

7. OR 32, 3:87.

8. David P. Conyngham, *Sherman's March Through the South with Sketches and Incidents of the Campaign* (New York: Sheldon, 1865), pp. 51, 380; George Ward Nichols, *The Story of the Great March From the Diary of A Staff Officer* (New York: Harper & Brothers, 1866), pp. 120–121; William F.G. Shanks, *Personal Recollections of Distinguished Generals* (New York: Harper & Brothers, 1866), pp. 25–26, 52, 56–57; *New York Times*, November 11, 1861.

9. Sherman, *Memoirs*, p. 343; U.S. Grant to W.T. Sherman, April 4, 1864, W.T. Sherman to U.S. Grant, April 10, 1864, both in OR 32, 3:245–246, 312–14.

10. OR 32, 3:245–246.

11. Unless otherwise noted, information on Union war policies was drawn from Mark Grimsley, *Hard Hand of War* (Cambridge: Cambridge University Press, 1995); Emmerich de Vattel, *The Law of Nations or Principles of the Law of Nature Applied to the Conduct and Affairs of Nations and Sovereigns*. Reprint. New York, 1982 [1863]), Chapter 8, Sections 138–145, Chapter 9, Section 172.

12. Grimsley, *Hard Hand*, p. 45; Constantin Grebner, *We Were the Ninth* (Kent, OH, and London: Kent State University Press 1987 [1907]), pp. 76–77.

13. Grimsley, *Hard Hand*, pp. 81–85; Warner, *Generals in Blue*, pp. 511–512; OR 16, 2:273–278.

14. General Order 100, April 24, 1863, OR Series 3, Vol. 3, pp. 148–164; Grimsley, *Hard Hand*, p. 149.

15. OR 64, 1:799 and 32, 2:281.

16. Simpson, *Civil War*, p. 587.

17. General Order, Number 45, June 21, 1862, OR 17, 2:23; General Order, Number 49, July 7, 1862, OR 17, 2:81.

18. Ibid., 17, 2:235–236, 261–262; ibid., 13:742.

19. Ibid., 24, 3:158.

20. Ibid., 24, 1:501–502, 3:209.

21. Ibid., 30, 3:401–404.

22. Ibid., 24, 2:526; *Brandon* [MS] *Republican* quoted in *Savannah Republican*, May 25, 1863.

23. OR 32,1:176.

24. Sherman, *Memoirs*, p. 329.

25. Ibid., p. 330.

26. General Orders, Number 6, OR 32, 3:279–280; General Orders, Number 8, OR 32, 3:420; OR 38, 4:25, 33–34; Sherman, *Memoirs*, pp. 330–331.

27. OR 38, 1:62–63, 115–117; Sherman, *Memoirs*, p. 342. For more information on the "effective strength" of both armies during the Atlanta Campaign, see Richard M. McMurry, *Atlanta 1864: Last Chance for the Confederacy*, pp. 194–196.

28. OR 38, 4:120; Sherman, *Memoirs*, p. 342; McMurry, *Atlanta*, pp. 35–36. For more information on the organization of Sherman's cavalry, see David Evans, *Sherman's Horsemen* (Bloomington and Indianapolis: Indiana University Press, 1996), pp. 2–4.

29. Sherman, *Memoirs*, p. 347.

30. Benjamin Ewell quoted in Steven H. Newton, *Joseph E. Johnston and the Defense of Richmond* (Lawrence: University Press of Kansas, 1998), p. 4; Walter Lord, ed., The *Fremantle Diary* (Boston: Little, Brown, 1954), p. 93; Eliza J. Warner, *Generals in Gray* (Baton Rouge: Louisiana State University Press, 1989), p. 161.

31. Ibid., 162; McMurry, *Atlanta*, p. 7–9; Richard M. McMurry, *Two Great Rebel Armies* (Chapel Hill: University of North Carolina Press), p. 127–128.

32. Joseph E. Johnston, *Narrative of Military Operations During the Civil War* (Reprint; New York: Da Capo Press, 1959 [1874]), p. 318.

33. Sherman, *Memoirs*, pp. 246, 345.

34. OR 38, 5:61; I.W. Avery, *The History of the State of Georgia from 1850 to 1881* (Reprint; New York: AMS Press, 1972 [1881]), p. 274.

6 — Innocent Pawns

The quote introducing this chapter is taken from Major-General Grenville M. Dodge, *Personal Recollections of President Abraham Lincoln, General Ulysses S. Grant and General William T. Sherman* (Council Bluffs, IA: Monarch, 1914), pp. 141–142.

1. Mary Rawson quoted in Katherine Jones, *When Sherman Came: Southern Women and the "Great March"* (Indianapolis: Bobbs-Merrill, 1964), p. 1.

2. Albert Castel, *Decision in the West* (Lawrence: University Press of Kansas, 1992), p. 196; "A Sketch of the Life of Major James Roberts Zearing, M.D.," *Transactions of the Illinois State Historical Society* 28 (1921), p. 178; Stephen A. Jordan Diary, May 19, 1864, Confederate Collection, Box 6, Folder 14, TSLA; Oliver C. Haskell Diary, May 20, 1864, Collection Number SC 0707, InHS.

3. OR 32, 2:279; George W. Pepper, *Personal Recollections of Sherman's Campaigns in Georgia and the Carolinas* (Zanesville, OH: Hugh Dunne, 1866), p. 246.

4. OR 32, 2:279; Conyngham, *Sherman's March*, p. 128.

5. Frances Thomas Howard, *In and Out of the Lines*

(Cartersville, GA: Etowah Valley Historical Society, 1998 [1905]), pp. 10–16.

6. Henry Hitchcock, *Marching with Sherman* (New Haven, CT: Yale University Press 1927), p. 157; Sherman to J. B. Fry, September 3, 1884, Letter Book, Papers of William T. Sherman Paper, Manuscript Division, DLC.

7. Rachel Thorndike Sherman, ed., *The Sherman Letters* (New York: Scribner's Sons, 1894), p. 185.

8. Jacob Dolson Cox, *Military Reminiscences of the Civil War* (New York: C. Scribner's Sons, 1900), pp. 233–234.

9. Special Field Order, Number 8, May 20, 1864, OR 38, 4:273.

10. Ibid., 4:297–298.

11. Sergeant David Nichol quoted in Castel, *Decision*, p. 207.

12. *Atlanta Daily Intelligencer*, July 9, 1864; Howard, *In and Out*, p. 39.

13. *Macon Telegraph*, July 2, 1864; Thomas P. Lowery, "Research Note: New Access to a Civil War Resource," *Civil War History* 49.1 (2003) *Questia*, 5 Dec 2006, <http://www.questia.com/PM.qst?a=o&d=500 1903384>; Charles Billingsley, Compiled Service Record, RG 94; Proceedings of U.S. Army Courts-martial and Military Commissions of Union Soldiers Executed by U.S. Military Authorities, File Number NN 2165, Records of the Adjutant General's Office, 1780s–1917, RG 94, M-1523, DNA.

14. James C. Bonner, *The Journal of a Milledgeville Girl 1861–1867* (Athens: University of Georgia Press, 1964), p. 63; Anne J. Bailey, *The Chessboard of War: Sherman and Hood in the Autumn Campaigns of 1864* (Lincoln: University of Nebraska Press, 2000), pp. 64–65.

15. Lowery, Research Note; Dayton to Steedman, August 12–13, 1864, Vol. 156/225, Department of the Cumberland, Records of the U.S. Army Continental Commands, 1821–1920, RG 393, DNA; Stockdale to Hunter Brooke, August 14, 1864, Vol. 21, Military Division of the Mississippi, Records of the U.S. Army Continental Commands, 1821–1920, RG 393, DNA; Sarah H. McConnell, Memoir, ca. 1923, *A Relic of the War 1860–1865*, Confederate Collection, Box 27, File 9, TSLA.

16. OR 39, 2: 135–136.

17. Ibid., 2: 131–132.

18. Ibid., 5: 42–70; John W. Geary to "My Dear Mary," July 8, 1864, in William Alan Blair, ed., *A Politician Goes to War* (University Park: Pennsylvania State University Press, 1995), p. 186; Sherman, *Memoirs*, pp. 380, 383. Although not specifically addressed in Sherman's order to Garrard, Sherman claimed that Garrard was ordered to secure possession of the Roswell factories.

7 — Hopeful to the Last

The quote introducing this chapter is from Barrington King to Archibald Smith, June 4, 1864, Smith Papers.

1. M.H. Wright to Capt. J.R. King, December 7, 1863, Letters Sent, Col. M.H. Wright, Commander of

Troops at Atlanta, July 1862–May 1864, Records of the Department and District of Georgia, Ch. 2, Vol. 186, War Department Collection of Confederate Records, RG 109, DNA.

2. Ibid., M.H. Wright to Col. George Wm. Brent, December 14, 1863, and M.H. Wright to Capt. J.R. King, February 2, 1864.

3. *Roche vs. U.S.*, Case 466.

4. Ibid.

5. Ibid.

6. Ibid.

7. OR 38, 4:726–27.

8. Capt. J.R. King to Col. M.H. Wright, May 28, 1864, Unfiled Papers and Slips Belonging to Confederate Compiled Service Records, M-347, reel 220, War Department Collection of Confederate Records, RG 109, DNA.

9. Anne Smith to My Dear Son, undated, Smith Papers. The letter appears to have been written in early February 1864.

10. Robert L. Rodgers, *A Historical Sketch of the Georgia Military Institute, Marietta, Georgia* (Atlanta: Kimsey's Book Shop, 1956), p. 83; Livingston, *Cradled in Glory*, pp. 87, 97.

11. Livingston, *Cradled in Glory*, pp. 97–99; James Oates, "Letter to the Editors," July 8, 1887, in Robert Underwood Johnson and Clarence Clough Buell, eds., *Battles and Leaders of the Civil War*. Reprint Edition (Harrisburg, PA: The Archive Society, 1991 [1887–1888]), 4:298.

12. Livingston, *Cradled in Glory*, p. 101.

13. Anne Smith to My Dear Son, May 25, 1864, Smith Papers.

14. Barrington King to W.E. Baker, July 18, 1864, BKP.

15. Barrington King to W.E. Baker, May 30 1864, August 10, 1864, BKP; Deposition of James R. King, A.S. Atkinson and Others, Executor of *Charles J. McDonald vs. A.V. Brumby*, Case Number 9, 821, GAFC; Olney Eldredge to "My Dear Brother," November 21, 1866.

16. OR 38, 4:758, 770–771.

17. *Southern Confederacy*, June 19, 1864.

18. Martin, *Roswell Presbyterian*, pp. 42–43; Walsh, *Narrative History*, p. 36.

19. Will H. Clark to Ralph B. King, July 3, 1864, BKP; Pass signed by Will H. Clark, July 3, 1864, BKP.

20. Deposition of James Roswell King, *Atkinson vs. Brumby*, Case Number, 9,821.

21. Ibid.; Deposition of James Roswell, *Roche vs. U.S.*, Case Number 466.

8 — *"The Women Will Howl"*

The quote introducing this chapter is taken from W. T. Sherman to General Garrard, July 7, 1864, OR 38, 5:76–77.

1. Deposition of James Roswell King, *Atkinson vs. Brumby*, Case Number 9,821.

2. Atlanta *Daily Intelligencer*, July 8, 1864; OR 38, 1:130; Record of Events, Roswell Battalion, June 2–August 25, 1864, M-861, reel 13, War Department of Collection Records, RG 109, DNA.

3. Compiled Service Records of Volunteer Union Soldiers, Records of the Adjutant General's Office, 1780s–1917, RG 94; Warner, *Generals in Blue*, p. 167; Bvt. Maj. Gen. George W. Collum, *Biographical Register of the Officers and Graduates of the U.S. Military Academy at West Point, N.Y.* (Boston and New York: Houghton, Mifflin,), Vol. 2, pp. 441–442; OR 38, 4:125, 507.

4. OR 38, 2:838; Thomas Crofts, *History of the Service of the Third Ohio Veteran Volunteer Cavalry* (Toledo: Stoneman Press, 1910), pp. 152–153; John C. Fleming to My Dear Father, July 12, 1864, John C. Fleming Papers, ICNL; Alva C. Griest Diary, July 5, 1864, Harrisburg Civil War Round Table Collection, PCMI; William Kemper Diary, July 5, 1864, MSS 836, The William H. Kemper Collection, Civil War Diary, May 21–August 17, 1864, OHS; A.W. Lester Diary, July 5, 1864, ILPL; Benjamin F. Nourse Diary, July 5, 1864, Rare Book, Manuscript and Special Collections Library, NcDU; Henry Albert Potter Diary, July 5, 1864, and Henry Albert Potter to Dear Father, July 10, 1864, Henry Albert Potter Letters, Bentley Historical Library, MiUBL; William H. Records Diary, July 8, 1864, InSL; Isaac Skillman Diary, July 5, 1864, Isaac Skillman Papers, Center for Archival Collections, OBGU; Evans, *Sherman's Horsemen*, pp. 10–11; Regimental Return, July 1864, 4th Michigan Cavalry, M-594, reel 83, Compiled Records Showing Service of Military Units in Volunteer Union Organizations, Records of the Adjutant General's Office, 1780s to 1917, RG 94, DNA; Regimental Return, July 1864, 1st Ohio Cavalry, M-594, reel 140.

5. *American Tribune*, December 2, 1897; W.E. Doyle, *The Seventeenth Indiana, A History from its Organization to the End of the War* (New Albany, IN: Ed, White, Book and Job Printer, 1886), p. 22; Kemper Diary, July 5, 1864; John C. McLain's Civil War Diary, July 5, 1864, Archives & Historical Collections, MiSU; B.F. Magee, *History of the 72d Indiana Volunteer Infantry of the Mounted Lightning Brigade* (Lafayette, IN: S. Vater, 1882), pp. 331–332. Although Magee's regimental history records his surname as "McGee," his service record, pension file, and census records indicate the correct spelling is "Magee." This author has used "Magee" throughout this volume. Either is preferred to "Mager," which has been used erroneously in two other works.

6. Allen D. Candler and Clement A. Evans, eds., *Georgia, Comprising Sketches of Counties, Towns, Events, Institutions, and Persons, Arranged in Cyclopedic Form* (Atlanta: State Historical Association, 1906), v. 3:93–94; Evans, *Sherman's Horsemen*, p. 11.

7. Atlanta *Daily Intelligencer*, September 13, 1863; William R. Mitchell, Jr., Sope Creek Ruins and Marietta Paper Mills, National Register of Historic Places Nomination, 1973; Temple, *First Hundred Years*, pp. 153–154; Joel Munsell, *A Chronology of Paper and Papermaking* (Albany, NY: J. Munsell, 1864), p. 135; Marietta Paper Mills, Invoices 1862–1864, Confederate Papers, M-347, reels 122, 655. Some sources suggest that the mills also manufactured paper for Confederate currency and bonds, but there are no supporting documents. According to Cobb County historian Sarah Blackwell Gober Temple, Sope Creek, often spelled Soap Creek, was named for "Ole Sope," an old Cherokee Indian who lived near the creek and remained in

the area, even after the other Cherokee were forced from their homes.

8. OR 38, 5:60; *American Tribune*, December 2, 1897; Atlanta *Daily Intelligencer*, July 8, 1864; *Detroit Free Press*, July 19, 1864; William L. Curry, *Four Years in the Saddle: History of the First Regiment Ohio Volunteer Cavalry. War of the Rebellion 1861–1865* (Columbia, OH: Champlin Printing, 1898), p. 172; Doyle, *Seventeenth Indiana*, p. 22; Magee, *72d Indiana*, p. 332.

9. OR 38, 2:813, 5:60; *American Tribune*, December 2, 1897, Atlanta *Daily Intelligencer*, July 8, 1864; *The Miners' Daily Journal and Pottsville General Advertiser*, August 20, 1864; *National Tribune*, May 31, 1894; Crofts, *Third Ohio*, p. 153; Curry, *Four Years*, p. 172; Doyle, *Seventeenth Indiana*, p. 22; Nourse, Diary, July 5, 1864; Joseph G. Vale, *Minty and the Cavalry* (Harrisburg, PA: Edwin K. Meyers, 1886), p. 321.

10. OR 38, 2:838, 5:60; Evans, *Sherman's Horsemen*, p. 13.

11. OR 38, 5:60.

12. *The Miner's Daily Journal and Pottsville General*, August 20, 1864; *American Tribune*, May 31, 1894; Vale, *Minty*, p. 321. Roche testified that the "commanding officers" told him that no order had been issued to burn the mills, see *Roche vs. U.S.*, Case Number 466.

13. *Daily Sandusky Register*, July 22, 1864; Livermore to Kennedy, February 10, 1910, p. 1, photocopy, Civil War File, GRHL.

14. Livermore to Kennedy, February 10, 1910, p. 2, photocopy, Civil War File, GRHL.

15. Kennedy to Livermore, July 6, 1864, Civil War File, GRHL; Deposition of Theophile Roche, *Roche vs. U.S.*, Case Number 466.

16. Vale, *Minty*, pp. 321–322; *American Tribune*, December 2, 1897; *National Tribune*, May 31, 1894; *Detroit Free Press*, July 22, 1864.

17. *Daily Sandusky Register*, July 22, 1864; Kennedy to Livermore, July 6, 1864, and Livermore to Kennedy, February 10, 1910, Civil War File.

18. *National Tribune*, May 31, 1894; Crofts, *Third Ohio*, p. 153; Kennedy to Livermore, July 6, 1864, Civil War File; Roche vs. U.S., Case Number 466; Vale, *Minty*, pp. 321–322. Although one local historian claims that the mill workers were subsequently arrested for refusing to leave the premises, only Vale's account makes any mention of their alleged refusal to evacuate the buildings, and Vale was not an eyewitness by his own admission. Furthermore, there is no evidence that Sherman was ever informed of this refusal.

19. Information on the burning of the cotton mills was taken from the following sources: OR 38, 5:68; Silas C. Stevens to E.B. Stevens, January 7, 1905, Silas Curtis Stevens Papers, ICHS; Olney Eldredge to My Dear Brother, November 21, 1866; *Daily Toledo Blade*, July 23, 1864, and July 27, 1864; *National Tribune*, May 31, 1894; *Detroit Free Press*, July 22, 1864; Macon *Daily Intelligencer*, August 3, 1864; *Miners' Journal and Pottsville General Advertiser*, August 20, 1864; *Sandusky Daily Register*, July 22, 1864; *Ohio State Journal*, July 26, 1864, *Cincinnati Daily Commercial*, July 22, 1864; *Nashville Times and Union*, July 27, 1864; Fleming to

My Dear Father, July 12, 1864; Curry, *Four Years*, p. 172; Nourse Diary, July 7, 1864; Kemper Diary, July 9, 1864; Records Diary, July 8, 1864; *Roche vs. U.S.*, Case Number 466.

20. Silas Stevens to E.B. Stevens, January 7, 1905.

21. Ibid.

22. Ibid.

23. Olney Eldredge to My Dear Brother, November 21, 1866; Conyngham, *Sherman's March*, p. 145; *Louisville Daily Journal*, August 23, 1864.

24. *Daily Toledo Blade*, July 27, 1864; *Roswell Neighbor*, December 19, 1984.

25. OR 38, 5:68.

26. U.S. War Department, *The Official Military Atlas of the Civil War*, Plate LXIII, Number 5, Sherman Map #103, DLC.

27. W.T. Sherman quoted in Major-General Grenville M. Dodge, *The Battle of Atlanta and Other Campaigns, Addresses, Etc.* (Denver: Sage Books, 1965), p. 176; *Cincinnati Daily Commercial* quoted in Macon *Daily Intelligencer*, August 3, 1864; *Daily Toledo Blade*, July 23, 1864; *Hartford Courant* quoted in the New Albany *Daily Ledger*, August 1, 1864.

28. *Cincinnati Daily Commercial*, July 22, 1864.

29. H.B. Teetor to H.H. Siverd, July 6, 1864, Cavalry Corps Military Division of the Mississippi, Vol. 57/140, pp. 142–143, Records of the U.S. Army Continental Commands, 1821–1920, RG 393, DNA. Some Roswell citizens, most notably Barrington King, later blamed the mill workers for the destruction of private property. See Barrington King to Ralph Browne King, July 22, 1865, BKP.

30. J.C. Audenried to Sherman, July 7, 1864, Vol. 19/28, p. 70, Military Division of the Mississippi, Records of the U.S. Army Continental Commands, 1821–1920, RG 393, DNA; OR 38, 5:76.

31. Ibid.

32. Ibid., 5:76–77.

33. Ibid., 5:73.

34. Ibid., 24, 1:754; Ulysses S. Grant, *Memoirs and Selected Letters* (Reprint; New York: Literary Classics of the United States, 1990 [1885]), p. 338; *Savannah Republican*, 25 May 1863. This author has not been able to determine if Sherman kept his word to the workers at the Green Cotton Factory.

35. General Order 100, April 24, 1863, OR Series 3, Vol. 3, pp. 148–164.

36. Ibid.

37. Ibid., 38, 4:296, 298, 5:76–77; Compiled Service Records, RG 109.

38. OR 38 5:73, 76–77, 92–93.

39. Ibid.

40. Audenried to Sherman, July 7, 1864, RG 393.

41. OR 38, 5:76; T.F. Dornblaser, *Sabre Strokes of the Pennsylvania Dragoons in the War of 1861–1865* (Baltimore: Gateway Press, 1998 [1884]), p. 167; Crofts, *Third Ohio*, p. 153.

42. Roche deposition, *Roche vs. U.S.*, Case Number 466; Eldredge to My Dear Brother, November 21, 1866.

43. For accounts pertaining to the number of women see the following sources. OR 38, 5:68; *American Tribune*, December 2, 1897; *Cincinnati Daily Commercial*, July 19, 1864; *Daily Toledo Blade*, July 27, 1864; Macon

Daily Intelligencer, August 3, 1864; *Nashville Daily Time and True Union*, July 27, 1864; *New York Tribune*, July 21, 1864; Charles G. Brown, ed., *The Sherman Brigade Marches South* (Washington, D.C.: Charles G. Brown, 1995), p. 98; Conyngham, *Sherman's March*, p. 145; Crofts, *Third Ohio*, p. 153; Curry, *Four Years*, p. 172. Dornblaser, *Sabre Strokes*, p. 167; Fleming to My Dear Father, July 12, 1864; Griest Diary, July 12, 1864; Kemper Diary, July 9, 1864; Donald Osborn, ed., *A Union Soldier's Diary* (Independence, MO: Donald Lewis Osborn, 1964), p. 2; Nourse Diary, July 7, 1864; George W. Pepper, *Personal Recollections of Sherman's Campaigns in Georgia and the Carolinas*, p. 95; Records Diary, July 8, 1864; James P. Snell Diary, July 10, 1864, James P. Snell Papers, ILPL; H.G. Stratton to "Dear Sister P.," July 17, 1864, in Frederick C. Cross, ed., *Nobly They Served the Union*, unpublished manuscript, p. 101, PCMI; Mary E. Kellogg, ed., *Army Life of an Illinois Soldier including a Day to Day Record of Sherman's March to the Sea; Letters and Diary of the Late Charles W. Wills* (Washington D.C.: Globe Printing Company, 1906), p. 279; Edwin Woodworth to Dear Mother, July 14, 1864, Civil War Collection, MSS 645, Kenan Research Center, GAHC.

44. Roche deposition, *Roche vs. U.S.*, Case Number 466; Eldredge to My Dear Brother, November 21, 1866.

45. Captain William Van Antwerp quoted in *Detroit Free Press*, July 22, 1864; *Nashville Dispatch*, July 28, 1864; *Daily Toledo Blade*, July 27, 1864; Dornblaser, *Sabre Strokes*, p. 167.

46. List of Rebel Citizens Arrested and Lists of Deserters, May–September 1864, Vol. 57/142, Cavalry Corps Military Division of the Mississippi, RG 393, Records of the U.S. Army Continental Commands, 1821–1920, DNA; Compiled Service Records, RG 109.

47. OR 38, 5:68; *American Tribune*, December 2, 1897; *The Aurora Register*, September 1, 1864; *Cincinnati Daily Commercial*, July 19, 1864; *Daily Toledo Blade*, July 27, 1864; *Nashville Daily Times and True Union*, July 27, 1864; Brown, *Sherman Brigade*, p. 98; Conyngham, *Sherman's March*, p. 145; Crofts, *Third Ohio*, p. 153; Dodge, *Personal Recollections*, p. 150; Dornblaser, *Sabre Strokes*, p. 167; Fleming to My Dear Father, July 12, 1864; Griest Diary, July 12, 1864; Hedley, *Marching Through Georgia*, p. 138; Osborn, *Soldier's Diary*, p. 2; Records Diary, 8 July 1864; H. P. Stratton to Dear Sister P., July 17, 1864; Kellogg, *Army Life*, p. 279.

48. Doyle in *American Tribune*, December 2, 1897.

49. Magee, *72d Indiana*, p. 337; Pepper, *Personal Recollections*, p. 95; Kellogg, *Army Life*, p. 280.

50. Snell Diary, July 10, 1864; Magee, *72d Indiana*, p. 337; D. Lee Woelk, *A Pilgrimage of Faith and Devotion: A History of the Roswell United Methodist Church, 1836–1984* (Roswell, GA: n.p., 1984), p. 10; Evans, *Sherman's Horsemen*, p. 22; William E. Crane Diary, July 8–9, 1864, Mss 980, OCMC; Nathaniel A. Pratt to My Dear Nephew, December 15, 1864; Pratt File, GRHL.

51. Nourse Diary, July 8, 1864; John W. Tuttle Diary, July 9, 1864, John W. Tuttle Papers, 1860–1867, 1F51M-45, AAP2201LM, Special Collections and Digital Programs, KyU.

52. Magee, *72d Indiana*, p. 333.

53. Ibid., pp. 333–334; OR 38, 2:850–851; Crane Diary, July 9, 1864; Crofts, *Third Ohio*, p. 153; Kemper Diary, July 9, 1864; Nourse Diary, July 9, 1864; Records Diary, July 8, 1864.

54. OR 38, 2:804, 813, 850–851, 854; *Miners' Journal and Pottsville General Advertiser*, August 20, 1864; *National Tribune*, May 31, 1894; Crane Diary, July 9, 1864; Crofts, *Third Ohio*, p. 153; Dornblaser, *Sabre Strokes*, pp. 167–168; Doyle, *Seventeenth Indiana*, p. 22; Fleming to My Dear Father, July 12, 1864; Othniel Gooding Letter, July 10, 1864, Othniel Gooding Papers, 1862–1865, Archives & Historical Collections, MiSU; Griest Diary, July 9, 1864; Kemper Diary, July 9, 1864; Magee, *72d Indiana*, pp. 335–337; Nourse Diary, July 9, 1864; Records Diary, July 8, 1864; Sipes, *Seventh Pennsylvania*, p. 114; Vale, *Minty*, pp. 322–323.

55. OR 38, 1:200, 2:813, 851; Macon *Daily Intelligencer*, August 3, 1864; Fleming to My Dear Father, July 12, 1864; Griest Diary, July 9, 1864; Kemper Diary, July 9, 1864; Magee, *72d Indiana*, p. 336; Nourse Diary, July 9, 1864; Records Diary, July 9, 1864; Snell Diary, July 10, 1864; Tuttle Diary, July 9, 1864; Vale, *Minty*, p. 323.

56. Magee, *72d Indiana*, p. 337; Records Diary, July 10, 1864; Crane Diary, July 10, 1864.

57. Magee, *72d Indiana*, pp. 337–338.

58. Zearing to Dear Wife, July 11, 1864, p. 182.

59. Magee, *72d Indiana*, p. 338; Kemper Diary, July 10, 1864; Temple, *First Hundred*, p 335.

60. OR 38, 5:117–119; Dodge, *Personal Recollections*, pp. 150–151.

61. Compiled Service Records, RG 94; Crane Diary, July 10, 1864; *Bryan Weekly Democrat*, August 4, 1864.

62. Tilmon D. Kyger, quoted in Illinois Infantry, *A History of the Seventy-Third Regiment of Illinois Infantry Volunteers* (Springfield, IL: Regimental Reunion Association of Survivors of the 73d Illinois Infantry Volunteers, 1890), p. 320; Kellogg, *Army Life*, p. 280.

63. Dodge, *Personal Recollections*, pp. 150–151. Dodge states that the women were taken to Marietta on horseback. This has been widely accepted as true although there is much evidence to the contrary. By all credible accounts, most of the women were gone by the time Dodge arrived. If he actually witnessed any women taken out of town on horseback, it was most likely the few women that remained after the 10th. And Garrard may have decided to send them out on horseback, rather than wait for the wagons, given the recent events involving the drunken soldiers. For evidence the women were taken by wagon, see Crofts, *Third Ohio*, p. 153; Dornblaser, *Sabre Strokes*, p. 167, *Detroit Free Press*, July 22, 1864. Some writers have gone so far as to attribute this incident to the events at New Manchester.

64. OR 38, 1:130, 3:383; J.P. Austin, *The Blue and The Gray* (Atlanta: Franklin Printing and Publishing, 1899), p. 128; Dodge, *Personal Recollections*, pp. 151–152.

65. Rev. E.C. Washington, comp., and Mary Wright Hawkins, ed., *Roswell Area Churches: The First Hundred Years* (Roswell, GA: Roswell Bicentennial Committee, 1973), p. 3; Bessie King to Barrington S. King, February 9, 1865, KFP; Woelk, *Pilgrimage*, p. 10; Martin, *Roswell Presbyterian*, p. 43. The checkerboard is still visible on the cabinet door.

66. Pratt to My Dear Nephew, December 15, 1864, Pratt File.

67. *Ohio State Journal*, July 26, 1864. The accounts of the individual mill workers are discussed in a later chapter. See "Mystery of the Lost Mill Workers."

9 — *Sweetwater Factory*

The quote introducing this chapter is taken from W. T. Sherman to General Webster, July 9, 1864, OR 38, 5:92.

1. Deposition of Henry Lovern, March 27, 1868, *Atkinson vs. Brumby*, Case Number 9,821.

2. Ibid.; OR 38, 2:514–515, 5:21–25.

3. *Atlanta Appeal* quoted in the *Macon Telegraph*, July 14, 1864; Miles G. Moseley, Case Number 6,218, Southern Claims Commission, RG 217 (hereinafter cited as SCC). Moseley is often spelled Mosely and Mozley. The author uses Moseley as it appears in this document.

4. Miles G. Moseley, Case Number 6,218, Southern Claims Commission, RG 217.

5. Isaiah J. Moseley, Case Number 3,599, SCC.

6. Eliza Tucker, Case Number 6,165; John Humphries, Case Number 7,180; Nancy Stewart, Case Number 7,189; Frederick Aderhold, Case Number 11,442; Eliza Causey, Case Number 7,174; Aaron Turner, Case Number 7813; William Strickland, Case Number 7,190; Benjamin Cooper, Case Number 7,778; Celie Joiner, Case Number 7,180; and Mary Mitchell, Case Number 7,184, all in SCC.

7. Deposition of Isaiah Love, Aderhold, Case Number 11,442.

8. Fannie Mae Davis, *Douglas County, Georgia* (Roswell, GA: W.H. Wolfe Associates, 1987), pp. 53; George White, *Statistics of the State of Georgia* (New York: W. Thorne Williams, 1855), p. 144; Somerset Publishers, *Georgia Biographical Dictionary* (New York, 1994), pp. 320–321; James F. Cook, *The Governors of Georgia, 1754–1995*, (Macon, GA: Mercer University Press, 1995) pp. 115–118.

9. Deposition of James King, June 2, 1869, *Atkinson vs. Brumby*, Case Number 9,821.

10. Davis, *Douglas County*, p. 54; White, *Historical Collections*, p. 293.

11. White, *Historical Collections*, p. 293; Davis, *Douglas County*, p. 54; Deposition of William J. Russell, *Atkinson vs. Brumby*, Case Number 9,821.

12. Nonpopulation Census, Georgia, 1850–1880; Davis, *Douglas County*, p. 54.

13. *Angus Ferguson vs. New Manchester Manufacturing Company*, Case Number A-13, GCSC; Tucker, Case Number 6,165, SCC; Margaret White to My Dear Husband, December 7, 1862, Andrew J. White Papers, 1861–1864, Rare Book, Manuscript and Special Collections Library, NcDU.

14. Russell Deposition, *Atkinson vs. Brumby*, Case Number 9,821.

15. Ibid.; *Ferguson vs. New Manchester*, Case Number A-13.

16. Deposition of Joshua Welch, *Atkinson vs. Brumby*, Case Number 9,821.

17. Ibid., Lovern Deposition.

18. Rawlinson, *Stewart Family*, pp. 342–343; Compiled Service Records, RG 109.

19. Lillian Henderson, comp., *Roster of the Confederate Soldiers of Georgia 1861–1865* (Georgia: Georgia Division, United Daughters of the Confederacy, 1994 [1959]), pp. 840–850, 882–888.

20. Ibid., pp. 533–543; Compiled Service Records, RG 109.

21. Henderson, *Confederate Soldiers*, pp. 499–507; Compiled Service Records, RG 109.

22. Compiled Service Records, RG 109.

23. Tucker, Case Number 6,165; Isaiah Moseley, Case Number 3,599; Miles Moseley, Case Number 6,218; Stewart, Case Number 7,189; and Aderhold, Case Number 11,442; Compiled Service Records, RG 109.

24. Tucker, Case Number 6,165.

25. Ibid.

26. Ibid.

27. Deposition of Perry Stewart in Stewart, Case Number 7,189; Tucker, Case Number 6,165; Compiled Service Records, RG 109.

28. Miles Moseley, Case Number 6218; Tucker, Case Number 6,165; Nancy Jones Cornell, comp., *1864 Census for Re-Organizing the Georgia Militia* (Baltimore: Genealogical Publishing, 2000), pp. 76–78; Wade White to A.J. White, September 6, 1982, White Papers.

29. New Manchester Manufacturing Company, Invoices 1863–1864, Confederate Papers, M-347, reel 893, RG 109; Augusta [GA] *Daily Chronicle & Sentinel*, August 10, 1861; *Savannah News* quoted in the *Natchez Daily Courier*, October 19, 1861.

30. Russell Deposition, *Atkinson vs. Brumby*, Case 9,821.

31. Compiled Service Records, RG 109.

32. Joshua Welch, Affidavit, January 30, 1864, Telamon Cuyler Collection, 1754–1951, MS 1170, Box 20, GUGL.

33. Ibid.; A.V. Brumby to "His Excellency Joseph E. Brown," January 30, 1864, Telamon Cuyler Collection, 1754–1951, MS 1170, Box 20, GUGL.

34. Rawlinson, *Stewart Family*, pp. 342–343.

35. Margaret White to Dear Husband, June 8, 1864, White Papers; Henderson, *Confederate Soldiers*, p. 542.

36. Welch Deposition, *Atkinson vs. Brumby*, Case Number 9,821.

37. Russell Deposition and Welch Deposition, *Atkinson vs. Brumby*, Case Number 9,821.

38. *Macon Telegraph*, July 7, 1864.

39. Lovern Deposition, *Atkinson vs. Brumby*, Case Number 9,821; Lewis C. Russell, "Sweetwater History," in the *Atlanta Journal*, April, 28, 1932.

40. *Angus Ferguson vs. New Manchester Manufacturing*, Case Number A-13; Lovern Deposition, *Atkinson vs. Brumby*, Case Number 9,821; OR 38, 5:76–77.

41. See appendix for complete arrest list. Although the arrest list shows M.H. Humphries, it is most likely N.H. Humphries (Nathaniel Harbin Humphries) as he was associated with the mill, and there is no record of an M.H. Humphries in the area at that time. Roll of Political Prisoners, Selected Records of the War Department Relating to Confederate Prisoners of War 1861–

1865, M-598, reel 95, RG; Lovern Deposition, *Atkinson vs. Brumby*, Case Number 9,821.

42. Charlene Humphries Herreid, *The Humphries Family of Campbell and Douglas Counties, Georgia, Part I* (June 2003), p. 18. Charlene Herreid provided me with a copy of this unpublished family history.

43. Compiled Service Records, RG 109; Eliza Tucker, Case Number 6,165.

44. Davis, *Douglas County*, p. 58.

45. Rawlinson, *Stewart Family*, pp. 342–343; Bell Family Genealogy, History Files, GSSP; Herreid, *Humphries Family*, pp. 18–19; Eighth Census, 1860, Georgia; U.S. Census Office. Tenth Census, 1880, Population of the United States, Texas, T-9, Records of the Bureau of the Census, RG 29, DNA; Russell, *Atlanta Journal*, April, 28, 1932; John Causey, Confederate Pension Application, January 5, 1898, GDAH; Synthia Catherine Boyd Stewart, *Civil War Oral History*, April 13, 1947, MSS 441f, Stewart Family Collection, GAHC.

46. Tolbert Family History, History Files, GSSP.

47. Indiana *Daily Express*, July 27, 1864; Thomas M. Robertson Diary, July 10, 1864, InCHS; Boyd, *Oral History*.

48. *Nashville Daily Times*, July 20, 1864.

10 — Precious Cargo

1. Benjamin F. Nourse Diary, July 3, 1864; OR 38, 5:141–142; *Cincinnati Daily Commercial*, August 2, 1864; *New York Tribune*, July 21, 1864.

2. William King Diary, July 10, 1864, #2985, Southern History Collection, Wilson Library, NcCH; Colonel Newell Gleason to General W.D. Whipple, July 6, 1864, Union Provost Marshal's File of Papers Relating to Two or More Civilians, M-416, reel 39, War Department Collection of Confederate Records, RG 109, DNA, hereinafter cited as Provost Marshal's Papers.

3. OR 38, 5:113, 141–142; *Cincinnati Daily Commercial*, August 2, 1864.

4. OR 38, 1:790, 796, 5:62–63, 141–142.

5. OR 38, 5:32; Sherman to Commanding Officer, July 9, 1864, and Sherman to General J.D. Webster, July 9, 1864, both in Sherman's Letter Book, Entry 159, General's Papers and Orders, Records of the Adjutant General's Office, RG 94, DNA; Evans, *Sherman's Horsemen*, p. 52; Lane, *Times That Prove People's Principles: Civil War in Georgia* (Savannah: Beehive Foundation, 1993), pp. 175–176.

6. William H. Ray quoted in the *National Tribune*, February 22, 1883; Evans, *Sherman's Horsemen*, p. 52; Theodore F. Upson, *With Sherman to the Sea* (Bloomington: Indiana University Press, 1958), pp. 118–119.

7. OR 38, 5:104.

8. *Louisville Daily Journal*, August 4, 1864.

9. OR 39, 2:210–211.

10. King Diary, July 3, 9–10, 1864.

11. Ibid.

12. Snell Diary, July 11, 1864; *Cincinnati Daily Commercial*, July 20, 1864.

13. *New York Tribune*, July 21, 1864; Upson, *With Sherman*, p. 119.

14. *Cincinnati Daily Commercial*, July 21, 1864; *New York Tribune*, July 21, 1864; Osborn, *Soldier's Diary*, p. 2.

15. *Cincinnati Daily Commercial*, July 21, 1864; Olney Eldredge to My Dear Brother, November 21, 1866.

16. *Richmond Sentinel* quoted in the Augusta, GA, *Daily Constitutionalist*, August 10, 1864.

17. Harrisburg [PA] *Patriot and Union*, August 2, 1864. Although it is clearly prejudicial, this article is frequently cited.

18. *Cincinnati Daily Commercial*, July 19, 1864.

19. Ibid.

20. OR 38, 5:92–93; Sherman to Webster, July 9, 1864, Sherman's Letter Book; Eldredge to My Dear Brother, November 21, 1866; Roche Deposition, *Roche vs. U.S.*, Case Number 466.

21. S.A. Stockdale to Hunter Brooke, July 29, 1864, Military Division of the Mississippi, Vol. 21, p. 12, Records of the U.S. Army Continental Commands, 1821–1920, RG 393, DNA; *Louisville Daily Journal*, August 4, 1864.

22. Charles Messmer, "Louisville During the Civil War," *The Filson Club History Quarterly*, 52 (April 1978), p. 214.

23. *Louisville Daily Journal*, July 21, 1864; *Louisville Democrat*, July 21, 1864, August 24, 1864; *Nashville Dispatch*, July 9, 1864.

24. OR, Series 3, Vol. 5:587.

25. *Louisville Democrat*, July 21, 1864; Roll of Political Prisoners, RG 109.

26. Boyd, *Oral History*; OR, Series 2, Vol. 7:563; *Louisville Daily Journal*, August 24, 1864.

27. Boyd, *Oral History*; Compiled Service Records, RG 109.

28. Compiled Service Records, RG 109; Shelly, *Life Histories*.

29. Shelly, *Life Histories*.

30. Various Lists of Registers Relating to Prisoners, 1861–1866, Department of Kentucky, Entry 1640, Vol. 257, Book 536, Records of the U.S. Army Continental Commands, 1821–1920, RG 393, DNA.

31. Special Order Number 48, Union Provost Marshal's File of Papers Relating to Two or More Civilians, M-416, War Department Collection of Confederate Records, RG 109, DNA.

32. Harrisburg *Patriot and Union*, August 27, 1864.

33. *Louisville Daily Journal*, September 13, 1864.

34. Tommie Phillips LaCavera, *Heroines of Georgia 1861–1865: A Biographical Dictionary, Volume I* (Georgia: T.P. LaCavera, 2005), p. 238.

35. W.D. Pickett, "Why General Sherman's Name is Detested," *Confederate Veteran* 14 (September 1906), p. 397.

36. *Louisville Daily Journal*, August 14, 1864.

37. Louisville Refuge Commission, *Report of the Louisville Refugee Commission* (Louisville, KY, 1865); *Louisville Daily Journal*, August 24, 1864.

38. *Louisville Daily Journal*, August 23, 1864, September 23, 1864.

11 — Land of Plenty

1. OR 38, 5:73, 76–77; *Louisville Daily Journal*, August 4, 1864.

2. Evansville *Daily Journal*, July 8, 1864; New

Albany *Daily Ledger*, August 19, 1864, September 6, 1864; *Louisville Daily Journal*, August 19, 1864, August 24, 1864.

3. Emma Lou Thornbrough, *Indiana in the Civil War Era 1850–1880*, Vol. 3, The History of Indiana (Indianapolis: Indiana Historical Society, 1992), p. 170.

4. Ibid., pp. 175–176.

5. Ibid., 176.

6. Ibid., 177–178.

7. Ibid. 178–179.

8. *Evansville Daily Journal*, July 8, 1864.

9. Ibid., July 12, 1864.

10. Ibid., July 14, 1864.

11. New Albany *Daily Ledger*, July 21, 1864.

12. Ibid., September 6, 1864.

13. *Louisville Daily Journal*, August 19, 1864.

14. OR 38, 5:481.

15. New Albany *Daily Ledger*, August 19, 1864.

16. Ibid., December 1, 1864.

17. New Albany *Daily Ledger* quoted in *Louisville Daily Journal*, December 11, 1864.

18. New Albany *Daily Ledger*, December 30, 1864.

19. Ibid., December 29, 1864.

20. Indiana Adjutant General, *Report of the Adjutant General of the State of Indiana* (Indianapolis: Alexander H. Conner, W. R. Holloway, Samuel M. Douglass, State Printers, 1869), 1:368.

21. OR Series 3, Vol. 4:1019.

22. OR Series 3, Vol. 4:1019–1020.

23. New Albany *Daily Ledger*, January 9, 1865; *Journal of the Senate of the United States of America Being the Second Session of the Thirty-Eighth Congress; Begun and Held at the City of Washington, December 5, 1864, in the Eighty-Eighth Year of the Independence of the United States* (Washington, D.C.: Government Printing Office, 1864).

24. Two works were particularly helpful in providing information on the Cannelton Cotton Mill: Anita Ashendel, "Fabricating Independence: Industrial Labor in Antebellum Indiana," *Michigan Historical Review* 23:2 (Fall 1977) and Michael F. Rutherford, *Perry County: Then and Now* (Paducah, KY: Turner, 2000), pp. 63–80.

25. *Daily Toledo Blade*, July 16, 1864; Ashendel, *Fabricating Independence*, pp. 21–22.

26. Ashendel, op. cit., page 22; *Louisville Democrat*, September 30, 1864 and October, 10, 1864; *Cannelton Reporter* quoted in New Albany *Daily Ledger*, October 12, 1864, January 14, 1865.

27. Ashendel, *Fabricating Independence*, p. 22; U.S. Census Office. Ninth Census, 1870, Population of the United States, Indiana, M-593, Records of the Bureau of the Census, RG 29, DNA.

12 — News from the Homefront

The quote introducing this chapter is taken from a letter from Barrington S. King to Catherine Margaret Nephew King, July 25, 1864, KFP.

1. Barrington King to W.E. Baker, July 18 1864, and August 10, 1864, BKP.

2. Barrington S. King to Catharine Nephew King, July 20, 1864, July 25, 1864, KFP.

3. Anne Smith to William Smith, July 12, 1864, and George Camp to Archibald Smith, July 13, 1864, both in Smith Papers.

4. Barrington King to W.E. Baker, July 18, 1864, BKP; William Smith to Anne Smith, September 7, 1864, Smith Papers.

5. Smith Papers, Anne Smith to William Smith, September 9, 1864.

6. Ibid., Barrington King to Archibald Smith, September 16, 1864.

7. King Diary, July 9–10, 1864.

8. Barrington King to W.H. Bailey, Esquire, March 12, 1848, Barrington King to Stewart & Meredith, March 20, 1848, Barrington King to Eva King Baker, February 11, 1848, all in BKP.

9. Ledger, Negroes owned by B. King, January 1, 1860, to March 7, 1864, BKP.

10. Teetor to Siverd, July 6, 1864, CCMDM; *Cincinnati Daily Commercial*, July 22 1864.

11. Helen Smith to William Smith, November 4, 1864, Smith Papers; Nathaniel Pratt to My Dear Nephew, December 15, 1864, Pratt File.

12. Minutes of Stockholders' Meetings, July 19, 1865.

13 — Return to Roswell

The quote introducing this chapter is taken from a letter from Barrington King to Ralph B. King, July 22, 1865, BKP.

1. OR 38, 1:70; Sherman, *Memoirs*, pp. 384–385.

2. OR 47, 1:1045; Compiled Service Records, RG 109; Ralph Browne King to Fannie King Pratt, April 6, 1918, BKP; Wiley C. Howard, *Sketch of Cobb Legion Cavalry and Some Incidents and Scenes Remembered* (s.l.: s.n., 1901), p. 14.

3. Howard, *Sketch*, p. 14.

4. Compiled Service Records, RG 109; Nirenstein, *With Kindly Voices*, p. 145; Barrington King to Florie King, March 23, 1865, BKP.

5. Ralph Browne King to Fannie King Pratt, April 6, 1918, BKP; Compiled Service Records, RG 109.

6. Ralph Browne King to Fannie King Pratt, April 6, 1918, BKP; Compiled Service Records, RG 109.

7. Compiled Service Records, RG 109; Elizabeth Lockhart Davis and Ethel Warren Spruill, *The Story of Dunwoody*, (Alpharetta, GA: Alpharetta Historical Society, 1975), pp. 18–20.

8. Compiled Service Records, RG 109; Joseph M. Atkinson to Archibald Smith, July 10, 1865, Smith Papers; Skinner, *Confederate*, p. 200.

9. Skinner, *Confederate*, pp. 252, 266.

10. Compiled Service Records, RG 109. For information on James Dunwody Bulloch's military career, see Charles Grayso Summersell, *CSS Alabama: Builder, Captain, and Plans* (University, AL: University of Alabama Press, 1985), pp. 3–21.

11. Summersell, *CSS Alabama*, p. 21.

12. *The Washington Times*, January 16, 2001.

13. Ibid.; Summersell, *CSS Alabama*, p. 30.

14. *The Washington Times*, January 16, 2001.

15. Compiled Service Records, RG 109.

16. Minutes of Stockholder Meetings, July 19, 1865; Barrington King to Ralph King, July 22, 1865, BKP.

17. Cooper, *King*, p. 62; Telegram, D.A. Adams to Rev. C.B. King, January 17, 1866, BKP.

18. Temple, *First Hundred Years*, p. 406; Nirenstein, *Kindly Voices*, p. 147; Coleman, *Short History*, p. 10.

19. Coleman, *Short History*, pp. 10, 11, 13.

20. Ibid., p. 14.

21. Walsh, *Roswell*, p. 260; William R. Mitchell, Jr., *Historic Area Study Roswell, Georgia* (Atlanta: Kidd and Associates, 1973) pp. 11–12.

14 — The Mystery of the Lost Mill Workers

1. Columbus [GA] *Daily Sun*, December 12, 1867.

2. Eighth Census, 1860, Georgia.

3. Eighth Census, 1860, Georgia; Ninth Census, 1870, Georgia; Shelly, *Life Histories*; *Index to Marriage Records, Perry County, Indiana, 1850–1920, inclusive* (Indiana Work Projects Administration, 1941), book 3, pp. 239, 654.

4. Ninth Census, 1870, Indiana.

5. Barrington King to Charles King, July 20, 1865, and Barrington King to Ralph King, July 22, 1865, BKP. Interestingly, two local historians have seen fit to omit the most significant phrase from Barrington's letter to his son Ralph in their own works on the subject: "We are determined to have a new sett with very few exceptions." See Martin, *Roswell Presbyterian*, p. 47, and Michael Hitt, *Charged With Treason: Ordeal of 400 Mill Workers During Military Operations in Roswell, Georgia, 1864–1865* (Monroe, NY: Library Research Associates, 1992), p. 153.

6. Ninth Census, 1870, Indiana.

7. Olney Eldredge to My Dear Brother, November 21, 1866.

8. *Roche vs. U.S.*, Case Number 466.

9. Ninth Census, 1870, Kentucky; Shelly, *Life Histories*.

10. Shelly, *Life Histories*.

11. Compiled Service Records, RG 109; Don L. Shadburn and Ted O. Brooke, eds., *Crimson and Sabres: A Confederate Record of Forsyth County, Georgia* (Cumming, GA: D.L. Shadburn, 1997), Pioneer-Cherokee Heritage Series, v. 4, pp. 259, 330; Ninth Census, 1870, Georgia; Tenth Census, 1880, Georgia. The 1880 census indicates that two of the Buice children were born in Illinois between 1864 and 1867.

12. Ninth Census, 1870, Indiana; Tenth Census, 1880, Indiana; *Marriage Records, Perry County*, book 3, pp. 239, 654, and book 4, p. 231. Descendent George Kendley and his wife, Elizabeth, of Fairhope, Alabama, were very helpful in providing photographs and history of the Kendley family.

13. Compiled Service Records, RG 109; Eighth Census, 1860, Georgia; Ninth Census, 1870, Indiana.

14. Ninth Census, 1870, Indiana; 35th Senatorial District Georgia Militia, Enrollment of Present Militia Company, District Number 845, Cobb County, Georgia, December 14, 1863, Microfilm Library, Drawer 245, Box 5, Militia Enrollments Lists, Cobb County, GDAH.

15. Eighth Census, 1860, Georgia; Ninth Census,

1870, Indiana; *Marriage Records, Perry County*, Book 3, p. 577.

16. Eighth Census, 1860, Georgia; Ninth Census, 1870, Indiana; *Marriage Records, Perry County*, Book 3, p. 625.

17. Eighth Census, 1860, Georgia; Ninth Census, 1870, Indiana.

18. Farr family history provided by descendant Thomas Farr in personal interview on July 8, 2000, in Roswell, Georgia; Eighth Census, 1860, Georgia.

19. Ninth Census, 1870, Indiana; Compiled Service Records, RG 109.

20. Eighth Census, 1860, Georgia; Ninth Census, 1870, Indiana.

21. Eighth Census, 1860, Georgia; Ninth Census, 1870, Georgia; Compiled Service Records, RG 109.

22. List of Rebel Citizens, CCMDM; Ninth Census, 1870, Tennessee; Compiled Service Records, RG 109.

23. Ninth Census, 1870, Tennessee; Compiled Service Records, RG 109; Bobby Alford, *History of Lawrence County, Tennessee* (n.p., 1994), pp. 48–49. Copy of Lawrence County History provided by Bobby Alford of Lawrenceburg, Tennessee. Information on gravesite provided by William's descendent, Bonnie Weed Malburg of Lackawanna, New York.

24. *Atkinson vs. Brumby*, Case Number 9,821.

25. Bill Cahill of the Friends of Sweetwater Creek State Park, and Dan Emsweller, Sweetwater Creek State Park historian, were particularly helpful in providing information on the history of Sweetwater Creek National Park and the surrounding area.

26. *Marietta Daily Journal*, January 20, 1987; Roll of Political Prisoners, RG 109.

27. Ninth Census, 1870, Georgia.

28. Compiled Service Records, RG 94; James Carroll, Pension Application, Records of the Veterans Administration, RG 15, DNA; Tucker, Case Number 6,165.

29. Deposition of Henry Lovern, *Atkinson vs. Brumby*, Case Number 9,821.

30. Ibid., Deposition of William H. Bell; Bell Genealogy File, History Files, GSSP.

31. Eighth Census, 1860, Georgia; Tenth Census, 1880, Texas.

32. Clement A. Evans, ed., *Confederate Military History, Extended Edition* (Reprint; Wilmington, NC: Broadfoot, 1987) [1899], Volume 7:747–748; Ninth Census, 1870, Georgia; Compiled Service Records, RG 109.

33. Russell, *Atlanta Journal*, April 28, 1932.

34. Eighth Census, 1860, Georgia. Summerlin family history provided by descendent, Hazel Bailin of Atlanta, Georgia.

35. Ninth Census, 1870, Georgia.

36. LaCavera, *Georgia Heroines*, p. 320. Information on the Wright family provided courtesy of Tommie Phillips LaCavera of Athens, Georgia.

37. LaCavera, *Georgia Heroines*, p. 321; Jennings family history provided courtesy of Mauriel Joslyn of Sparta, Georgia and Tommie Phillips LaCavera. Tommie LaCavera also provided information on the Young family history.

38. LaCavera, *Georgia Heroines*, p. 238.

39. Rawlinson, *Stewart Family*, p. 336; Boyd, *Oral History*; Ninth Census, 1870, Georgia.

40. Ninth Census, 1870, Georgia; Boyd, *Oral History*; *Atlanta Journal Constitution*, January 7, 1999. The newspaper article contains some information edited out of the copy of the oral history provided to the Georgia Historical Society.

41. Rawlinson, *Stewart Family*, p. 333.

42. *Atlanta Journal Constitution*, January 7, 1999.

Epilogue

1. Mitchell, *Historic District*. For more information on the historic homes and churches of Roswell, see Walsh, ed., *Roswell: A Pictorial History*; Medora Field Perkerson, *White Columns in Georgia* (New York: Bonanza Books, 1956); Martin, *A History of Roswell Presbyterian Church*.

2. Mitchell, *Historic District*, entry 9.

3. Ibid., entry 2.

4. Ibid., entry 16.

5. Ibid., entry 11.

6. Ibid., entry 10.

7. Program, Dedication Service for the Lost Mill Workers of Roswell: Monument of Honor, July 8, 2000 [in author's possession].

Bibliography

Abbreviations

DLC   Library of Congress, Washington, D.C.
DNA   National Archives, Washington, D.C.
GAFC   Fulton County Superior Court, Atlanta, Georgia
GAHC   Atlanta History Center, Atlanta, Georgia
GCCL   Cobb County Library, Marietta, Georgia
GCSC   Campbell County Superior Court, Douglasville, Georgia
GDAH   Georgia Department of Archives and History, Morrow
GSSP   Sweetwater Creek State Conservation Park, Lithia Springs, Georgia
GRHL   Roswell Historical Library, Roswell, Georgia
GUGL   Hargrett Rare Book and Manuscript Library, University of Georgia Libraries, Athens
ICHS   Chicago Historical Society, Chicago, Illinois
ICNL   Newberry Library, Chicago, Illinois
ILPL   Abraham Lincoln Presidential Library & Museum, Springfield, Illinois
InCHS   Clay County Historical Society, Brazil, Indiana
InHS   Indiana Historical Society, Indianapolis
InSL   Indiana State Library, Indianapolis
KyU   University of Kentucky, Special Collections and Digital Programs, Lexington
MiSU   Michigan State University, East Lansing
MiUBL   University of Michigan, Bentley Historical Library, Ann Arbor
NcCH   University of North Carolina, Chapel Hill
NcDU   Duke University, Durham, North Carolina
OBGU   Bowling Green University, Bowling Green, Ohio
OCMC   Cincinnati Museum Center, Cincinnati, Ohio
OHS   Ohio Historical Society, Columbus
PCMI   U.S. Army Military History Institute, Carlisle, Pennsylvania
TSLA   Tennessee State Library and Archives, Nashville

Primary Sources

Manuscripts

Atkinson, A.S., and Others. Executors of Charles J. McDonald vs. A.V. Brumby. GAFC
Bell Family Genealogy. History Files. GSSP
Boyd, Synthia Catherine Stewart. Civil War Oral History, MSS 441f, Stewart Family Collection, Kenan Research Center. GAHC
Causey, John. Confederate Pension Application. GDAH
Crane, William E. Diary. OCMC
Cuyler, Telemon. Collection. GUGL
Eldredge, Olney. Letter, Nov. 21, 1866, to Michael Eldredge
Ferguson, Angus, vs. New Manchester Manufacturing Company. GCSC
Fleming, John C. Papers. ICNL
Gooding, Othniel. Papers, Archives & Historical Collections. MiSU
Griest, Alva C. Diary, Harrisburg Civil War Round Table Collection. PCMI
Haskell, Oliver C. Diary. InHS
Jordan, Stephen A. Diary. TSLA
Kemper, William. Civil War Diary, MSS 836, The William H. Kemper Collection. OHS
Kennedy, Robert P. Letter, July 6, 1864, Civil War File. GRHL
King, Barrington. Papers. GDAH
King Family Papers. MSS 753, Kenan Research Center. GAHC

King, William. Diary, Southern Historical Collection, Wilson Library. NcCH

Lester, A.W. Diary. ILPL

Livermore, Darius. Letter, Feb. 10, 1910. GRHL

McClain, John C. Civil War Diary, Archives & Historical Collections. MiSU

McConnell, Sarah M. "A Relic of the War 1860–1865." TSLA

Minutes of the Roswell Manufacturing Company Stockholder's Meetings, 1840–1900. GRHL

Nourse, Benjamin F. Diary, Rare Rook, Manuscript and Special Collections Library. NcDU

Potter, Henry Albert. Diary. MiUBL

Potter, Henry Albert. Letters. MiUBL

Pratt, Nathaniel. Pratt File. GRHL

Record Group 15, Records of the Veterans Administration. DNA

Record Group 56, General Records of the Department of the Treasury. DNA

Record Group 76, Records of the Department of State. DNA

Record Group 94, Records of the Adjutant General's Office. DNA

Record Group 109, War Department Collection of Confederate Records. DNA

Record Group 110, Records of the Provost Marshal General's Bureau. DNA

Record Group 217, Records of the General Accounting Office. DNA

Record Group 233, Records of the Southern Claims Commission. DNA

Record Group 393, Records of U.S. Army Continental Commands, 1821–1920. DNA

Records, William H. Diary, Manuscript Section. InSL

Reniker, Samuel D. Diary, Civil War Misc. Collection, 2nd Series. PCMI

Robertson, Thomas M. Diary. InCHS

Shelly, William Robert. "The Life Histories of James William Shelly and Lucinda Elizabeth Wood Shelly." Rome, Georgia, May 1928. Carmel Boswell [Private hands].

Sherman, William T. Papers. DLC

Skillman, Isaac. Papers, Center for Archival Collections. OBGU

Smith, Archibald. Papers. GDAH

Snell, James P. Papers. ILPL

Stevens, Silas Curtis. Papers. ICHS

Thomson, James. Diary. GDAH

Tolbert Family History. History Files. GSSP

Tuttle, John W. Papers, 1860–1867, 1F51M-45, AAP 2201LM, Special Collections and Digital Programs. KyU

West, Martin. Diary. ILPL

White, Andrew J. Papers, Rare Book, Manuscript and Special Collections Library. NcDU

Woodworth, Edwin. Civil War Collection, Kenan Research Center. GAHC

Newspapers

American Tribune

Athens [GA] *Southern Banner*

Atlanta Daily Intelligencer

Atlanta Journal

Atlanta Journal Constitution

[Atlanta] *Southern Confederacy*

Augusta Daily Chronicle and Sentinel

[Augusta, GA] *Daily Constitutionalist*

Aurora [IL] *Register*

Brandon [MS] *Republican*

Bryan [OH] *Weekly Democrat*

Charleston Courier

Cincinnati Daily Commercial

Columbus [GA] *Daily Sun*

Daily Sandusky [OH] *Register*

Daily Toledo Blade

Detroit Free Press

Evansville Daily Journal

[Harrisburg] *Patriot and Union*

[IN] *Daily Express*

Lafayette [IN] *Courier*

Louisville Daily Journal

Louisville Democrat

Macon Daily Intelligencer

Macon Telegraph

Marietta Daily Journal

Miners' Journal & Pottsville [PA] *General Advertiser*

Mobile Register and Advertiser

Nashville Daily Times and True Union

Nashville Dispatch

Natchez Daily Courier

National Tribune

New York Tribune

New Albany [IN] *Daily Ledger*

Ohio State Journal

Roswell [GA] *Neighbor*

Sandersville Central Georgian

Savannah [GA] *Republican*

Washington Times

Official Documents

Candler, Allen D., comp. *The Confederate Records of the State of Georgia.* 6 vols. Compiled and published under authority of the legislature by Allen D. Candler, Atlanta, 1909–1911. Vols. I, II, III, IV, and VI have been published. Vol. V consists of unpublished manuscripts in the Georgia State Department of Archives and History.

Georgia. Convention of the People. *Journal of the Public and Secret Proceedings of the Convention of the People of Georgia Held in Milledgeville, and Savannah, in 1861, Together with the Ordinances Adopted.* Milledgeville, GA: Boughton, Nisbet & Barnes, State Printers, 1861.

Georgia. General Assembly. *Acts of the General Assembly of the State of Georgia, passed in Milledgeville, at an annual session in November and December, 1839*. Atlanta, 1870.

Georgia. Records of the Governor and the Adjutant and Inspector General. Thirty-Fifth Senatorial District Georgia Militia, Enrollment of Present Militia Company, District Number 845, Cobb County, Georgia, December 14, 1863. GDAH

Indiana Adjutant General. *Report of the Adjutant General of the State of Indiana*. 8 vols. Indianapolis: Alexander H. Conner, W.R. Holloway, Samuel M. Douglass, State Printers, 1865–1869.

U.S. Census Office. Eighth Census, 1860. Manufactures of the United States in 1860. Washington: Government Printing Office, 1865.

_____. Eighth Census of the United States, 1860: Population.

_____. Ninth Census of the United States, 1870: Population.

_____. Nonpopulation Census Schedules for Georgia, 1850–1880.

_____. Seventh Census of the United States, 1850: Population

_____. Sixth Census, 1840, *Compendium of the Enumeration of the Inhabitants and Statistics of the United States*. Washington: T. Allen, 1841.

_____. Tenth Census of the United States, 1880 Population.

United States. Congress. Senate. *Journal of the Senate of the United States of America Being the Second Session of the Thirty-Eighth Congress; Begun and Held at the City of Washington, December 5, 1864, in the Eighty-Eighth Year of the Independence of the United States*. Washington, D.C.: Government Printing Office, 1864.

_____. War Department. *The War of the Rebellion: A Compilation of the Official Records of the Union and Confederate Armies*. 128 volumes. Washington: 1880–1901.

Books and Articles

Austin, J.P. *The Blue and the Gray: Sketches of a Portion of the Unwritten History of the Great American Civil War, A Truthful Narrative of Adventure with Thrilling Reminiscences of the Great Struggle on Land and Sea*. Atlanta: Franklin Printing and Publishing, 1899.

Avery, I.W. *The History of the State of Georgia from 1850 to 1881*. Reprint. New York: AMS Press, 1972 [1881].

Blair, William Alan. *A Politician Goes to War: The Civil War Letters of John White Geary*. University Park: Pennsylvania State University Press, 1995.

Bonner, James C., ed. *Diary of a Milledgeville Girl, 1861–1867*. Athens: University of Georgia Press, 1964.

Brainard, Mary Genevie Green. *Campaigns of the 146th Regiment, New York State Volunteers*. New York, London: G.P. Putnam's Sons, 1915.

Brown, Charles G., ed. *The Sherman Brigade Marches South: The Civil War Memoirs of Colonel Robert Carson Brown*. Washington, D.C.: Charles G. Brown, 1995.

Buckingham, James Silk. *The Slave States of America*. London: Fisher, Son, 1842.

Bulloch, James Dunwody. *The Secret Service of the Confederate States in Europe; or, How the Confederate Cruisers Were Equipped*. New York: T. Yoseloff, 1959 [1884].

Byerly, Victoria. *Hard Times Cotton Mill Girls: Personal Histories and Poverty in the South*. New York: ILR Press, 1986.

Chicago Board of Trade Memorial Association. *Historical Sketch of the Chicago Board of Trade Battery, Horse Artillery Illinois Volunteers*. Chicago: Henneberry, 1902.

Conyngham, David P. *Sherman's March Through the South with Sketches and Incidents of the Campaign*. New York: Sheldon, 1865.

Cox, Jacob Dolson. *Military Reminiscences of the Civil War*. New York: C. Scribner's Sons, 1900.

_____. *Sherman's Battle for Atlanta*. Unabridged republication of the 1882 edition. New York: Da Capo Press, 1994 [1882].

Crofts, Thomas, comp. *History of the Service of the Third Ohio Veteran Volunteer Cavalry in the War for the Preservation of the Union From 1861–1865 Compiled from the Official Records and from Diaries of Members of the Regiment by Serg't Thos. Crofts, Company C, Regimental Historian*. Toledo: Stoneman Press, 1910.

Cross, Frederick C., ed. *Nobly They Served the Union*. Walnut Creek, CA: n.p., 1976. PCMI

Curry, William L., comp. *Four Years in the Saddle: History of the First Regiment Ohio Volunteer Cavalry. War of the Rebellion 1861–1865*. Columbus, OH: Champlin Printing, 1898.

Dodge, M. Grenville. *Personal Recollections of President Abraham Lincoln, General Ulysses S. Grant and General William T. Sherman*. Council Bluffs, IA: Monarch, 1914.

_____. *The Battle of Atlanta and Other Campaigns, Addresses, Etc.* Denver: Sage Books, 1965

Dornblaser, T.F. *Sabre Strokes of the Pennsylvania Dragoons in the War of 1861–1865*. Reprint. Baltimore: Gateway Press, 1998 [1884].

Doyle, William E. *The Seventeenth Indiana, A History From its Organization to the End of the War; Giving Each Days Action, Lists of Killed and Wounded, Descriptions of Battles; Also, Lists of All* the Officers, and the Roll of the Regiment on February 28, 1865. New Albany, IN: Ed, White, Book and Job Printer, 1886.

Evans, Clement A., ed. *Confederate Military History: A Library of Confederate States History, in Twelve Volumes, Written by Distinguished Men of the South, and Edited by Gen. Clement A. Evans of Georgia.* 17 vols. Reprint. Harrisburg, PA: Archive Society, 1994 (1899).

Foner, Philip S., ed. *The Factory Girls: A Collection of Writings on Life and Struggles in the New England Factories of the 1840s by the Factory Girls Themselves, and the Story, in Their Own Words, of the First Trade Unions of Women Workers in the United States.* Urbana: University of Illinois Press, 1977.

Grant, Ulysses S. *Memoirs and Selected Letters: Personal Memoirs of U.S. Grant, Selected Letters 1839–1865.* New York: Literary Classics of the United States, 1990.

Grebner, Constantin. *We were the Ninth: A History of the Ninth Regiment, Ohio Volunteer Infantry, April 17, 1861, to June 7, 1864.* Trans. and ed. by Frederic Trautmann. Kent, OH, and London: Kent State University Press, 1987 [1907].

Gross, Luelja Zearing. "A Sketch of the Life of Major James Roberts Zearing, M.D." *Transactions of the Illinois State Historical Library* (1921) pp. 139–202.

Hancock, Louise. "A Southern Woman's Heroism." *Confederate Veteran* 22 (October 1915) p. 445.

Hedley, Fenwick Y. *Marching Through Georgia: Pen-Pictures of Every-Day Life in General Sherman's Army, From the Beginning of the Atlanta Campaign Until the Close of the War.* Chicago: R.R. Donnelley & Sons, The Lakeside Press, 1885.

Hitchcock, Henry. *Marching with Sherman.* New Haven, CT: Yale University Press, 1927.

Howard, Frances Thomas. *In and Out of the Lines.* Cartersville, GA: Etowah Valley Historical Society, 1997 [1905].

Howard, Wiley C. *Sketch of Cobb Legion Cavalry and Some Incidents and Scenes Remembered.* S.l.: s.n., 1901.

Howe, M.A. DeWolfe, ed. *Home Letters of General Sherman.* New York: Charles Scribner's Sons, 1909.

Illinois Infantry. *A History of the Seventy-Third Regiment of Illinois Infantry Volunteers: Its Services and Experiences in Camp, on the March, on the Pickett and Skirmish Lines, and in Many Battles of the War, 1861–1865, Including A Sketch in Full of the Valuable and Indispensable Services Rendered by Opdycke's First Brigade, Second Division, Fourth Army Corps, in the Campaign in Tennessee in the Fall of 1864, Embracing an Account of the Movement from* Columbia to Nashville, and the Battles of Spring Hill and Franklin. Also, Including Many other Interesting Miscellaneous Sketches, the Latter Being Made up of Recitals of Individual Experiences of Capture, Imprisonment, and Escape, and an Account of the Visit of James F Jaquess, Colonel of the Seventy-Third, to Richmond, Virginia, in the Summer of 1864. Springfield, IL: Regimental Reunion Association of Survivors of the 73d Illinois Infantry Volunteers, 1890.

Johnston, General Joseph E. *Narrative of Military Operations During the Civil War.* Reprint. New York: Da Capo Press, 1959 [1874].

Kellogg, Mary E., ed. *Army Life of an Illinois Soldier including a Day by Day Record of Sherman's March to the Sea: Letters and Diary of the Late Charles W. Wills.* Washington, D.C.: Globe Printing, 1906.

Kemble, Frances A., and Frances A. Butler Leigh. *Principles and Privilege: Two Women's Lives on a Georgia Plantation.* Ann Arbor: University of Michigan Press, 1995.

Lane, Miles, ed. *Times That Prove People's Principles: Civil War in Georgia.* Savannah: Beehive Foundation, 1993.

Linvill, Dale Edward. *Battles, Skirmishes, Events and Scenes: The Letters and Memorandum of Ambrose Remley.* Crawfordsville, IN: Montgomery County Historical Society, 1997.

Louisville Refugee Commission, *Report of the Louisville Refugee Commission.* Louisville, KY: Civill & Calvert, 1865.

Lyell, Sir Charles. *A Second Visit to the United States of North America.* New York: Harper & Brothers, 1849.

Magee, Benjamin F. *History of the 72d Indiana Volunteer Infantry of the Mounted Lightning Brigade.* Lafayette, IN: S. Vater, 1882.

Myers, Robert Manson, ed. *The Children of Pride: A True Story of Georgia and the Civil War.* New Haven and London: Yale University Press, 1972.

Nichols, George Ward. *The Story of the Great March from the Diary of a Staff Officer.* New York: Harper & Brothers, 1866.

Oates, James. "Letter to the Editors." In *Battles and Leaders of the Civil War.* 4:298. 4 vols. Edited by Robert Underwood Johnson and Clarence Clough Buell. Reprint Edition. Harrisburg, PA: The Archive Society, 1991 [1887–1888].

Osborn, Donald Lewis, ed. *A Union Soldier's Diary.* Independence, MO: Donald Lewis Osborn, 1964.

Partridge, Charles Addison. *History of the Ninety-sixth regiment, Illinois volunteer infantry, pub. Under the auspices of the Historical society of the regiment.* Chicago: Brown, Pettibone, Printers, 1887.

Pepper, George W. *Personal Recollections of Sherman's Campaigns in Georgia and the Carolinas.* Zanesville, OH: Hugh Dunne, 1866.

Pickett, W.D. "Why General Sherman's Name is Detested." *Confederate Veteran* 14 (September 1906) p. 397.

Rawlinson, Mary Stewart, ed. *The Walter Stewart Family History.* Columbia, S.C.: State Printing, 1982.

Rodgers, Robert L. *An Historical Sketch of the Georgia Military Institute, Marietta, Georgia.* Atlanta: Kimsey's Book Shop, 1956 [1890].

Roth, Margaret Brobst, ed. *Well Mary: Civil War Letters of a Wisconsin Volunteer.* Madison: University of Wisconsin Press, 1960.

Shanks, William F.G. *Personal Recollections of Distinguished Generals.* New York: Harper & Brothers, 1866.

Sherman, William T. *Memoirs of General William T. Sherman.* New York: The Great Commanders, 1994 [1875].

Simpson, Brooks D., and Jean V. Berlin, eds. *Sherman's Civil War: Selected Correspondence of William T. Sherman, 1860–1865.* Chapel Hill: University of North Carolina Press, 1999.

Sipes, William B. *The Seventh Pennsylvania Veteran Volunteer Cavalry: Its Record, Reminiscences and Roster with an Appendix.* Pottsville, PA: Miners' Journal Print, 1906.

Skinner, Arthur N., and James L. Skinner, eds. *The Death of a Confederate: Selections from the Letters of the Archibald Smith Family of Roswell, Georgia, 1864–1956.* Athens: University of Georgia Press, 1996.

Skinner, James L. III, ed. *The Autobiography of Henry Merrell: Industrial Missionary to the South.* Athens: University of Georgia Press, 1991.

Smith, Gustuvas W. "The Georgia Militia About Atlanta." In *Battles and Leaders of the Civil War.* 4:331–335. 4 vols. Edited by Robert Underwood Johnson and Clarence Clough Buell. Reprint Edition. Harrisburg, PA: The Archive Society, 1991 [1887–1888].

Stiles, Joseph C. *Capt. Thomas E. King, or a Word to the Army and the Country.* Charleston: South Carolina Tract Society, 1864.

Tarrant, Eastham. *The Wild Riders of the First Kentucky Cavalry: A History of the Regiment in the Great War of the Rebellion 1861–1865, Telling of Its Origin and Organization; A Hard Service, and Fierce Conflicts on Many a Bloody Field.* Louisville, KY: Press of R.H. Carothers, 1894.

Thorndike, Rachel Sherman, ed. *The Sherman Letters: Correspondence Between General and Senator Sherman from 1837 to 1891.* New York: Scribner's Sons, 1894.

Vale, Joseph G. *Minty and the Cavalry: A History of*

Cavalry Campaigns in the Western Armies.* Harrisburg, PA: Edwin K. Meyers, 1886.

de Vattel, Emmerich. *The Law of Nations, or, Principles of the Law of Nature Applied to the Conduct and Affairs of Nations and Sovereigns.* Revised. London: G.G. and J. Robinson, 1797. Reprint. New York, 1982.

Walsh, Darlene M., ed. *Natalie Heath Merrill's Narrative History of Roswell, Georgia.* Roswell, GA: Walsh House, 1996.

Williams' Atlanta Georgia Directory, City Guide & Business Mirror. Atlanta: M. Lynch successor to Wm. Kay, 1859.

Winther, Oscar Osburn, ed. *With Sherman to the Sea: The Civil War Letters, Diaries & Reminiscences of Theodore F. Upson.* Bloomington: Indiana University Press, 1958.

Secondary Sources

Books and Articles

Alford, Bobby. *History of Lawrence County, Tennessee.* Lawrence County, TN: n.p., 1994.

Anderson, William L., ed. *Cherokee Removal: Before and After.* Athens and London: University of Georgia Press, 1991.

Ashendel, Anita. "Fabricating Independence: Industrial Labor in Antebellum Indiana." *Michigan Historical Review* 23:2 (Fall 1977) pp. 1–24.

Bailey, Anne J. *The Chessboard of War: Sherman and Hood in the Autumn Campaigns of 1864.* Lincoln: University of Nebraska Press, 2000.

Bell, Malcom Jr. *Major Butler's Legacy: Five Generations of a Slaveholding Family.* Athens: University of Georgia Press, 1987.

Bryan, T. Conn. *Confederate Georgia.* Athens: University of Georgia Press, 1953.

Candler, Allen D., and Clement A. Evans, eds. *Georgia, Comprising Sketches of Counties, Towns, Events, Institutions, and Persons, Arranged in Cyclopedic Form.* Atlanta: State Historical Association, 1906.

Cash, W.J. *The Mind of the South.* New York: Vintage Books, 1991.

Castel, Albert. *Decision in the West: The Atlanta Campaign of 1864.* Lawrence: University Press of Kansas, 1992.

_____. "Mary Walker: Samaritan or Charlatan?" *Winning or Losing in the Civil War: Essays and Stories.* Columbia, University of South Carolina Press, 1996.

Cate, Margaret Davis. *Our Todays and Yesterdays: A Story of Brunswick and the Coastal Islands.* Revised Edition. Spartanburg, NC: The Reprint Company, 1979.

Coleman, Richard. *A Short History of the Roswell*

Manufacturing Company of Roswell, Georgia: Home of "Roswell Grey." Atlanta: Richard Coleman, 1982.

Conrad, James Lee. *The Young Lions: Confederate Cadets at War*. Mechanicsburg, PA: Stackpole Books, 1997.

Cook, James F. *The Governors of Georgia, 1754–1995*. Macon, GA: Mercer University Press, 1995.

Cooper, Sarah Joyce King. *King and Allied Families*. Athens: Agee Publishers, 1992.

Cornell, Nancy Jones, comp. *1864 Census for Reorganizing the Georgia Militia*. Baltimore: Genealogical Publishing, 2000.

Coulter, E. Merton. *Auraria: The Story of a Georgia Gold-Mining Town*. Athens: University of Georgia Press, 1956.

_____, ed. *Georgia's Disputed Ruins*. Chapel Hill: University of North Carolina Press, 1937.

Cullum, Maj-Gen. George W. *Biographical Register of the Officers and Graduates of the U.S. Military Academy at West Point, N.Y. From Its Establishment, in 1802, to 1890 with the Early History of the United States Military Academy*. Boston and New York: Houghton, Mifflin, 1891.

Davis, Elizabeth Lockhart, and Ethel Warren Spruill. *The Story of Dunwoody: Its Heritage and Horizons*. Alpharetta, GA: Alpharetta Historical Society, 1975.

Davis, Fannie Mae. *Douglas County, Georgia: From Indian Trail to Interstate 20*. Roswell, GA: WH Wolfe Associates, 1987.

DeCredico, Mary A. *Patriotism for Profit: Georgia's Urban Entrepreneurs and the Confederate War Effort*. Chapel Hill: University of North Carolina Press, 1990.

Dillman, Caroline. *Days Gone By in Alpharetta and Roswell Georgia*. Roswell: Chattahoochee Press, 1992.

Evans, Clement A., ed., *Confederate Military History, Extended Edition*. Reprint. Wilmington, NC: Broadfoot, 1987 [1899].

Evans, David. *Sherman's Horsemen: Union Cavalry Operations in the Atlanta Campaign*. Bloomington and Indianapolis: Indiana University Press, 1996.

Fishback, Price Van Meter, and Shawn Everett Kantor. *A Prelude to the Welfare State*. Chicago: University of Chicago Press, 2000.

Georgia Biographical Dictionary: People of All Times and Places Who have Been Important to the History and Life of the State. New York: Somerset, 1994.

Goodrich, Thomas. *Black Flag: Guerilla Warfare on the Western Border, 1861–1865*. Bloomington and Indianapolis: Indiana University Press, 1995.

_____. *Bloody Dawn: The Story of the Lawrence Massacre*. Kent, OH: Kent State University Press, 1991.

Graf, Mercedes. *A Woman of Honor: Dr. Mary Walker and the Civil War*. Gettysburg: Thomas, 2001.

Griffin, Richard. "The Origins of the Industrial Revolution in Georgia: Cotton Textiles 1810–1865." *Georgia Historical Quarterly* 42, (1958) pp. 355–375.

Grimsley, Mark. *The Hard Hand of War: Union Military Policy Toward Southern Civilians, 1861–1865*. Cambridge: Cambridge University Press, 1995.

Hawk, Emory Q. *Economic History of the South*. New York: Prentice-Hall, 1934.

Henderson, Lillian, comp. *Roster of the Confederate Soldiers of Georgia 1861–1865*. Georgia: Georgia Division, United Daughters of the Confederacy, 1994.

Herreid, Charlene H. *The Humphries Family of Campbell and Douglas Counties, Georgia, Part I*. N.p., 2003.

Hindle, Brooke, and Steven Lubar. *Engines of Change: The American Industrial Revolution, 1790–1860*. Washington, D.C.: Smithsonian Institution Press, 1986.

Hitt, Michael D. *Charged with Treason: Ordeal of 400 Mill Workers During Military Operations in Roswell, Georgia, 1864–1865*. Monroe, NY: Library Research Associates, 1992.

Hoehling, A.A. *Last Train From Atlanta*. New York: Thomas Yoseloff, 1958.

Holland, Lynwood M. "Georgia Military Institute, The West Point of Georgia: 1851–1864." *Georgia Historical Quarterly* 43 (September, 1959) pp. 225–47.

Holland, Ruth. *Mill Child: The Story of Child Labor in America*. New York: Crowell-Collier Press, 1970.

Howard, Annie Hornady, ed. *Georgia Homes and Landmarks*. Atlanta: Southern Features Syndicate, 1929.

Hudson, Leonne M. *The Odyssey of a Southerner: The Life and Times of Gustavus Woodson Smith*. Macon: Mercer University Press, 1998.

Jones, Katherine. *When Sherman Came: Southern Women and the "Great March."* Indianapolis: Bobbs-Merrill, 1964.

Kennett, Lee. *Marching Through Georgia: The Story of Soldiers & Civilians During Sherman's Campaign*. New York: Harper Collins, 1995.

King, Monroe. *Destruction of New Manchester, Georgia: The Story behind the Ruins at Sweetwater Creek State Park*. Douglasville, GA: Monroe M. King, 1982.

Knight, Lucian Lamar. *Georgia's Landmarks, Memorials and Legends*. Atlanta: Byrd Printing Co., State Printers, 1913–1914.

LaCavera, Tommie Phillips. *Heroines of Georgia, 1861–1865: A Biographical Dictionary*. Volume I. Georgia: T.P. LaCavera, 2005.

Leonard, Elizabeth D. *Yankee Women: Gender Battles in the Civil War*. New York: Norton, 1994.

Lewis, Lloyd. *Sherman: Fighting Prophet*. New York: Harcourt Brace, 1932.

Livingston, Gary. *Cradled in Glory: Georgia Military Institute, 1851–1865.* Cooperstown, NY: Caisson Press, 1997.

Lord, Walter, ed. *The Fremantle Diary.* Boston: Little, Brown, 1954.

Lowry, Thomas P. "Research Note: New Access to a Civil War Resource" *Civil War History* 49.1 (March 2003) Questia, 5 Dec. 2006, <http://www.questia.com/PM.qst?a=o&d=5001903384>.

Marszalek, John F. *Sherman: A Soldier's Passion for Order.* First Vintage Civil War Library Edition. New York: Vintage Books, © 1993, reprinted, 1994.

Martin, Clarence. *A Glimpse of the Past: The History of Bulloch Hall and Roswell, Georgia.* Roswell, GA: Lake Publications, 1996.

_____. *History of the Roswell Presbyterian Church.* Dallas: Taylor, 1984.

Massey, Mary Elizabeth. *Women in the Civil War.* Lincoln: University of Nebraska Press, 1994.

McCall, Mrs. Howard H., comp. *Roster of Revolutionary War Soldiers in Georgia.* Atlanta: Georgia Society, Daughters of the America Revolution, 1941.

McMurry, Richard M. *Atlanta 1864: Last Chance for the Confederacy.* Lincoln and London: University of Nebraska Press, 2000.

_____. *Two Great Rebel Armies: An Essay in Confederate Military History.* Chapel Hill & London: The University of North Carolina Press, 1989.

Messmer, Charles. "Louisville During the Civil War." *The Filson Club Quarterly* 52 (April 1978), pp. 206–233.

Mitchell, Broadus. *William Gregg: Factory Master of the Old South.* Chapel Hill: University of North Carolina Press, 1928.

_____. *The Rise of Cotton Mills in the South,* © 1921, reprinted 1966. Gloucester, MA: Peter Smith, 1966.

Mitchell, William R. Jr. *Historic Area Study Roswell, Georgia: A Plan to Preserve Roswell's Historic Character.* Atlanta: Kidd and Associates, 1973.

_____. Roswell Historic District, National Register of Historic Places Nomination, 1973.

_____. Sope Creek Ruins and Marietta Paper Mills, National Register of Historic Places Nomination, 1973.

Munsell, Joel. *A Chronology of Paper and Papermaking.* Albany, NY: J. Munsell, 1864.

Newton, Steven H. *Joseph E. Johnston and the Defense of Richmond.* Lawrence: University Press of Kansas, 1998.

Nichols, Frederick Doveton. *Early Architecture of Georgia.* Chapel Hill: University of North Carolina Press, 1957.

Nirenstein, Virgina King. *With Kindly Voices: A Nineteenth Century Georgia Family.* Macon, GA: Tullous Books, 1984.

Perkerson, Medora Field. *White Columns in Georgia.* New York: Bonanza Books, 1952.

Podmore, Frank. *Robert Owen: A Biography.* Reprint Edition. London: George Allen & Unwin, 1923 [1906].

Pope, Mark Cooper III. *Mark Anthony Cooper: The Iron Man of Georgia, A Biography.* Atlanta: Graphic, 2000.

Ranta, Judith A. *Women and Children of the Mills: An Annotated Guide to Nineteenth-Century American Textile Factory Literature.* Westport, CT: Greenwood Press, 1999.

Rhyne, Jennings J. *Some Southern Cotton Mill Workers and Their Villages.* Chapel Hill: University of North Carolina Press, 1930.

Royster, Charles. *Destructive War: William Tecumseh Sherman, Stonewall Jackson, and the Americans.* New York: Alfred A. Knopf, 1991.

Rutherford, Michael F. *Perry County: Then And Now.* Paducah, KY: Turner, 2000.

Scaife, William R. *The Campaign for Atlanta.* Atlanta: W.R. Scaife, 1985.

Shadburn, Don L., and Ted O. Brooke, eds. *Crimson and Sabres: A Confederate Record of Forsyth County, Georgia.* Cumming, GA: D. L. Shadburn, 1997.

Snyder, Charles McCool. *Dr. Mary Walker: The Little Lady in Pants.* New York: Arno Press, 1974.

Starr, Stephen Z. *The Union Cavalry in the Civil War.* 3 vols. Baton Rouge: Louisiana State University Press, 1979–1985.

Summersell, Charles Grayson. *CSS Alabama: Builder, Captain, and Plans.* University, AL: University of Alabama Press, 1985.

Temple, Sarah Blackwell Gober. *The First Hundred Years: A Short History of Cobb County, in Georgia.* Atlanta: Walter W. Brown, 1935.

Thomas, Martha. "Amazing Mary." *Civil War Times Illustrated* 23 (March, 1984), pp. 37–41.

Thomas, Samuel W. *Cave Hill Cemetery: A Pictorial Guide and Its History.* Louisville, KY: Cave Hill Cemetery Co., 1985.

Thornbrough, Emma Lou. *The History of Indiana.* 3 vols. Indianapolis: Indiana Historical Society, 1992.

Walsh, Darlene M., ed. *A Pictorial History of Roswell.* Revised Edition. Roswell: Roswell Historical Society, 1994.

Ware, Caroline F. *The Early New England Cotton Manufacture: A Study in Industrial Beginnings.* New York: Russell & Russell, 1966.

Warner, Ezra J. *Generals in Blue: Lives of the Union Commanders.* Baton Rouge: Louisiana State University Press, 1964.

_____. *Generals in Gray: Lives of the Confederate Commanders.* Baton Rouge: Louisiana State University Press, 1959.

Washington, Rev. E.C., and Mary Wright Hawkins, eds., *Roswell Area Churches: The First Hundred*

Bibliography

Years. Roswell, GA: Roswell Bicentennial Committee, 1976.

White, George. *Historical Collections of Georgia: Containing the Most Interesting Facts, Traditions, Biographical Sketches, Anecdotes, etc., Relating to Its History and Antiquities, From its First Settlement to the Present Time*. New York: Pudney & Russell, 1855.

___. *Statistics of the State of Georgia: Including an Account of its Natural, Civil, and Ecclesiastical History; Together With a Description of Each County, Notices of the Manners and Customs of its Aboriginal Tribes, and a Correct Map of the State*. Savannah: W. Thorne Williams, 1849.

Williams, David. *The Georgia Gold Rush: Twenty-Niners, Cherokees, and Gold Fever*. Columbia: University of South Carolina Press, 1993.

Williams, Harry T. *McClellan, Sherman and Grant* New Brunswick, N.J.: Rutgers University Press, 1962.

Woelk, D. Lee. *A Pilgrimage of Faith and Devotion: A History of the Roswell United Methodist Church, 1836–1984*. Commissioned by The Bicentennial Committee as part of the celebration of the founding of Methodism in America. Roswell: n.p., 1984.

Index

185

Index